AF420974

# PRAISE FOR
# *All Things Hidden*

"This is the breathtaking and daring story of one woman's relatively innocent entry into a benevolent Maya community building experience in Guatemala where she discovers a deep and dangerous complexity of American involvement in arms dealing, proxy wars, and genocide. Her journey leads her to want to piece back together 'what happened' for herself and for other survivors, to unearth what is buried underneath American 'aid' projects."

—Lidia Yuknavitch, national bestselling author of the *Chronology of Water*

"This is a book bathed in tears. A testimony to a piece of our Guatemalan history with international proportions. It couldn't have felt the same if you had not been there as a witness at its very beginnings."

—Ricardo Falla, anthropologist and Jesuit priest and author of *Massacres in the Jungle: Ixcán, Guatemala, 1975-1982*

"Lesley Miles' *All Things Hidden* is both a thrilling page-turner and a deeply moving monument of love to a people who did not get to tell their own beautiful and tragic story. This memoir of witnessing, community, and survival pulls back veils of American empire and global greed, and truly reminds us that no two-minute news story can ever convey the truths of people's lives."

—Jordan Rosenfeld, author of *Fallout* and nine other books.

"Lesley Miles' *All Things Hidden* is the powerful story of her experience as an agricultural volunteer living for two years in a remote Guatemalan village in the 1970s during a period that began idyllically and ended in genocide. The depth of the relationships Miles developed with the villagers is beautifully described as is the horror of the murder of a great many of them by the Guatemalan Army with American support. Miles is a gifted storyteller who brings readers with her asking them only to keep their eyes open and not turn away, for there are important lessons to be learned in facing what is happening today."

—Dr. Thomas Ogden, Psychoanalyst and author of *What Alive Means: Psychoanalytic Explorations* and *Aunt Birdie and Other Stories*


"An idealistic young American agronomist joins her boyfriend in an isolated Maya village in the sweltering tropical forests of Guatemala and remains with the Maya after the Catholic Church is driven out and the Guatemalan Army seizes control. Miles reveals her own physical struggle to survive in isolation and make sense of daily life incrementally shifted by threats and whispers of violence, then suddenly engulfed by the Army's genocidal terror. A great story of cross-cultural love and friendship, and a must read to understand Ixcan life before the genocidal massacres."

—Victoria Sanford, PhD, anthropologist, senior research fellow and writer of *Buried Secrets Truth and Human rights in Guatemala* and *Textures of Terror*

# All Things Hidden

## A Witness to
## Paradise Lost

*A Memoir*

LESLEY LUCINDA MILES

Sibylline Press

Copyright © 2026 by Lesley Lucinda Miles
All Rights Reserved.

Published in the United States by Sibylline Press,
an imprint of All Things Book LLC, California.

Sibylline Press is dedicated to publishing the
brilliant work of women authors ages 50 and older.
www.sibyllinepress.com

Sibylline Digital First Edition
eBook ISBN: 9798897409495
Print ISBN: 9798897409501

Cover Design: Alicia Feltman
Book Production: Aaron Laughlin

This memoir reflects the author's current recollections of experiences over time. Most names and personal characteristics have been altered to protect privacy and anonymity, and dialogue has been recreated.

**HUMAN AUTHORED:** Any use of this publication to train artificial intelligence (AI) technologies to generate text is expressly prohibited.

Sibylline
Press

*In memory of those killed, the survivors and their children,*
*and the virgin jungle.*

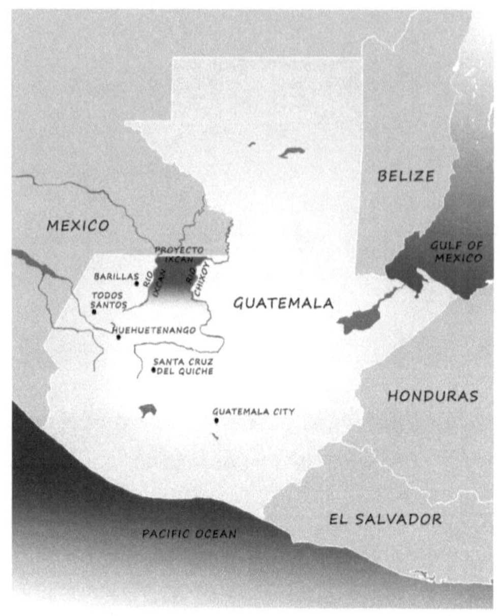



Map of Guatemala

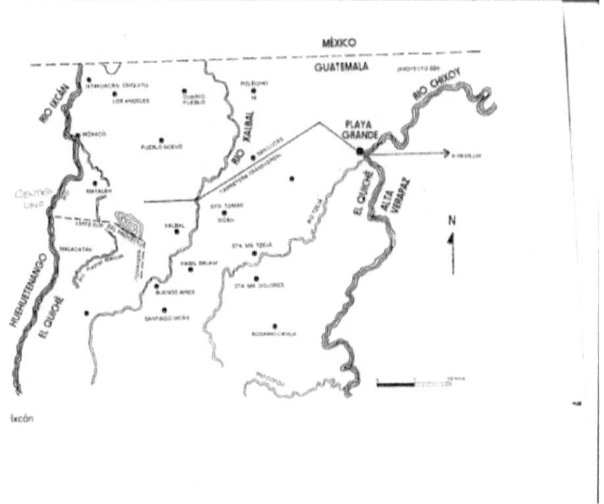

Map of Ixcán Grande

Ixcán Grande was comprised of the main cooperative centers: Mayalan, Los Ángeles, Pueblo Nuevo (La Resurrección), Cuarto Pueblo and Xalbal. Centro Uno was one of several small villages in the Mayalan co-op area. Map courtesy of Ricardo Falla

## List of Abbreviations

CIA - U.S. Central Intelligence Agency
DRF - Direct Relief Foundation
DID - Direct International Development
EGP - Ejército Guerrillero de los Pobres (Guerrilla Army of the Poor)
FAR - Fuerzas Armadas Rebeldes (Rebel Armed Forces)
INAFOR - Instituto Nacional Forestal (Guatemala)
MOSSAD - Intelligence Agency of Israel
NGO - non-governmental organization
UN - United Nations
USAID - United States Agency for International Development

# CHAPTER 1

Spring of 2000

I pulled over to the side of the road shaking and reached for my Nextel phone. Just seconds before, the KGO San Francisco talk show host had said, "Well, we–as in the U.S.–we have never been in a clandestine war."

I grabbed my phone and dialed in, pressing the buttons hard.

"What do you want to add to the conversation?" The producer asked.

"That's a lie," I said too fast. "That isn't true. I lived in Guatemala in 1978 when the U.S. was 'not' involved in any war in Central America. I was at the build-up of a U.S. supported genocide."

"Okay, I'll put you on hold and right before your air time, I'll tell you when you're up next."

I waited, holding my breath. *How do I share this story?* I wanted to be clear and tell just the facts. I tried to focus out the windshield, but the sky was dark. My reflection looked back at me clutching the phone, hunched over, waiting, my teeth clenched. Tears of anger and sadness trickled down my cheeks as I remembered how vulnerable we were, sitting fucking ducks.

But how could I say all that in a minute on air? I pressed the red receiver icon and hung up.

Hours later, I awakened at 2:00 a.m. heart racing, expecting to find myself alone looking out the rusted screen window at the dark jungle beyond. Instead, my husband lay next to me snoring. My border collie, Lucy, lying on the floor, looked up, always attentive. The children were in their rooms but I was back in Ixcán. I inhaled and exhaled slowly, trying to relax. *I am here. I am alive.* But how many of my friends from Guatemala could say the same?

# THE CRASH

The Crash large photo Flying into
Centro Uno over the Río Ixcán

# CHAPTER 2

November 20, 1976

It was a clear, hot and humid day when the plane didn't come, my boyfriend Ernest would tell me later. They'd expected the red and white Cessna 182 piloted by Maryknoll Father Bill Woods, Padre Guillermo, as he was known to the community, in the early afternoon. The thick bladed grass of the pista was cut short by machetes, ready for the plane to land. The cicadas had cranked up their whirring. The parrots weren't due back to their towering ceiba tree until early evening.

Before they'd see the almost comically tiny plane, the single prop engine would echo across the broad forested valley above the continual cicadas whirring and the calls of jungle birds.

From the air, he'd told me, the ground held no hint of soil, no space to see the jagged karst rocks below, just the deep, dark green of hundreds of miles of virgin rainforest, broad dark leaves of every shape and tone. Two wide cerulean rivers hugged the area of Ixcán Grande in a big abrazo. The settlement was bordered by the Río Ixcán on the west and the Río Xalbal on the east; rivers wild, sinuous and free and at the north end of the valley, the southern border of Mexico, an arbitrary line in the dark, wet rainforest.

Ernest, my boyfriend of several years, waited with the fifteen families of Centro Uno, who were now successful farmers and ranchers. With him was Larry Sawyer, tall and blonde, but Ann Kerndt, dark haired and experienced in community medicine as well as trained in French Intensive/Biodynamic farming was on the plane. They were volunteers working with Direct International Development (DID) an offshoot of the Direct Relief Foundation (DRF) a well-known NGO. The plane was scheduled to arrive with Padre Guillermo and Ann who was to live with Ernest and Larry in the Padre's house at the end of the high plateau above the small runway.

Ernest and the villagers heard no echo, no sound of a motor, engine, or any other sound beside the cicadas. The sky was clear until early afternoon. Given the days of pouring rain that typically fed this deep jungle and roaring rivers, it was unusual.

Dependent on Padre Guillermo to bring in medicine, sugar, salt and benedictions, the people waited, trusting that he would come. Maryknoll priest Padre Eduardo Doheny was the progenitor of the Ixcán Grande project having penetrated the virgin jungle a decade earlier with a group of co-op members and new landowners from the highland town of Todos Santos Cuchumatan, whose over-farmed land was barren and unable to support them. But, early on, a towering tree fell on the rustic church canopy of wood and cane while he was saying Mass, killing his assistant, a catequista, and mortally wounding the Padre.

Padre Guillermo, a priest and bush pilot, was posted nearby at the Barillas parish. He was quick to pick up the task of negotiating land titles and safety for the co-op members. Although the co-op was a joint project with the Guatemalan Government, oil and minerals had recently been discovered by U.S. and Canadian prospectors and the Ixcán basin was looking more promising for development than just a project to give the poor unoccupied land.

The pista was the only connection with the community other than a two-to-three foot wide muddy and rocky trail winding thirty kilometers down from the highland town of Barillas. Then, one still had to cross the Río Ixcán in a cayuco and follow the trail up a slight rise to the plateau of Centro Uno, Ixcán, the First Center.

Centro Uno was the first stop on a necklace of small communities, each with a grass pista, connected by a thin chain of a trail weaving in and out of the rainforest and jungle.

In Santa Barbara, California at the time, I knew nothing about them waiting. As evening descended over the red tile roofs and palm trees, I wrote down my thoughts of the day on the blue single fold paper and airmail envelope to send to Ernest. I imagined Padre Guillermo delivering it with a joke about me "maybe coming sometime soon." Ernest had said, "He is a force with his cowboy boots and hat...a real Texan...he is so focused on helping the people and he always has a smile and the kids run down when he flies in."

I wrote, "I made a salad of French lettuces, watercress and heirloom tomatoes from the garden that were incredibly sweet and tart at the same time! The food co-op is still as great as ever and I picked up raw almonds and sunflower seeds to top off my salad, yumm." Our letters had become a welcome and almost nightly ritual. Eventually, I pulled up the light blanket under my chin and drifted off to sleep.

In the predawn dark I jolted awake to the sound of the heavy black dial phone next to the bed ringing. The coiled cord was a tangle and I struggled to separate the receiver enough to answer it. When I did, I could barely understand the voice on the other end of the line. Groggy with sleep, I finally realized it was Ernest's father's choked and sobbing voice. "Plane crash ... Ixcán jungle. Ernest on plane ... went to get visa ... killed in crash ... seven people killed ... pilot ... Father Bill Woods, the Maryknoll priest."

I heard a strange, strangled scream in such a high pitch that I didn't recognize it as my own voice at first. I tried to focus on Ernest Sr.'s words, but I was above myself, an observer. Watching as though from afar I saw myself lurch out of bed with my hands shaking, and the receiver falling, silencing the call. Deep sobs racked my body. I felt like I would throw up. I randomly reached out, flailing for something unknown.

Fumbling, I struggled to pull on my jeans and rough leather boots and grabbed a T-shirt and sweatshirt from the pile on the chair. My legs did not respond as I tried to push up off the bed.

It was so early I didn't know what to do. I just needed to move as far away from that heavy black phone as I could. I didn't want to hear more. I threw open the door and walked unsteadily in the darkness of the uneven concrete pathway to where my bike was parked, mounted it and started riding. Without direction, I rode as fast as I could. The day's breaking, light shifted through the trees on De La Vina Street, creating patterns on the vacant roadway. All of a sudden, I remembered falling the day before when I was planting herbs in little pots. It was not just a trip or fall but a sensation of dropping from a great height followed by a feeling as though someone had died. I had written it off as the result of dehydration from working too hard in the sun, but now, I reconsidered—had I sensed the crash? I turned around and headed to the DID program's office.

The light from the window of the otherwise darkened building lit up the interior of the office. I could see the profiles of the two DID Program Directors, Edwin Thomas and Stephen Gibbons, and I contemplated the activity in the window. Both were bureaucrats—not your typical nonprofit leaders—both older white men, who were well-entrenched in California government jobs working with Governor Ronald Reagan before joining the USAID-supported DID. I tossed my bike to the side of the front steps, ran up the stairs, and pushed open the door. Ed was on the phone with the U.S. State Department. I grabbed the back of the chair closest to me to steady myself and asked, my voice catching in my throat, "When will we know what happened?"

"I have no idea. No one does," Steve said.

It would be hours before we would learn anything more. Pouring rain in the Ixcán jungle and the mountainous terrain made it impossible to travel to the crash site and investigate.

Still waiting at the office in the late afternoon, not knowing what to do and not wanting to be alone, I jumped at the sound of the ringing phone. Ed lifted the handset, held it briefly to his ear and turned to us, covering the receiver with his palm, "It's the State Department." He listened some more, and then filled us in, "A team has made it to the site, and they are investigating and not sure how many people have died."

"Maybe Ann carried Ernest's and Larry's passports with her on the plane to get their visas re-stamped?" Ed wondered aloud, "She had told us that she was flying out of Ixcán to visit the hospital where she had worked in San Juan Comalapa with her brother before she decided to work in Ixcán." This gave us some hope that Ernest and Larry might be alive. All was confusing and the flight manifest was not readily available. Waiting with Ed and Steve in the starkly furnished government-standard conference room, I was numb but tried to maintain hope.

I called my mother from a small office. She was very close to Ernest. I just choked it out, "They think Ernest is dead." She was too shocked to cry and dropped the receiver saying, "Come home," the sound of her voice diminishing as the receiver fell. But it was an eight-hour drive, and I wanted to be by the phone and with the group trying to make sense of what was happening. I also wasn't sure that I could drive.

Gradually information began to roll in over the next few hours that first day—a telegram from the embassy, a call, but nothing concrete. I didn't know it then, but La Prensa, the main Guatemalan daily, reported that American volunteers, Ernest Cole and Larry Sawyer were killed in the crash.

Over the next few days, preliminary information from the State Department seemed to indicate that the crash might not have been accidental. Weeks later, field investigators from both USAID and the FAA investigating in conjunction with the Guatemalan government had discovered that parts of the crashed plane were missing. There would never be any final agreement of what had happened. But campesinos and farmers around the crash site said that it had been a clear and beautiful day and that the plane had plunged to earth appearing to have been forced down by army helicopters and planes into the rocky mountainside.

In Centro Uno, on the narrow muddy Ixcán trail from the highlands, the clear sky gave way to rain falling with a vengeance. Clouds obscured visibility too much for planes to fly. Centro Uno was isolated and the wild Río Ixcán was too rough to pass in the cayuco. With no plane or communication and the unceasing rains, Ernest and Larry could not be reached. It took until the next day before the operator in the Aero Ixcán hangar in Guatemala City was able to contact the radio operator in Mayalan, Ixcán, via the two-way radio, the only communication. Once the connection was made, the co-op would send a runner to Centro Uno to see if Ernest and Larry were there, check, run back and relay that information.

With a brief break in the storm came a static radio connection. "Ay que ir a Centro Uno imedíamente para ver si los gringos están allí ... cambio." With that call, a runner sprinted to Centro Uno, his direction clear—run as fast as you can to Centro Uno to see if the gringos are there. Yet the eight-kilometer trail, the only way to make contact, was slick and slippery deep with mud.

The runner returned to Mayalan after checking quickly, and the radio operator called in "Estan bien, cambio,"—"They are well, over."

The transmission was forwarded to the Maryknoll house, and they called the DID office to share the news. Could Ernest be alive? I had felt the rapid descent of the plane and the energy of loss surging through my body. Was this now a cruel joke? I had been holding my breath, holding myself together. I waited, disbelief superseding that moment of happiness. How could he be alive?

Ernest told me later, "We were expecting Bill and Ann, and we waited, looking up at the clear blue sky, and then it started to pour. Larry and I kept waiting but we knew no one was flying in that day. Finally, on the third day, we looked up from our work in the garden to see a stranger jogging down the muddy path from the village toward us with Tomás, our neighbor and head of the Ixcán Cooperative. He looked stricken. We'd heard his wife Pabla scream and the children crying and we knew that something terrible had happened."

I was at the DID office again when Ernesto's call finally came from the Maryknoll residence almost a week later. He and Larry had been able to fly out with Guy Gervais, a bush pilot with Wings of Hope. I clutched the handset and tried to listen through the bad connection and clicking in the background. Before I could say anything, a sob rose in my throat and all I could choke out was, "You are alive, you are alive," over and over again. The relief I felt at hearing Ernest's voice was only a brief reprieve—he was alive, but he had a new shock for me.

"I can't believe that you and my parents thought I was dead ... I can't even think of how that must have been for you. I love you, but I want to stay here. I feel like I am really helping for once in my life. You would love it. The work we are doing is even more important now that Bill and Ann are dead. The people need our help."

At 21, Ernest—now Ernesto—was my first serious boyfriend. When he decided to go to Guatemala after taking the French Intensive/Biodynamic training program, I was surprised, but we had also drifted apart. As an only child I felt that the world rotated around me. I hadn't been sure how to respond but since I didn't have much else going on, I decided to take the program and join him.

Since I'd been studying horticulture at Cal Poly San Luis Obispo, I was fairly experienced in the basics of plant growth. My first job transplanting petunias in a small Sebastopol, California nursery had awakened an interest in plants and gardening.

When I heard about the plane crash, I was living in a tiny one-room backyard cottage that must have been a tool shed years before. Dirty white shelves were full of herbs planted in the smallest terracotta pots, ready to sell at the Santa Barbara flea market.

Shocked by Ernesto's decision to stay, I was surprised when DID Director Steve told me, "Lesley, we just trained you for four months you can't just quit, it's just like when I was in the Army, you signed up you're taking the class, you need to go."

Didn't he realize that a young woman, our volunteer, my age, had just been killed? This was not the Army, we were volunteers. On the other hand, when I asked Ed if I should go, he said, "I don't know what I would do. Don't feel pressured to go."

I didn't have anyone questioning or helping me to make the decision. My parents were doing their own thing, deeply involved with the self-help program EST my father left our family of three and embarked on a search for his "real and true family." My mother, depressed and confused, was unable to think clearly enough about anyone or anything beyond that. Ernesto was so intent on staying it was hard to think clearly.

Jimmy Carter was president, and the Vietnam war had just wound down. We held ourselves high as a country and didn't provide funding to Guatemala due to the serious humanitarian issues. That was the story, although it was just that—a story.

By the end of February 1977, I was emotionally and physically ready for the trip. Our letters had stalled since there wasn't the nearly daily Maryknoll mail delivery by plane. Ernesto and I had talked twice more before I was scheduled to leave.

"Lesley, the garden is really coming along but we're having a hard time getting seeds. The seed store in Guatemala City stinks with pesticides and half the time the seeds don't germinate."

This was right up my alley, "Got it, what seeds do you need? Do you need books or tools?"

"Yes, particularly with Ann gone we don't have any books on health or medicine, and I'd really like a book or two on tropical crops. As the garden is starting to grow people are getting interested and asking for all sorts of information. The longest anyone has been here is 10 years and the people are only familiar with the crops from their highland villages, not the tropical lowlands."

I bought the British standard, *Tropical Crops* by Purseglove. I knew we'd get a kick out of repeating his name with a funny accent as we toiled in the garden. I bought both volumes: *Monocots* and *Dicots*. There was no way to find things quickly or research things in the 1970's so

I had driven up to Cal Poly and found a professor in the Fruit Science Department. He just so happened to have a small farm, a coffee finca, in the highlands of Guatemala, a ten-hour drive from Guatemala City and he recommended the Purseglove books.

Then I returned to Sebastopol to get ready. My mom raised herself from her overwhelming malaise and drove with me to Berkeley in search of waterproof boots. She had gone to school there but now it was a "radical hot bed" so she hadn't been back in a while. We searched the phone book and found an army Surplus store with a mannequin in front dressed in fatigues wearing a gas mask that looked like it was from WWI. Inside, the narrow shop expanded vertically with rows of sagging and broken cardboard boxes and army green everywhere. In their ad it said it was the only place to find jungle boots.

"These look sturdy and the combo of canvas and is this… leather or plastic? Either way they look comfortable," my mom said while weighing one boot in her right hand as she passed it to me.

"Yeah, it says that they are 'Vietnam' boots, which sounds perfect for the jungle. Not sure if they're the real thing but they look good."

We bought them and a couple of sturdy waterproof duffle bags then wandered next door to a hippie-ish clothing store. "I think I need something lighter than my usual jeans and work boots, let's see if we can find some light weight yoga pants. Also T-shirts. Ernest, I forgot to tell you he is no longer Ernest. He is now Ernesto…told me no shorts, just long pants, skirts and dresses. He said the women in the village all weave their clothes and only wear traje or the clothes from their village, which are mostly red and white striped. And he said 'whatever you do, don't forget: bring lots of film. The film here is expensive.' Oh, and binoculars, we could use those too."

I wanted to understand who the people were. I had never even heard of the town of Todos Santos Cuchumatan. My mom, whose degree was in history and anthropology, suggested that we check the University bookstore for books about Todos Santos. We found the *Two Crosses of Todos Santos* by Maud Oakes tucked behind the *Popol Vuh*, the Mayan sacred text.

Oakes' field work and research into the indigenous Maya chimanes, or shamans, and her stay in Todos Santos in the 1940's was mesmerizing. I became instantly curious about the community in Centro Uno and why they would move so far away from Todos Santos. Ernesto had told me that they had moved as a group to their own cooperatively owned land because they were overpopulated in the highlands, but I wanted to know them more deeply. I later found out that everyone in the 15 Centro Uno families were related somehow.

Even with my curiosity and interest piqued and Ernesto's glowing descriptions, I wasn't sure it made sense to risk my life trying to help people I didn't know learn how to grow vegetables.

My doubts were compounded by rumors that our group of student trainees discussed over and over again: why were we were going into clearly dangerous areas? Ernesto and Larry were in Guatemala and other volunteers with my group were slated to go to Honduras at the border of El Salvador and others to the Dominican Republic.

Perched on tree stumps in a small circle surrounded by lush garden beds at the Mesa Garden our student group watched as the sun set over the Pacific Ocean while munching on tiny alpine strawberries. Pete, a volunteer who was going to the Dominican Republic said, "It's only been 22 years since the CIA carried out a covert operation to depose democratically elected President Jacobo Arbenz in 1954 in Guatemala, where you're going Lesley. And just two years ago, in 1974, the CIA infiltrated the Peace Corps in Peru. Peru was the only left-wing government in Central and South America that was pushing for agrarian reform just as Arbenz had put into place in Guatemala… I hope we are all not walking into something crazy."

Providing land to small subsistence farmers did not align with the goals of corporations that needed large tracts of land and an inexpensive workforce. Peru expelled the Peace Corps hoping to turn the tide of the U.S. meddling in the country.

Years later I would find out that the U.S. Ambassador Francis E. Meloy Jr. had met with Bill Woods and warned him that the army believed that he was working with the Ejército Guerrillero de los Pobres (EGP) the leftist guerrillas. He had also followed up with the Maryknoll Order in Guatemala, reinforcing the clear threat and danger of flying into Ixcán. Bill Woods told family members that if the Guatemalan army wanted to assassinate him, it would be in the foothills of the Santa Cruz Quiche Ixcán divide, exactly where the crash occurred. Unknown to me at the time, DID, with direct connections to USAID, had also been warned by the U.S. Embassy that flying with Father Bill Woods was not safe.

How naïve it was to even assume that I could help. I would find out later, there is no "helping" when there is the potential for oil, minerals and agriculture. There is no helping when governments claim that they are acting on a left-wing threat. No helping when the people are considered dispensable and in the way of Western progress.

# CHAPTER 3

February 1977

As the Boeing 707 hit altitude and cruised to Guatemala City, I contemplated my current place between lives. The past was just that—behind me. I was completely on my own for these few hours, and I settled in, buoyed by the realization that soon enough I would be joining Ernesto.

Then it struck me that this was not just a trip to visit Ernesto. People had died and I knew nothing about gardening in the jungle. My contemplation turned to worry and I closed my eyes, took a deep breath, and tried to relax.

"We are now crossing into Guatemala," the captain announced, and then half an hour later, "we are passing over Lake Atitlán." I caught a glimmer as the sun hit the lake's surface, its pristine clarity sparkling. Having read any books I could find on Guatemala, Aldous Huxley's musing came to mind that, ringed by volcanoes, Lake Atitlán was the most beautiful lake in the world—I couldn't disagree. We flew by Volcán de Fuego, capped with a thin puff of smoke rising from the uppermost crater above the historic colonial city of Antigua. Both were centers of tourism and not on my itinerary.

The plane dropped lower circling Guatemala City, flying over miles of homes perched on the sides of deep, steep and forested canyons strewn with a rainbow of trash, plastic ollas to carry water and pieces of plastic called nylo, fluorescent colors that bloomed like fields of flowers below. Dirty white colonial buildings and gray and turquoise multi-story offices and apartments rose on broad boulevards in the middle of these fields of poverty. I watched with hesitancy over the lap of my seatmate, as he leaned back to give me a view.

The landing was quick without much taxiing. I leaned over again and looked out the window to the tiny Aurora airport. There were no real gates. We parked on the tarmac. Standing up and grabbing my knapsack, I walked unsteadily down the aisle to the metal stairs, pausing at the top of the platform to search the crowd assembled at the front of the building for Ernesto.

I saw his long red hair first, and then the sweat-stained T-shirt and a rose that he was waving above the heads of the mostly shorter Guatemalans. Gesturing wildly, he yelled, "Lesley, Lesley." I ran into his arms, still not believing that he was alive. Incredible relief and a resounding flash of passion passed between us. The waiting was over, we were together, and our heated letters were in the past. I reached out to hug him again, but he tripped back into the person standing behind him, mumbling, "I have lice."

Soon I too had "piojos."

And so I moved into this new life unaware of what was to come and how my life would be forever changed.

It was well over six months since I had seen Ernesto. Leaning into each other, we walked to the baggage claim to pick up the giant duffels and retrieve the boxes of books. Staggering under the weight, we took a cab to drop off everything but a few essentials at the Ixcán Grande hangar on the other side of the airport. Ernesto had been bunking there the past few days, and we could safely leave everything that I brought while we prepared to fly in.

Taking the bus downtown and without much thought, we checked into the first reasonable hotel that we saw. At $1.50 a night, the tiny room looked out onto a five-by-five air shaft with sewer and water pipes providing a background ambiance of flushing toilets and running water. Covering the straw mattresses were rough muslin sheets and scratchy gray blankets.

We sat down on the edges of the beds facing each other after peeking out the window hoping for a view, laughed and then just looked at each other. Holding hands and gently crying, the full realization that I was there and that we were together finally settled in. I hadn't realized how nervous I was about seeing him. I needn't have worried because I immediately felt at home.

"Lesson number one: always ask to see the room first before you pay," I cracked and we fell on the bed laughing.

The next morning, I already felt tiny lice running through my hair. I quickly began to understand that this was no vacation as we checked our funds to see if we could go to another more expensive hotel. Hopefully one with a regular mattress and our own bathroom.

We moved to Le Colonial. At $8.00 a night, it felt luxurious. Our room on the second floor had a large, white-tiled bathroom and over the balustrade a view of the interior courtyard with a tinkling tiered fountain, terra cotta pots of pink geraniums and deep red mahogany benches with colorful striped cushions brightening the patio below.

I took a quick shower, drenched my head with a toxic lice shampoo and wrapped a white fluffy towel around my wet hair. I peeked out the door of our room. There was a small round table and two wooden chairs overlooking the courtyard. Ernesto was sitting in one of the chairs. I quickly brushed my wet hair, put on clean clothes and went out to sit with him.

Ernesto stretched his legs out, crossed his ankles and said, "Things have changed dramatically from just a few months ago. The support and enthusiasm for the Ixcán has really disappeared." Originally the

Maryknoll order had been supportive both in Guatemala and in the U.S., he related, but by the time I arrived in Guatemala, the Health Resource Centers in Mayalan and Centro Uno and the relationship between DID and the Maryknolls was not expected to continue. Ernesto said, "I scheduled a visit to the Guatemala City Maryknoll residence later in the week to talk about next steps. It is hard to know what the outcome will be."

With a few days free we explored the city. A bustling international hub, Guatemala City was the unofficial capital of Central America. The diversity of peoples and businesses reminded me of Los Angeles, but Guatemala was much more vibrant. Diesel buses and trucks filled the air with sharp acidic smog and the constant high-pitched whine of gears shifting and screeching brakes. Small children selling chicle, tiny packages of multi-colored squares of gum, swarmed the sidewalks, dodging between pedestrians and the mostly Maya women kneeling on striped mantellas, hand woven fabric, with huipiles from their village and jewelry spread out to sell. Newspaper hawkers selling pink, green and white newspapers with gruesome photos yelled. One photo has stayed with me—legs and one shoeless foot extending out of a sewer manhole with the sensational title, "Sewer explosion kills three!"

We found places to eat, shop, and buy Penguin books in English. These books were not available in the U.S. except at colleges, and we both loved to read so we were excited to see a whole bookstore devoted to Penguin books. On the front counter sat a book that looked interesting, *Guatemala—Another Vietnam?* by Thomas and Margarita (Marjorie) Melville, so we bought it. Finding information about Guatemala in the U.S. was difficult, and we thought this might give us some perspective.

At our now favorite restaurant, Auto Mariscos, we thumbed through the book. Thomas Melville, had been a Maryknoll priest, and Marjorie Peter Melville, had been Sister Luisan Peter, a Maryknoll nun. Thomas Melville was asked to leave Guatemala in 1971 due to his meeting with the guerrillas. They left the Maryknoll order and married, and wrote the book documenting the similarities of the U.S. intervention in Vietnam and what was beginning in Guatemala. I was surprised and relieved that books that questioned the status quo were available. Perhaps my concerns were not as big of a deal as I thought.

Taking a sip of my Cerveza Gallo I asked, "What about the people in the village? Who are they? I'm nervous as you know I'm not great with children."

Ernesto laughed, "Didn't you even babysit?

"No, never!"

"Well, there are fifteen families and they all came from down from the highlands of Todos Santos with Padre Eduardo. He later died and was replaced with Padre Guillermo…Bill and he's dead." Ernesto paused and looked away.

"I'm sorry. We haven't talked about what happened." The distance between us grew as he disappeared into his thoughts. I reached for the book and tried to read while really waiting for him to tell me more.

He cleared his throat and said, "It's a small village made of thatched huts and some mahogany board and batten one-room houses with lamina roofs, oh that is metal, and two houses have concrete floors, the others are all dirt. They mill all of the boards with handsaws. The other day I was out in the jungle and came upon two men with a giant two-person saw. One was standing on top of the downed tree the other below it sawing back and forth. It was incredible—the sound, the rhythm of the saw and they were singing."

I took a sip of Gallo and reached for the crispy fried fish that the waiter had just slipped onto the table. It sounds like something from the 1700's. "What was it like in Todos Santos?"

"Over cropped and not enough land for growing families. Because there wasn't arable land people traveled to the coast to work on large fincas where they were paid pennies a day. Big flatbed trucks with plank sides would show up in the center of Todos Santos and if anyone owed money to the store or the bank, they had to work it off on the coast. Men, women and young kids lined up and climbed in and stood packed in for the twelve-hour drive to the coast. No one made any money and then they returned, ended up in debt again and within months they had to go back. So, the Ixcán Grande project is an incredible opportunity for them."

"How did they get from the highlands to Ixcán?"

"The land was set up by the Maryknolls and the Guatemalan government as cooperatives, with individual properties radiating out from the center of the villages like spokes on a wheel. The titles are held collectively. That was what Bill was working on when he was killed. Now it's all in limbo."

He hesitated and looked away again. I considered how the shock of the crash, and thinking that Ernesto was dead, had left me numb—what must he be feeling? I reached over and forked a piece of his tomato-smothered pescado Veracruz chewing until he started again. "So, each family was vetted by Tomás, our neighbor and then, if approved, admitted to the co-op." He smiled. "Everyone is so unique, just like our neighbors in Sebastopol, each with their own history. But one of the weirder things is that there are no older people, just families with children. They weren't allowed since they couldn't work the land as well as younger families and yet elders are really important in their culture. You might find the language barrier difficult. The women only speak Mam but the men all speak Spanish. It was a requirement to join the co-op but it is their second language so most people in the community speak slowly."

I took my last sip of Gallo not realizing that I was on number three until I saw the six bottles on the table. I hadn't anticipated that I wouldn't be able to talk with the women or that Ernesto would slip into an unreachable place or that I might be moving somewhere that was about to be the next Vietnam. But there was no time to think or worry—we had to get down to business.

# CHAPTER 4

Checking in at the DID attorney's office was like stepping back in time. We walked down the narrow hallway where the rippled opaque glass transom and door panel with gold and black letters announced the office of Licenciado Oriano. I fully expected Dashiell Hammett's Sam Spade when I opened the door and tripped over an oak and brass coat rack. Sr. Oriano would help with the paperwork necessary to allow me to stay for more than the three months allotted by a tourist visa. I had been thinking this would be a quick process, but with the raft of papers that he gave me, I knew it would be anything but. As we left, he smiled and laughed, "¡Buena suerte!"

The bureaucratic process was endless and included waiting for at least two hours per line in five separate buildings, and then the inevitable two-hour siesta that ensued just when we reached the head of the line. Finally, we figured it out, and three days later we were able to get my visa. I now understood why Ann had carried Larry's and Ernesto's passports to get them stamped out. It could have been weeks away from the garden, setting back their progress.

The Ixcán region was now a no-entry military zone. We all needed a letter from Colonel Castillo, the air force and military commander, to be able to work there. That required a trip to the air force offices at the airport by the Maryknoll hangar.

I had my visa by the time we met Father Ron Hennessy, the Maryknoll regional superior, and Brother Dave Holstegge at the Maryknoll house in

Zona 18. The house sat in a neighborhood of walls, secure steel locked gates and graceful large-leafed trees. The high walls capped with broken glass were draped in magenta and orange bougainvillea. The concrete main house had a mid-century meets the tropics feel. We rang the bell to enter the compound and then knocked at the door. The door was opened by a priest.

Ernesto introduced us and announced that we were there to see Father Ron.

"Let me find him," he said tersely.

We waited in the cool and beautifully appointed foyer with a tile floor and polished natural dark mahogany wall paneling. Ernesto warned me, "Although they're a liberal group, that doesn't extend to being unmarried." Two older priests shot us looks of disgust as they walked by on their way up the stairs. Was it that I was a young woman or did we just look like a couple of young messy hippies?

Father Ron, wearing khakis that hung loosely on his hips and an open collared shirt, bounded toward us immediately, smiling broadly and stretching out a hand. Tall and thin, he ushered us into a large room that looked out on a tropical garden. We sat together for a few minutes chatting about my trip down and the trials and tribulations of getting a visa. He had stories about waiting for even longer, and we laughed about the "efficiency!" Fifteen minutes later we were joined by Brother Dave Holstegge. Dave had lived and worked with Father Bill and Father Eduardo as an engineer surveying and developing the individual lots and the overall co-operative boundaries. He and his wife now lived in San Juan Sacatepéquez, a small town outside of the city.

After Bill's death, no one in the Maryknoll order was interested or able to follow in his footsteps. The Ixcán mission was viewed as just too dangerous and uncertain. Dark shadows ringed Dave's eyes, and his tone was bleak but forceful. "I don't want to be involved now, not without Bill, and there is no way that you should even consider going into Ixcán. You will be completely on your own, and it is getting more and more dangerous."

Ernesto made a scoffing sound, but Father Ron pressed on, "You will have no ability to communicate with the capital and no support even if you have an emergency. Although I am still supportive of DID doing this project, there are others who believe that we should not even voice support. It's really too dangerous. Let's meet again when you have taken time to really think about the danger," Father Ron said.

It was still hard to conceptualize what that meant. How remote was the selva, the Ixcán jungle? I wasn't sure what I had anticipated, but I'd at least thought that there would be some support or interest in what we were doing.

Ernesto brushed it off as we drank our second beers at Auto Mariscos. "It'll be fine, everything has been peaceful...since then," he said. After a moment he added, "Not saying that it isn't very retirado."

"What does that mean?"

"Remote. Far away from everything."

I had no idea at all what I would face. Ernesto had spent almost three months without much support and summed up his view. "I feel safer there than anywhere I've ever lived, and the people are incredibly kind. On top of that it is the most beautiful place you've ever seen. You will love it, and wait until you meet Chaya, Luisa, and tiny Esperanza. You will even learn to like children."

"Ha, that will be the day. Okay, let's do it then. One more beer and then off to the Maryknoll house to tell Father Ron that we'll continue." We clinked bottles.

A few days later we discovered that the Maryknolls were trying to hire a temporary new pilot to finalize some things in Ixcán. Jerry Key was an adventurer who was excited by the danger of flying into the remote grass airstrips and dirt pastures. We hoped that they had perhaps relented and agreed to provide support. But his plane was so small that it could accommodate only one passenger, so it wasn't particularly useful.

Jerry said, "I'm just here until my next job. I won't fly in to rescue you if you need help. Only here to take the padres out to the cooperatives on an as-needed basis while I wait."

In three months, he would fly his small plane to Suriname so it was just a fleeting possibility that he could actually fly us in. Ernesto didn't see the lack of flights as a problem; perhaps because he'd had good experiences with the Maryknolls so far. I trusted him.

A few days later, we checked our cash and decided we needed to move from the Colonial to the small apartment at the back of the hangar for the Aero Ixcán project to save money. We had dropped my bags there when I flew in. It was one of the few areas of support that the Maryknolls provided us. The pilots had used the hangar in between flights, and now it was vacant except for the two-way radio operators and occasional agronomist volunteers Tonino and Christina from Switzerland who lived in a village on the other side of Ixcán. When they flew out to the city, they parked their small Piper cub plane in the hangar. That plane and Jerry Keys' small plane were the only two planes that ever used the hangar when we were there.

The hangar, well known to the local Guatemalan air force and army, was under constant surveillance. Guards carried Israeli machine guns, Uzis, and stood just far enough away to be threatening without being openly hostile as we waited, trying to figure out our next steps.

We would visit the Maryknoll house only once or twice in the ensuing two years to check in with Father Ron. We did visit Dave and his wife in San Juan Sacatepéquez once, but we never saw anyone from the Maryknoll order in Ixcán and never saw a priest in Centro Uno. The devout community was left without spiritual guidance.

There was another option to fly into the Ixcán: Wings of Hope, an NGO in Quiche. DID worked out an agreement with them to fly us in. Quiche was a good ten hours by bus, but they were the only NGO with a plane that was still flying into Ixcán. Wings of Hope, focused on humanitarian missions around the world, responded to emergencies and had been working in the area for several years helping the cooperatives.

Ernesto had flown out on the small Wings of Hope plane, so we set our sights on going to Santa Cruz del Quiche, a Maya town high in the mountains.

# CHAPTER 5

We took the bus to Zona Uno where we bought pan integral, whole-wheat bread that was so dense it would last two weeks even in the humidity of Ixcán. We also bought short, thick candles, "non-absorbent" toilet paper (apparently the only kind in Guatemala), rice, cottonseed cooking oil, and salt and pepper at the open mercado. In Ixcán our staples would be black beans and corn tortillas, all grown there, but nothing else. I liked beans and was not too worried about the lack of meat or fish.

Provisions needed to be simple and require no refrigeration, to last for at least three to four months, and to occupy a space no larger than the two knapsacks we were carrying. There was no space for cookies, candy bars or even trail mix. I thought about the food co-op in Santa Barbara and the myriads of organic snacks and nuts that I munched on daily. I had been hoping at the very least to be able pack in some dried fruit. I couldn't imagine what it would be like to have no market or store. The inability to even bring in a snack set me back. Who was this man, Ernesto? He was definitely not the Ernest I had known. He would have said "Sure let's get some cookies." Never one to ponder or even think about what could happen I forged ahead. I told myself: I am here, I made my choice, and I guess it doesn't include snacks, regular food or safety for starters. After loading our limited purchases into a thick plastic bag, we hopped a bus to our next stop, the agricultural products store.

Seeds for the garden were the highest priority, and I had brought quite a few packets from Santa Barbara, but Ernesto insisted we go to the seed store. "They have mustard by the pound and radishes too...our main crops right now." The store was as he had told me, an old building that stank of pesticides and chemical fertilizers and had mostly temperate crop seeds that were of questionable viability in the lowlands.

Ernesto asked the man behind the counter, "¿Dónde está la semilla de mostaza?"

To me, he said, "Mustard grows like a weed, that and radish, so we need to get a lot of those. Elena is asking for cabbage because she says that it is the only vegetable that she really likes, and Demetria wants tomatoes, but it's way too hot and humid. I'll get a different variety so we can try them out but didn't you bring some tomato seeds?"

When I said I had, he told me we'd test the seeds first in the garden and then if they grew well we'd sell the seeds in small packages to the *campesinos* for less than what we paid for them. He loaded the tiny black seeds into a plastic tub to take to the counter.

The next day, the trip was finally upon us. Lugging our boxes and my duffels, we took a cab to the Terminal Central de Buses in Guatemala City. Puddles of rancid water and rotting vegetables punctuated the parking area, and we lifted and dragged everything to a riotously decorated bus with "Quiche" and "Nebaj" written in fanciful script. This was no ordinary bus. "Joyfully painted!" I laughed. "This is our bus?"

Ernesto looked at me with an eyebrow raised. "You were expecting a Greyhound?"

I laughed again. "Guess not!" and realized that I was looking over everyone's head and that my white skin and brown hair were an anomaly. Surrounded by women wearing exquisite huipiles from many different pueblos and carrying babies on their backs with brightly striped manteles, I felt very tall, very white, and drab but excited. I wondered what it would feel like to live in a small village with all my neighbors looking different and speaking a language that I couldn't understand but the excitement overtook my worry. I heard whispers, "Ay gringos, ¿Adónde van ellos?" Where are the gringos going?

The bus was piled high with boxes of every shape and size and large white woven bags or bultas. We squeezed in with chickens, dogs and many children, our boxes and duffels stashed above and our knapsacks on our feet.

Off to a screeching start, the bus wove in and out of the bus station tapestry, colors and sizes of buses changing with names of places I wanted to know more about, like Xela, Santa Luisa and Huehue. I'd left my paper map in the big duffle, but there wasn't any space to unfold it anyway. I asked Ernesto, "Where is Huehue?"

"It's at the other end of Ixcán on the northern border of Guatemala and Mexico. It's Huehuetenango; they just call it Huehue for short. I got you that purple and orange striped huipil in the mercado there."

Years later I would read another Melville book, *Through the Glass Darkly*, about Ron Hennessy and find out that right after we left, Father Ron took a position as the priest in the small town of San Mateo. San Mateo was on the long winding and sometimes dirt road from Huehuetenango to the Ixcán trailhead. It would be one of the first places that the army would target in the highlands after Ixcán Grande, killing everyone in the tiny highland pueblos surrounding San Mateo, including women, babies, and children.

For now, however, I remained innocent, rocking to sleep just like a baby to the motion of the bus on Ernesto's shoulder and awoke to the sound of grinding gears as we slowly lumbered up a mountain pass, then another. The road hugged the mountain on one side and the other side dropped to the edge of Lake Atitlán. I saw the majestic Volcán Tolimán with a halo of mist across the lake. Smaller volcanos dotted the shoreline. Aldous Huxley was right—it was magnificent even though the dark blue waters were choppy. Waves and whitecaps almost concealed tiny boats as they headed to the other side.

After a brief stop in Sololá, the main village on the eastern shore, the bus turned for the last leg, up and over the mountains to

Chichicastenango. When the bus listed dangerously, I leaned away from the precipitous cliff and gripped Ernesto's knee, as if my shift of weight would make a difference as we ascended the narrow winding road up to Chichi and then to Quiche.

High in the sparsely populated pine-covered Sierras, there was a noticeable chill in the air. The deep clear blue sky was dotted with white cumulus puffs. The invigorating scent of pinon filled the bus via a crack in the window. The blue gray smoke of wood cooking fires wafted through the towns along the road, weaving between the pines and small adobe homes perched along the hillsides. I caught the musky perfume of copal resin incense and the lanolin of damp wool as men and women climbed onto the bus wearing heavy wool ponchos and the men short wool skirts over their hand-woven pants.

Everywhere the indigenous Maya wore hand-loomed traje, each village or aldea with its unique style. I was struck by the beauty of the stark white rocks and cobblestones of the ancient roadway and the contrast of bright reds, blues and purples tightly woven in stripes or textured lush floral bodices worn by the women walking alongside the bus. I soon was able to identify the villages and peoples based on their traje.

Bouncing over the cobbles, we finally arrived in Quiche. Ernesto slid down the cracked window and pointed at the dilapidated hangar, the grass and gravel airstrip, and the plane parked outside, a red and white Cessna 185, "That's Guy's plane." It looked so small.

The brakes caught and squealed, and we came to a rocking stop. Untangling ourselves from the straps of our packs and stepping over two dogs lying in the exit path, we climbed off. I staggered a bit as I got out and turned as the mozo tossed our duffels off the roof and the boxes too. I jumped sideways, dodging their fall. Glad that nothing was fragile, we hefted them to our shoulders and set off. The next stop for the bus was the small village of Nebaj, with many interim stops along the side of the road. Small groups of ranchos sprinkled the steep hillsides until the end of the line and the beginning of the lowlands.

Quiche was not a tourist destination, so there were no hotels and few places to stay while waiting for the plane the next day. Finally, after walking up and down and dragging our boxes and bags, we found a small pension. All of the other guests were single men. I went into the bathroom, which was a stall in the middle of a courtyard surrounded by the individual rooms. The toilet was overflowing, and the shower was located above and to the right of the toilet. The sink, to my disgust, was not connected to the drain. I brushed my teeth, and water, soap and saliva flowed out onto my canvas boots and down to a central drain. When the shower ran, the entire bathroom became the shower stall. So, no shower, even though I was dense with grime and sweat and had just started my period. The enchantment of the pine-scented colonial city with cobbled narrow roads almost overshadowed the squalor.

As the sun set, we walked to Fabiano's house—he was the liaison and organizer of the Ixcán flights out of the Quiche pista, Ernesto told me. Walking in the dusk along the meandering cobble roads, darkness descended quickly. High walls lined the narrow alleys, blocking out the light from inside the small homes and courtyards. Stumbling, we saw the light above the door of Fabiano's family's small adobe home at the end of the street beckoning us. Fabiano and his wife met us at the door.

Ernesto asked, "¿Con permiso?" The phrase, I had learned, was polite Guatemalan etiquette before entering a house.

"Sí pasen adelante." Welcoming us in, Fabiano's wife offered us sugary coffee. I welcomed the warmth flooding through my body. Their home was sparsely furnished with white washed adobe walls, blank except for a vibrant print of a tortured looking Jesus, sharp thorns and thick vines twined around his head as a crown. His heart was thrust to the front of the illustration, also wrapped in vines laden with even larger hooked thorns.

"Qué lindo," I said, how beautiful, and then I read the fanciful script below: "When heartburn rips through your chest...it is time for Mylanta." Struggling to contain my not always appropriate sense of humor, I choked out, "Qué alegre," how happy. Later, in other homes, I saw several versions of "The Last Supper" with the tagline, "Alka Seltzer when you really need it." Faith was central to the indigenous peoples, who were mostly Catholic and Evangelical Christians now. There were few non-believers, and no one would pass up the opportunity for a free print of Jesus!

The next morning, we would fly in with Guy Gervais, the French Canadian who worked for Wings of Hope. Fabiano told us, "Mañana Guy sale a las ocho en la mañana, hay que estar allí o sale sin ustedes." Tomorrow he will leave at 8 a.m. sharp. If you are not there, he will leave without you.

"Is it safe?" I asked in very broken Spanish.

"Solo Dios sabe." Only God knows. Looking back, it is hard to believe Fabiano would be viewed as a threat to the Guatemalan government and gunned down by the army. I had heard but did not believe it until I read Guy's account of escaping from Guatemala with his family in the middle of the night after seeing Fabiano's execution.

Fabiano reiterated as we left, "Eight a.m. sharp."

Years later, I realized that evening, as I hovered on the brink of flying into Ixcán, worrying about taking a shower, was my last night as a young woman with thoughts just about myself.

# CHAPTER 6

March 3, 1977

That next morning, we took a taxi back to the pista and met Fabiano. In the light of day, I studied him, a short, stocky Maya man who exuded powerful energy. He managed all the flights that went in and out of Ixcán, documenting what needed to be picked up or dropped off at the ten or so small pistas, and prioritizing the movement of goods and people. His forehead wrinkled as he squinted at the group waiting and looked back and forth from them to a wooden clipboard. I supposed that the pressure of how to fit so many into such a small plane and wondering if the weather would hold had taken a toll on him.

Before, Padre Guillermo would have also been flying from the Guatemala City hangar providing more access for people living in the northwestern jungle, Ixcán Grande, and the developing areas to the east. But now working with Guy, Fabiano determined the logistics of transporting families and items for the several thousand co-op members and residents.

The only way in was to fly with Guy or to hike a single-track trail, from Barillas in the highlands on the other side of Ixcán down 30 kilometers of mud and rocks through the jungle to cross the Río Ixcán and arrive in tiny Centro Uno. I hadn't realized then that the length of a trip wasn't described in miles and kilometers but in time—in the case from Barillas to Centro Uno, "como 12 horas." Alternatively, we could hike the even longer trail through Ixcán Chiquita, a narrow trail of over 120 kilometers of slipping and sliding in the mud, "como 50 horas." I much preferred the small Wings of Hope Cessna 185 sitting in front of us.

A group of families dressed in red and white striped traje sat on the ground by the small bodega that I had thought was a hangar. Once again, I was struck by the beauty and complexity of the huipiles of the women and pantalones of the men woven on a simple backstrap loom. The intricate design of each weaver's pattern shared the common colors of their village but also the weaver's artistic interpretations.

Piles of supplies were visible through the wide swinging doors. Inside everything was neatly arranged but had expanded to fill the central walkway.

When I reached the plane, I saw that all the interior seats had been removed except for the pilots. Cargo was to be stowed and wedged in the empty space and people were an afterthought.

A family of four anxiously joined us, peering into the plane. Weight and size took precedence. We too were cargo and, as a group, were evaluated and assessed to determine where and if we could all fit.

The father pleaded with Fabiano, "Tenemos que ir, ya estamos aquí hace tiempo." "We have to go; we have been waiting here for a long time." I hung back, sensing that they, camped at the bodega for a week, were concerned that we gringos would get to go first, and they would yet again be waiting.

Fabiano and his helper, another Maya man with large rough hands and an incredible ability to heft a 100-pound bulta, started packing the plane methodically. He tossed the sagging white plastic mesh bags filled with rice onto the floorboards of the cabin and then filled every open space only leaving room for people to perch on top of the boxes and bultas. Our boxes and packs were unwieldy and caused loading problems. Ultimately, we ended up leaving one box that Guy said he would deliver later. It contained my books on tropical agriculture, fruit trees, citrus and spices. I hoped that I would see it again.

The mother with long black braids hanging down her back looked at me and smiled and then patted me on the shoulder, a Maya greeting. She carried a live flapping chicken swinging upside down from a rawhide strap and sat on a box of sugar, tucking the hen under her arm as she climbed in. I jumped in next, taking a short leap into the plane. At the open door, the father lifted up the small boy and then the girl to me one at a time. I caught their tiny hands and pulled them into the plane. The boy immediately hid behind his mother, and the chicken squawked and flapped. The little girl, a bony toddler wearing a hand-woven huipil, was told to sit on my lap. She leaned away from me as far as she possibly could while still barely sitting on my lap. I reached out gently to hold her. Ernesto squatted in front on a large white bulta filled with rice, his chin resting on his bent knees. The father squeezed in next to me, his sharp machete blade turned away between his raised knees seemed a bit dangerous. Fabiano closed the door tightly and flipped the handle up.

Guy arrived, resplendent in a beret with a cigarette hanging out of the left side of his mouth. He performed his pre-flight check walking around the plane. Making conversation to assuage my fear, I asked, "What's next on your bucket list of things to do?"

"Maytag repairman," he said with a smile as he climbed in. For a moment I was back home watching the ad on TV with the Maytag repairman relaxing. Then I looked out the plastic window and felt an urge to open the door and climb out. But it was too late.

The single propeller began to rotate and the engine buzzed, sounding a bit tinny until it roared, then the entire plane vibrated before lumbering down the rocky runway. Gravel kicked up from the wheels and clattered against the body of the plane. Finally, we lifted off, heading due north toward Ixcán. I looked down to see the sparse pines and what looked like oaks dotting the hillsides, as well as small ranchos, and a few horses and pigs outside the clustered pueblos. Gliding, we followed the road down past the last vestiges of civilization.

I didn't know how we would communicate again with the small hangar in Quiche or the Aero Ixcán hangar in Guatemala with no electricity, batteries nor radio. Although Ernesto seemed comfortable and acclimated to the current situation, suddenly terror flooded me. I had never flown in a small plane. My thoughts about the plane crash, the lack of seats, and the strangeness of everything came together at the same time, and even though the morning was brisk, I broke out in a sweat from head to toe. Ernesto twisted his head toward me in the back, not noticing the beads of sweat on my forehead, and said, "See, it's going to be fine!"

With that, the plane shuddered. I was unnerved by the squeaking of metal upon metal and the high pitch of the engine throbbing, like it was coming apart. It was hard to know if that was a common occurrence in a small plane or if it was truly falling apart. Guy seemed proficient and jovial, as he threw out enthusiastic comments. "It is a great day for a flight. Here we come Xalbal!"

This helped our small group relax a bit, but I looked at my hands and realized that white knuckles are a real thing. I exhaled my tightly held breath. My palms were sweaty, and as I unclenched them, the imprint of my fingernails marred my palms. Hidden beneath the terror and newness of everything was excitement. The adventure was beginning. What lay ahead?

As we dropped over a ridge, Guy said more quietly, "It is here."

The end of the road transitioned from pine covered mountains plunging to rainforest, jungle and the broad Ixcán Valley extending across the border and far into Mexico. Sheared off and broken tree branches remained from the not-so-distant crash. We quickly passed over. The engine droned on, and we flew deeper and deeper over the undulating rocky karst hills and outcroppings completely obliterated by deep dark ever-stretching green. No roads, just solid vegetation and green broccoli-like treetops. No glimpse of grass or earth.

The brisk temperatures of the highland night had cooled the cabin but the temperature climbed rapidly with the sweltering heat and humidity of the lowlands. The plane lifted up on thermals above the jungle only to drop sharply as lighter hot air swirled up from the jungle floor.

Amidst endless jungle stretching forever, Guy pointed out what we passed. "There's the foot trail connecting the five main cooperative centers of Cuarto Pueblo, Xalbal, Los Angeles, Mayalan and La Union," Guy said.

The towns appeared only as small orange-red clearings punctuating miles of green jungle.

When the plane bucked, the little girl sitting on my lap started crying and then threw up frijol negro and cookies onto the floor and my shiny new jungle boots. Equally nauseated, I grabbed the plastic bag holding the pan integral from my pack, dumped it quickly and vomited into the empty bag. The acid stench hung thickly in the hot and now humid unventilated cabin. Ernesto turned and weakly patted my shoulder.

The plane slowed as we approached the first stop, the trimmed grass runway of Xalbal. We dropped down to the pista, the engine roaring as the propeller reversed, and came to a stop. I mopped up the vomit with a rag that Guy had handy just for that purpose, and we all clambered out. I was hit by overwhelming heat and humidity as stifling as a steam room. By the time we helped unload the families' morales and cardboard boxes, I was drenched. Even my breath felt heavy and wet. And the noise! The cicadas' high-pitched shrill buzzing enveloped us. Their manic mating dance drilled into my brain. I reached up to cover my ears.

The bodega at Xalbal, a rusted corrugated metal structure, sat at the edge of the pista, the compacted earth ringing it, naked was an iridescent reddish orange. The trees, just green tops from the air, were a towering 100-foot-tall rain forest from the ground, branching high above lower shrubbier trees at the edge of the clearing. A small office space at the front of the bodega was occupied by a co-op member manning the radio. A member of the cooperativa received goods and sold a few things to children waiting patiently, younger siblings tied hammock-style on their backs. A 1,000 square foot storage area to the rear was piled five-high with bultas, 100 pound quintals of coffee and cardamom to be exported, Ernesto explained. Campesino cooperativistas grappled with the weight as they lifted a few bags into the plane.

We struggled to fit back in, once again shifting our weight on top of the new quintals and the reorganized boxes. With the family gone, we welcomed two men carrying machetes, who politely asked permission to join us on their way out of Ixcán. They squatted on the bags next to me. I shifted my weight, the dried cardamom pods that had just been loaded crushed slightly, releasing a cleansing scent, spicy, slightly nutty, aromatic and sweet. It almost obscured the vomit. I wriggled a bit more to get comfortable and finally gave up.

From the air the property below looked like a large pizza of individual and varied pieces, some with milpa or corn fields, some with virgin forest, some with coffee or cardamom planted below tall trees and some with cattle placidly grazing the bright green grass. Ernesto yelled over his shoulder, "Each family owns 28 acres radiating out from their rancho at the center of the pie, the village center."

By the time we descended into the tiny dot of Centro Uno, I was exhausted and nauseated again, aggravated by my period, prickly with anxiety, and ready to get my feet on the ground. We followed a ribbon of strikingly beautiful white sand and rocks and the alternating clear turquoise and then muddy brown waters of the Río Ixcán winding gently for miles in front of us.

The plane banked and circled Centro Uno. I saw a flash of white water, splashing over submerged rocks, white sand beaches and rocky outcrops at the verdant forest edge. The contrast of color and beauty was everywhere. My upset stomach took a backseat to the remarkable colors of the world below me. The stately trees, the narrow path winding from one side of the village to the other, a thin red line of lateritic clay, the thatched roofs on either side broken by an occasional metal or corrugated roof. The sky was a cloudless deep blue as the plane banked and came around, preparing for landing on the rough grass pista.

As we circled Centro Uno, Ernest pointed out our house, the houses of our neighbors, the market and the church. It was just a small clearing with what looked like six or seven small thatched buildings and a few corrugated roofs. It was not really a village, just a few huts in the expanse of jungle. There was no bodega by the pista, nothing. The grass on the runway didn't look cut, and as we flew down for a closer look, I realized it was almost a foot tall. The children below danced and ran, twirling in a swirl of red and white stripes and dark blue skirts waiting for our arrival, their joy and excitement palpable even at 100 feet above the runway. As we descended, they turned their faces up to the plane in expectation. Ernesto called over his shoulder, "They are so looking forward to meeting you. Look, see the tall girl? That's Luisa, and there is Chaya!"

Circling again and finally landing, we jolted down the pista, bouncing from one large grass bunch to the next.

Guy, frustrated by the condition of the airstrip, exploded, waving his arms to no one in particular and said, "There's no way I will fly into this runway again unless you are able to keep it mowed."

I didn't realize what this meant until later when I learned that there was no mower; the small pista was cut by hand with machetes.

I pushed open the flimsy door. The heat burned, searing my uncovered head as I poked it out of the plane, the air even more oppressive than Xalbal. I jumped down and was immediately surrounded by children. Here there were no men to help since there was no bodega and not really an airstrip, but there were children, perhaps the entire village's worth.

Considered "la esposa de Don Ernesto" with my height and my fine auburn hair that was a different texture than the villagers, I immediately provided both curiosity and entertainment. Although not actually Don Ernesto's wife, our living together made us a family.

We unloaded my duffle bags and our purchases from the city, including the box of different types of seeds to test for the garden. On the ground at last, I looked around. The low hills and vegetation on the eastside of the pista were not rolling hills but a vertical climb up to the village. The plateau where we had just landed dropped to the river below on the west side. The tall slender trees, intensely dark green, were spiked with lime colored shoots of fresh growth. The rusty red of the soil of the trail leading to the village and the serrated grass of the pista lent a somewhat formal and manicured edge in contrast to the riotous greens.

The children pressed closer and closer, reaching out to touch me. In chorus they asked, "¿Cómo se llama?" and followed up with a number of words that I couldn't understand. Unsteady, I sat down on the box of seeds as I watched Guy prepare the plane for its return flight. I hadn't registered initially, but Larry, Ernesto's volunteer partner, was standing to one side, moving quickly toward the plane. Tall, lanky and slightly hunched over, his blond hair ragged and dirty he put his foot on the metal step and pulled himself up, ducked in, waved and slammed the door.

"Where's he going?" I asked.

"Huehuetenango, then Mayalan," Ernesto said.

I wondered if he'd be back.

Guy said, "I need to get going," and with that, the propeller began to turn. The plane rolled and rocked quickly down the grass. The children took off running behind it until, lurching up and down, it finally lifted off into the air. Guy had just barely cleared the trees at the end of the pista and the creek beyond.

It was cool for those brief seconds as the breeze kicked up from the propeller. The children ran to the end of the pista, and with their braids still whipping from the wind, they turned and ran back toward me laughing and dancing down the runway.

The sound of the plane's engine roaring, then humming, hauntingly echoed all the way across the jungle until it climbed the mountains to the southwest, an echo of emptiness and distance. There was no room for the thoughts that typically raced through my mind. Just like that, I left behind all contact with the world I had known.

# CHAPTER 7

## Ixcán, March 1977

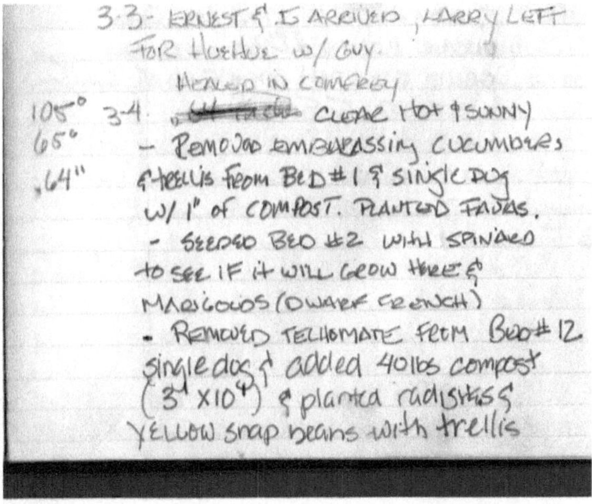

3-3- ERNEST & I ARRIVED, LARRY LEFT
FOR HUEHUE w/ GUY.
HEALED IN COMFREY
105° 3-4. CLEAR HOT & SUNNY
65° - REMOVED EMBARRASSING CUCUMBERS
.64" & TRELLIS FROM BED #1 & SINGLE DUG
W/ 1" OF COMPOST. PLANTED FAVAS.
- SEEDED BED #2 WITH SPINACH
TO SEE IF IT WILL GROW THERE &
MARIGOLDS (DWARF FRENCH)
- REMOVED TELHOMATE FROM BED #12
single dug & added 40lbs compost
(3' x10') & planted radishes &
YELLOW snap beans with trellis

Excerpt from the Hortaliza Anna Garden Journal- March 1977

As the plane disappeared into the late afternoon sky, I felt a wave of nausea and chills despite the heat and humidity. Guy had opened the plane window and yelled over the sound of the engine as he was leaving, "If you want to fly out, cut the pista, hike to Mayalan and radio Fabiano and ask for a flight."

I'd known that we would be alone but had not cemented just how completely disconnected we would be from the outside world. I glanced at Ernesto to connect for a second, but he was laughing and kidding with the children with a joy I had not seen before. Speaking quickly, I heard him mention "la hortaliza y la gata" and the children laughing in response, "Están bien."

I took a deep breath of the humid air. Surrounded by every dazzling shade of green imaginable and a deep rich terracotta earth, the bright red and white of the children's traje a vivid kaleidoscope. To the west, the edge of the pista dropped down to the roaring muddy Río Ixcán with white-capped rapids, and to the south, a quieter, slow bright aqua spring-fed creek. To the east stood my home for the next two years at the far edge of the village. Remote from the other houses, it stood stark against the clear deep blue cloudless sky.

The extremely helpful children ranging from three to about 14 years old darted up the red rocky trail from the pista to the house about 100 yards in front of us, laughing and yelling questions as they dragged and hefted our knapsacks, boxes and duffels. "¿Tiene niños?" "¿Va a vivir junto con Don Ernesto?"

"No, I don't have children," I replied and, "Yes, I am going to be living here with Don Ernesto."

The two tallest girls, Luisa and Chaya, grabbed the heaviest boxes and lifted them gracefully to their heads. All the girls wore dark blue heavy cotton skirts with wide coarsely woven red wool belts and red and white striped huipiles. The younger girls balanced the smaller boxes on their heads. The boys wore ripped red and white striped pants and shirts, some with the Todos Santos collar, others just a long-sleeved shirt with the tails tied tightly around their waists. They wrestled each other to get close to us. It was also the first time I had been surrounded by a group of children.

Slipping and sliding in the slick mud and dodging the rocks, I followed them up the hill to the concrete front porch of my house affording a grand view of the lowland jungle and the Río Ixcán. Endless trees and green stretched before us to the southern and western mountains. I laughed in amazement at the sight of a flock of toucans in a 25-foot rubber tree, cocking their heads and flashing their immense bright yellow curved bills at us.

Crossing the Río Ixcán below us was a cayuco, a long canoe. Struggling horses swam across the river alongside the cayuco. A man wearing Todos Santos traje stood holding a long oar and paddling hard, fighting the current. I said to Ernesto, "That must be Santiago who you were telling me about!"

Crossing the river laden with large bultas and cardboard boxes as well as a family of three hunkered down low, he balanced and moved with the river toward the Centro Uno trail connection on the other side of the river. It was the only way to get from one leg of the trail at Barillas to the cooperative communities of Ixcán Grande and beyond. No road, no bridge and soon there would be no small airplane flying into the thick high grass of the pista, just the cayuco.

The house originally used by the padres for brief visits was a low 20' by 40' structure built of hand-hewn planks with gouging teeth marks, milled from the wood of the tropical hardwood forest by hand with axes and handsaws. The gray corrugated asbestos roof was unnerving given the cancer connection I had just read about in the newspaper, particularly since there was a gutter to catch the rainwater and divert it to a fiberglass storage tank on the garden side of the house that fed into the house taps. The bottom four feet of the four exterior walls were constructed of the board and batten rough shellacked mahogany siding. Above, wall to roof, the house was encircled by screen windows. The screen was surrounded by citrus trees pressing in on one side and pure jungle on the other.

The children dropped the packages and duffels on the porch and ran away. The only other gringa woman that they had ever seen was Ann when she had flown in with Bill, Ernesto and Larry to look at Centro Uno. I wasn't sure why they had left until I heard them running to the center of the village calling to their friends to come and see the gringa!

I waited on the stoop while Ernesto picked up a heavy box. "I can't believe I'm really here!" I said opening the solid plank door. I stepped across the threshold into the house, our home. Ernesto had described the kitchen and the open screened windows, but I couldn't imagine it.

The scarred wooden kitchen counter faced the door and was broken by a large once-white chipped enamel porcelain sink with a faucet, though no running water. A two-burner portable gas cooktop sat on the counter to the left of the sink with a five-gallon rusted propane tank below the counter on the concrete floor. The waist high screened windows were open to the elements. Soon the next wave of children arrived, peering in. A small bird in a cage, I was visible to all, completely exposed. Ernesto squinting as if to peer out of the windows cracked, "Not much privacy, it wasn't a problem before!"

I squatted down and touched the rough and slightly cool concrete floor, which held the history of settling the jungle and the tragedy of the two priests who had died: Padre Eduardo and Padre Guillermo, as well as Ann who had died. I said, "There has been so much sadness here maybe the garden will bring new life."

"Oh, I forgot to tell you, one other pilot died too, John Stork, he is buried in the garden there is a stone where he was buried..."

I stood up, shaking the thoughts of death from my mind and brushed my hands off on my pants. In the months and years ahead, I felt the terror of being completely vulnerable and living in this screen cage at the end of the plateau. But for now, it was all new. Shocked I said, "I thought it was a real house, but there are no windows and no lock on the door—just this rusty screen for half the wall!"

"Good point. I've gotten used to it," Ernesto said. "Padre Eduardo, the first padre here, built this house eleven years ago as the center of planning for the Proyecto Ixcán Grande cooperatives."

What an incredible feat it had been for formerly landless campesinos to own and farm their own land. It was a new frontier; there was plenty of excitement to build Centro Uno, the First Center or Belen, Bethlehem, the birthplace of the first village on the trail from Barillas to the Ixcán. Now, Ernesto and I were living in the place where it had all begun.

"So it never was a real house?"

"I guess not. But compared to everyone else's houses, or ranchos as they call them, this is really nice and we even have running water when it rains!"

The mahogany door in the middle of the main room was ajar, and I was surprised to find a bathroom complete with a mirror, sink, toilet and shower. The padres must have once had a generator and a pump to bring up water from the spring fed creek below the house, but now that was long gone—there wasn't even a shed where the pump may have sat. Looking in the mirror above the porcelain sink, I caught a glimpse of myself. My hair was stringy and limp with the humidity and my round wire glasses were steamed up. I felt uncertain and tired but a thrum of excitement spurred me on even in this small, strange village in a house with no electricity and no running water. I took off my glasses and wiped them on my T-shirt, took a deep breath and pulled my shoulders back watching my reflection morph as I raised an eyebrow and laughed. I reached down automatically to turn on the faucet, but there was not even a drop of water. A waterless bathroom! I caught sight of a cockroach sitting on Ernesto's toothbrush as though awaiting my tooth brush to savor. The insects prevailed here. I would soon learn there was no fearful scurrying; lethargy in the humid heat and their sheer numbers gave them authority.

I plopped down on one of the two bunks that were covered with rough seersucker sheets tucked in the thin mattress above metal frames that were used as couches and guest beds for visitors. The sharp smell of mold permeated everything. Exhausted and unrefreshed, I would have given anything for a cold glass of water, or even better, a Hercules Flip, frozen strawberries and buttermilk from the health food store in Santa Barbara. But there was no refrigeration, nothing cold and certainly no hope for a Flip. "Where is the health food store and the food co-op?" I joked as I flopped down on the bunk.

Then, the house was overrun by children, giggling and exclaiming. Pushing and shoving, they forced their way into the house with so much excitement it was hard not to laugh with them. "¿Qué es esto?" What is this Don Ernesto? "¿Cómo se llama?" What is your name? "Lesley" didn't work; it was impossible to pronounce. But my middle name Lucinda was perfecto. I became Doña Lucinda. As they helped unpack our books and the food from the market in Guatemala City, I began to relax. Although I couldn't understand everything they said, their joy was infectious. Soon enough they had ripped through my belongings, and turned their focus on me. Laughing with them, I quickly forgot the lack of amenities.

Eventually, I needed a few minutes to take it all in and said in broken Spanish, "Hasta mañana en el mercado voy a vender." "See you tomorrow at the market, I will come down to sell." Ernesto had somehow convinced me that selling at the market would be a great way to meet the community. He and Larry had been selling at the Sunday market to introduce vegetables to the pueblo.

Spanish was a second language for all of us; Mam was their first language, so we all muddled through my broken Spanish, and the children eventually skipped off with a bright, "¡Adiós, adiós, adiós, hasta mañana!"

As they left, I walked out to look at my surroundings. A large concrete platform that had housed another of the Maryknoll priests stood to the side of the house, facing the valley and the mountains beyond. Since everything rotted quickly in the high humidity and the 200 inches of annual rainfall, just a concrete slab broken by vining plants and thick grasses remained of the house. It was as though the house had dissolved. Next to it and in a grove of mandarinas, tart orange-like citrus fruit, sat a small house that was used by the co-op as a meeting place. Since it was still in use, it was maintained. Eventually a teacher would move in and live there, bringing with him his guitar and songs, both triste and alegre. This small compound stood at the farthest edge of the village between the trail head leading to the pista and the creek below and a trail that arrived at the Sunday market stand.

Behind the house and to the east was la hortaliza, the vegetable garden. Ernest and Larry had worked hard to organize the garden with pathways and four-foot-wide garden beds thoroughly planted with bright-green fresh mustard, blue-green radish leaves, and then some sunburned and shriveled plants that were unrecognizable. Another tall, broad rubber tree shaded a large compost pile beneath its large-leafed branches.

The church and school sat between the garden and the center of the village and our neighbors, Tomás and Pabla's house. The open-sided rock and corrugated asbestos-roofed building, about 40 feet square, served both functions—school during the week when there was a teacher and church, when a priest would come. Depending on use, the children or parishioners sat in rows on rough-hewn mahogany benches, worn smooth with years of use. I wondered if this is where Padre Eduardo had been killed by the fallen tree.

We couldn't have known it then as we looked at the canopy and imagined Sunday church services, but the padres would no longer come. It was as Father Ron had said: we would be without support, physical or spiritual. The spiritual didn't bother me since I wasn't religious, but the physical was incredibly challenging. Sometimes I couldn't draw a breath; the humidity was so high I felt under water. The remoteness, even with the activity of my first day, started to sink in as I stared at the narrow path to the small cluster of village houses in the distance. The separation of our house from the village proper increased this sense of isolation.

The closest communication was the two-way radio in Mayalan, an eight-and-a-half-kilometer walk, a trek between three and six hours, depending on the weather. The trail led from Centro Uno, winding through the low hills to pass through Segundo Centro and Tercero Centro, a short trail off to the east, to finally arrive in Mayalan. Once in Mayalan, if the weather was bad, the radio often didn't connect and the planes didn't fly. If the radio didn't work you were even farther from the end of the road at Barillas and deeper in the jungle. If an accident or an emergency occurred, there was little hope for survival. The closest clinic, staffed by a young and enthusiastic medic, was also in Mayalan and only open when he wasn't working his crops. None of this worried me; although when I was 17, I had been very sick with toxic shock syndrome, I was otherwise healthy and strong and in that phase of youth when I viewed myself as invincible.

The children left and the garden beckoned. The tiny lath house was packed with seed flats and seedlings and the beds were laid out with a formality that was central to the French Intensive/ Biodynamic method. The beauty of the regularity of the beds brimming with greens was striking. I could see how, even in this short period of time, Ernesto and Larry had created a productive and organized garden that could supply produce for the market, and a few greens for us. Looping the garden Ernesto pointed out the successes and failures, like the tomatoes, limp and discolored. We talked about the importance of keeping track of planting and transplanting and harvesting and of course, the weather. The little journal on the desk at the front of the house was essential and we walked back to the house, pausing to look at the garden in the gathering dusk to write, Ernest and I arrived, Larry left for Huehue with guy.

That first night I was surprised how quickly darkness descended. It was as though a light switch had been turned off, dark all at once. I lit the two kerosene lanterns and a brighter lamp, the Aladdin. Dimly illuminating the interior, the flames attracted four-to five-inch flying cockroaches, which Ernesto called avionetas, little airplanes, that flew and crashed into the lamps, walls and the screens. Equally large speckled moths burned the edges of their wings to a frayed scallop as they dashed against the glass chimneys.

I am not sure whether the sounds of the jungle were actually greater at night or if it was the combination of human silence and nocturnal animal activity, but all sounds were amplified, including the tree frogs in the tank. After blowing out the lamps, the house descended into pitch darkness. I climbed up onto the platform bed lifted high above the concrete floor on wooden posts to keep snakes from climbing into the bed, slid into the damp, coarse sheets, and laid my head on the hard foam pillow reeking of mold. A slight breeze drifted through the high screen, a relief from the oppressive day's heat, and I lit candles on the windowsill. In the flickering light I took in the room, wondering what my life would hold. I turned to Ernesto, propping my head on my hand and said, "When you wrote about the incredible beauty and the children, I thought you were exaggerating. I've never seen a place like this, and you never know, I may even learn to like children!"

The next day was Market Day, and I kept my promise to the children. Ernesto and Larry had a bumper crop of radish greens and mustard greens. The radish bulbs didn't grow as well as hopped, but the greens flourished, providing an excellent source of iron added to the stark daily diet of black beans and thick four-inch tortillas for breakfast, lunch and dinner.

Given Ernesto's direction and thinking nothing of it, I made my way alone down the muddy narrow path toward the main stall built of tree branches and cane. He decided to stay at the house in case anyone came by the garden. I had no idea that I would be the main attraction as I carried the bright pink plastic tub down to the small festive market, outdoing the ox head hung with a heavy rusty hook from the main beam of the single thatched market stall.

The stench of putrefying meat in the heat hit me first. The ox's glazed eyes were covered with shiny blue flies. The head was important, I would learn, so whomever was buying meat could look at it and see that it was a healthy ox. Large quarters were also hung on steel meat hooks off the beam over a rough wooden table that served as the cutting board and sales counter.

Other vendors set up on the ground around the main stall with their wares spread out in front of them on hand-woven colorful manteles. A Ladina, a Spanish speaker, not an indigenous Maya woman, sat behind a hand-woven basket with small round breads and fresh unpasteurized milk in used glass bottles with corn cob stoppers. A child in Todos Santos traje sat next to her with a basket of eggs wrapped in cornhusks and tied with thin strings of husk to protect the eggs from breaking. Eggs were precious and sold individually, not by the dozen.

The village women were all wearing their Todos Santos huipiles and the men their hand-woven shirts or camisas with long patterned collars reminiscent of the women's huipiles and some wore the red and white striped pantalones. The villagers selling or visiting the market from Segundo Centro wore Ixtahuacán traje from their original village of Ixtahuacán. I thought that this must be their Sunday best but soon realized that they wove daily and wore only their hand loomed traje as did all the women in Centro Uno.

I sat down in the thick bladed recently cut grass, placed my pink round plastic dishpan mounded with radish greens in front of me, and was immediately mobbed. Everyone wanted to touch me, particularly my hair, talk to me, buy my radish greens, and some wanted seeds as well. My rudimentary Spanish was lost in the panic and I clearly didn't speak Mam, so we pantomimed. One woman demanded, "¡Quéro todo!", "I want it all," but I had to defer to the other ten women in line who started arguing in Mam. I sold out in minutes, struggled to my feet and was followed back to the house by a crowd of men, women and children, eager to figure out who I was and, more importantly, to buy more radish and mustard greens. Ernesto and Larry had set up an improvised sales counter for selling or giving away seeds and dispensing information on the hortaliza right inside the door to the house. The seeds that we had just brought in from the city went quickly, but the main interest was not in sowing their own but in buying vegetables from the garden.

The hortaliza was the center of interest mainly for people from other pueblos and particularly on Market Day. The fifteen local families had all been living in the village for eleven years and were both very successful and somewhat jaded about the potential of yet another group of do-gooders. Ernesto said, "Initially everyone ignored us, they thought we were here to stay for a week or two, dropped off by plane and picked up by plane with no intention of staying long term. But with the crash and our decision to stay, we're no longer just passing through."

The grass runway and the planes had made Centro Uno relatively easy to access. Volunteers and people interested in the progressive development landed there first. The fifteen families from Todos Santos were very formal and their history and culture was insular, so although the children were friendly and outgoing, their parents were not open or effusive. Given the previous comings and goings of the padres and volunteers, it was easy to understand that forging friendships didn't make sense since people regularly left. They focused their energies on their family and the overall community. The one Ladino family in town that rented space, however, was friendly and open. Demetria and her daughter came by and invited us immediately upon my arrival.

The next day we went "downtown" to their comedor for lunch, where I was to be introduced to some of the families living there. Chickens pecked at the masa, puppies and piglets rooted under the table, and the children did their best to get themselves and everything else filthy. Ernesto and I were sitting and eating the standard black beans and tortillas when a tiny boy toddled by with a huge distended stomach and began urinating and picking his nose. I said, "¡Ay Dios!" and everyone laughed.

Someone pointed at me and asked, "¿Ella es enfermera o trabaja con la iglesia?" I was not a nurse, and I didn't work with the church, so I wasn't sure how to explain my role.

When we walked back to the house, I said to Ernesto, "It's really odd to be working in a place where everyone is religious except us."

Ernesto said, "Yea, and neither one of us has the slightest knowledge about church or the Bible."

I nodded. "I never really thought about it, but it's true. My parents never wanted to go to church, so I went two days to Sunday school but that was it. Will it make a difference?"

Ernesto laughed. "¡Saber!" To know, or in this case, who knows, was the standard answer for any question.

We had no real end game other than helping the villagers grow vegetables organically. Vegetables were the most important thing, and we gradually adapted the program to the environment.

Ernesto and Larry had already been there for four months when I arrived, and shared the horror and sadness of the plane crash with the community, which embraced them in mutual sorrow. They initially had been viewed like the young pilots who had frequently lived in the house, as temporary visitors who came and went. Once I joined Ernesto, he was viewed differently: we were seen as a family. I would soon come to learn that living as a family here meant acceptance. The longer we stayed, the more trust grew, and the more we became part of the community.

# CHAPTER 8

The neighbor women rose every day from the family bed at 4 a.m. to start the cooking fires. I smelled burning kindling and the morning fires before I could see them, and then at daybreak, the smoke hovered over the village down the trail from my house. Depending on the day and wood type, the smoke would nestle over the village like a white cloud or dance with wispy blue gray fingers between the trees.

The fire was built on a waist-high timber table that served as a stove. If there was no fire, there would be no breakfast. I asked Demetria how to cook black beans and got a quick lesson. I had started a pot of beans for breakfast at 7 a.m. on the sputtering gas hotplate and they weren't ready until almost noon. I realized that my day would also have to start much earlier, perhaps 4:30 a.m.

Dressing was simple for the Todos Santos women in Centro Uno. Wearing a long single piece of heavy blue cotton with the narrow characteristic white stripe of the Todos Santos, a corte, skirt, was wrapped tightly around their hips and secured over a unique red and white striped huipil that each woman had woven. It was held in place with a wide red wool belt. Their cortes and belts, imported from the Cuchumatanes mountain town of Todos los Santos, were just like what their great-grandmothers, grandmothers, mothers and now their daughters wore. They dressed for the day early and plaited their long hair into two braids tied together with a fresh ribbon at the braid ends, a classic and centuries' old style. They kept their hair in braids from their first year of life, so they rarely cut or trimmed their hair.

Cooking was laborious and there were no shortcuts. The black beans took a minimum of two hours to cook after soaking due to the unpredictability of the fire. Dried light-yellow corn kernels were mixed with lime and soaked overnight for nixtamal, the softened corn for the small, thick tortillas. The nixtamal was ground in a metal hand cranked mill and then finished with a metate, formed into tortillas and toasted on a comal over the open fire. Tiny, quarter-inch red chilies were soaked in lemon, water, and salt and set in a small bowl to marinate. Smoke from the wood cooking fires hung in the house on a wet day but filtered through the blackened thatch when the sun came out and a breeze picked up.

Without refrigeration in the thick, hot humidity, the beans rapidly rotted, becoming fetid and inedible in just a few hours. Continual cooking, from before dawn to after dusk, and preparing the nixtamal for the following morning was the rhythm of survival. I had burned the beans so many times, or we hadn't eaten them fast enough and had to toss them on the compost pile, that I was thankful that my life did not completely depend on this daily rhythm. Although we cooked beans and our vegetables, we bought hot tortillas from either Elena or Demetria daily. For the families, one misstep and they could go hungry.

There was no running water and no water close by. In synchrony with the cooking, water was collected at daybreak at the pozo, a small spring a quarter mile away, and carried in bright pink, yellow and blue plastic ollas on rag ring cushions atop the women's and children's heads. Boiling drinking water was a necessity: the blue and white speckled enamel pot sat above the fire filled with sweetened watery coffee that the entire family drank all day long. We were lucky during the rainy months to collect water on our roof and store it in the tank, but in the dry months, we too went to the pozo.

Un-occupied for at least 600 years, nature had completely taken over following the mysterious disappearance of the indigenous Maya lowland population. While digging in the garden, I surmised that the house was built on an old Maya ruin, as I discovered obsidian shaped arrow points, chunks of odd green glazed pottery, and red clay pottery feet from centuries before.

The hot, humid jungle floor received more than 200 inches of rain a year, a perfect habitat for the malarial mosquito, yellow fever, the barba amarilla or fer-de-lance, the coral snake, bright green tree vipers, and continual jungle rot, where a small scratch rapidly became a raging skin infection. It could not have been more different from the chill bareness of the highlands and for me, from my comfortable existence back in the United States.

Creating a vegetable garden was also a struggle. The daily temperature ranged in the low 90's to 100's with 80 to 90% humidity and rain almost every day. Our time to work in the garden was limited from daybreak to the early morning hours and late afternoons. The hours from 10:30 am to 3:30 pm were off limits, which I found out when I came down with heatstroke my second month.

During the first week, I was harvesting the radish greens and doing some watering but missed the sensual feeling of the soil in my hands and under my feet, so I went out into the garden. I dug both hands deep into the soil of the raised, mounded vegetable bed, hoping to recapture the soft moist texture and scent of a well-composted garden bed. Small black ants immediately rushed to my fingers, ran up my arms and started stinging furiously. I yanked my hands out of the dirt, jumped up and hit the lemon tree branch above my head knocking fire ants onto my bare sweaty back and shoulders. Sticking to the sweat, they stung repeatedly, like multiple cigarette burns. I screamed in pain and Ernesto came running out of the house. "What's wrong?"

"Red ants!" I yelled trying to brush them off. But that didn't work—I could only pick individual ants off.

"Well, I am glad it wasn't a snake. Just be careful putting your hands in the soil!" he said as he went back in the house. I followed him and retreated to the safe mildewed cot, my skin still burning and a few ants with incisors still attached pumping in venom, my foray into the garden aborted. This was not the soil that I was used to. There was nothing magical and spiritual about it, alive with all manner of creatures from ants to nematodes and the unknown.

As if stinging ants weren't alarming enough, small striped coral snakes hid by the rock at the corner of the garden in an intertwined pile, their orange and black stripes woven together like a colorful basket. They weren't too dangerous because although highly venomous, their tiny heads and teeth would have to grip the skin and chew for a while, so I viewed them as cute but deadly in that order. On the other hand, the cantil, a mini rattlesnake that usually concealed itself behind the wood pile, was a version of the pit viper rattler in California, just smaller, more aggressive and ubiquitous. At one point I was surprised by a cantil as I squatted by a garden bed. Usually, I made sure that the garden was clear of snakes before I started weeding. This time I had somehow missed it. Surprised, panic overtook me. I grabbed a rake nearby and beat it to death and beyond until it was an unrecognizable bloody pulp. I stopped, stepped back with my heart racing and looked with horror at what I had done. How did fear turn into such vicious anger? Gradually the continual fear of my immediate environment had morphed into a heightened awareness that prompted a fight or flight reaction to everything. The awareness became visceral, humming throughout my body and mind day and night and stayed with me.

In addition to snakes slithering and insects crawling and hiding beneath leaves and branches on the ground in the garden, I always needed to look up above me into the citrus tree to see if the bright lime-green Guatemalan palm pit viper happened to be wrapped around a branch. Highly venomous and hard to see with excellent camouflage, it was the same color as the lime-green leaves. We pruned the lemon away from the screen windows as it was a rather flimsy separation between restful sleep and death in an hour or so. Vigilance was imperative.

While biting ants and venomous snakes made sense to fear, the first time I saw a soft looking fluffy caterpillar meandering along a branch,

I was enchanted and reached out. I admired the beautiful spiky white and green hair, assuming it was not unlike the soft black caterpillars that I used to capture and watch pupate as a child. Instead, it stung my hand repeatedly, marking my palm with raised purple tracks running from one side to the other.

In my third week I took on an additional role that I was not prepared for. The community assumed that I, a white woman, must certainly be a nurse even though I told everyone that I wasn't. I had no training in nursing and, more importantly, was not particularly adept at ministering to anyone, especially the sick or children. I was trained as an agronomist. At home, I had never babysat or been around small children, nor had I felt the absence of such experiences to be a loss.

Mariano was one of three brothers who had migrated to Centro Uno as a young family when it was first settled. He was the first person who came to our house expecting me to have a level of medical competence that I clearly lacked. He cried, "Hay que venir a mi casa inmedíatamente mi hijo, Eric, está muy enfermo y no está tomando leche." I had to come to his house immediately to help; the baby would not nurse. The urgency in his voice when he spoke of his sick child was unmistakable even though my Spanish was still limited. I had never held a baby, much less helped nurse one to health.

"I'll come to your house soon," I told him.

Meanwhile Ernesto and I pulled out the *Donde No Hay Doctor* paperback and the *Merck* manual and went to work trying to determine how we could help.

*Donde No Hay Doctor, Where There is No Doctor,* suggested feeding the baby sterilized sugar water to help with rehydration. Having learned this, I walked hesitantly down the trail and through the empty market toward Mariano's home, rancho. The one-room house was built of cane walls bound together vertically and topped with a thatched roof of thick-leafed grass.

Children were waiting for us outside when we arrived. Three- and four-year-olds were caring for infants, carrying them on their backs like little mothers. We were invited in by Mariano but the women were reserved and did not welcome us. I was so unsure of myself I could understand their hesitancy—how could this young woman who had no children possibly help? I was sure they could feel my lack of experience.

Ernesto and I entered Mariano's rancho, stepping carefully from the rough dirt outside to the swept and compacted dirt floor. We uttered the polite, "Con permiso." The room held the raised fire, a table and the large family bed, which consisted of a wooden platform that was wide enough for the whole family to sleep together. Mariano's wife and several of the other village women were gathered in the corner surrounding the baby. The infant cried softly, his skin hanging loosely on his arms. His mother kept him at a distance from me, speaking softly in Mam to the others. Mariano, changing from Spanish spoke to them sharply in Mam. I thought he was telling them that I was there to heal the baby.

I tried to assume the role of woman and healer. I had practiced a sort of grounding when I was nervous or under stress—I now inhaled deeply in an effort to dispel my anxiety. I then felt sort of okay and reached out and offered to hold the baby boy. I felt my only hope was to ask for guidance from somewhere—where that might be was not at all apparent. The baby's mother reluctantly placed him in my arms, and I focused my mind and body on him. The feeling came to me that the baby might have a blockage in his intestines. I focused deeply on the blockage, trying to turn it into a green healing field, an image that I had only recently learned about in a healing class in Santa Barbara.

I handed Eric back and recited the *Donde No Hay Doctor* recommendations of sterilized water with sugar on a spoon twice every 15 minutes to hydrate the body. Since his wife averted her eyes and shook her head, I was concerned that she still didn't trust my involvement. I showed Mariano how to sterilize the spoon by putting it into the fire, boil the water for five minutes and gently spoon the sugar water into the baby's slack lips. I then gave the baby back to his mother, and Ernesto and I went home and fell into a deep sleep.

Dreaming I saw the baby, now a boy, running and jumping, leading other children down the trail. Several days later Mariano returned and told us, "Eric, está bien, usted hizo la cura." He said that I had cured his son and that he was very grateful to me. He told me that he would do anything he could to help Ernesto and me in our work with the village and community. This proved to be a small foothold into the closed, traditional Mam-speaking women's lives as I gradually became part of the village.

My naïve vision quickly shifted from wiling away my days planting a lush tropical organic vegetable garden and feeding the masses to realizing how fragile we were and just surviving was all we could hope for.

# CHAPTER 9

Excerpt from the Hortaliza Anna Garden Journal-March 1977

We had not seen Larry since he'd left on Guy's plane and hadn't thought much about visiting Mayalan until we heard from a family on their way out of Ixcán that they'd just seen him. Ernesto suggested a hike to Mayalan to check on him and see how he was doing.

I had yet to walk or hike much as I was still adjusting to the heat and humidity but a change in our routine sounded fun.

The village was surrounded by a towering virgin rainforest that very few people have or will ever see, dense with huge ceiba, breadfruit or ramon nut and 250-foot majestic mahogany trees. Demetria had pointed out the trail from the front of her comedor the previous week, a thin line of dark-red sinuous mud that was obscured by the shadow of tall trees. It was the same trail that the runner had taken to find Ernesto and Larry after the crash.

Starting out early, we hoped to avoid the strongest heat of the day and made our way through the short stiff grass of the market to the trailhead. Even so, the humidity had started to rise and sweat was already making my back damp beneath my knapsack.

Once on the trail I was as enchanted as if I had just stepped into the glass conservatory at Golden Gate Park in San Francisco. The tree branches reaching to the sky were draped with bromeliads, ferns with their fronds tightly furled and tiny white orchid flowers. Creating its own moisture, the forest dripped and where the trail had been cut, leaf mold steamed. Large evergreen leaves stretched to umbrella over the path, shading and softening the ferocity of the sun and dampening the sound of the rain that had just started to fall.

Pausing to look up, I called out to Ernesto, "Look, a begonia up at the top by that huge fern. I've never seen a begonia growing without soil!" As he moved down the trail I pointed out epiphytic orchids and bromeliads all over the branches, a horticulturist's paradise.

With the continual rain, and insects and birds fertilizing them, the wild houseplants had multiplied and flourished, magically balancing on twigs high above the forest floor.

He called back, "We have a long hike, you need to stop looking and walk!"

Where the trail wound through a small hamlet, an aldea, the tree canopy had been felled, and fifteen-foot cane with razor sharp leaves made the sides of the trail impenetrable to passage. The rain ceased for a moment and in the uncovered space the heat blazed down like a furnace. Children ran out from a smattering of small cane houses surrounded by barren red soil and gawked as we passed. We all shared the polite, "¡Adiós, adiós, adiós!" both hello and goodbye. As we left the aldea we transitioned back into dark cool shade but the humidity remained thick.

Aerial roots as thick as fire hoses dropped from high branches where they captured water, channeling it into puddles that the roots of other large trees had woven into dense baskets spanning the trail. Strangler figs wound up into the canopy hundreds of feet in the air and wrapped tightly around tall thin trees. Deep puddles formed in the root baskets hiding deeper mud beneath. The hooves of horses and mules, heavily laden with supplies, slipped and sunk into the muck, churning it to slop.

Rotting plants, leaves, flowers and wood combined to make a heady earthy scent a bit like mushrooms but also reminiscent of greenhouses I had worked in to support myself at school. I stopped and closed my eyes for a second, breathing in, not believing what I was seeing and smelling.

Ernesto relayed that in the eleven years since the first trail and pista were carved into the forest, the residents had made just a dent in the rainforest and jungle understory. Campesinos used axes and the big toothed two-man saws to clear the forest and make room for planting coffee, cardamom and corn and beans. As families moved in across the Ixcán and beyond the confines of the co-op, they felled the large ancient forest trees more quickly, but with basic hand tools the impact was gradual. Smoke rose from the fires of this slash and burn and was caught creating a hazy brown inversion layer hovering just above the trees. Sometimes it was hard to see blue sky for weeks with all the smoke from the continual burning. But for this first walk, the sky was a clear deep blue.

Yet uncertainty was deeply interlaced with the beauty of the forest. Life-threatening sounds presaged danger around any corner—a rustle from above followed by a faint slap meant a snake dropping to the jungle floor. The challenge was to accurately calculate the location of these and the innumerable other sounds that might be a sign of extreme danger. A move to the right to avoid the shower of red ants might push me toward a caterpillar magnificent and soft with stinging hairs. Due to this constant vigilance, that initial feeling of managed awe gave way to fear as the unrelenting jungle surrounded us. Every once in a while, the deep rich scent of rot was broken by the perfume of a sweet flower. I even discovered a new plant blooming to the side of the trail whose flowers looked just like the red waxed lips I had gotten at the candy store as a child.

This was no easy hiking. Stepping cautiously, balancing on roots, jumping over rocks, slipping and sliding, my rubber boots were frequently sucked off, the tops left gaping filled quickly with water and muck. My sweaty hands slipped off the shaft of my boots as I tried to yank them out of the mud. Wiping my hands on my pants I pulled hard and almost fell over backwards when the mud released them. Moving from trees and shade to open areas of sun, the heat burned and the humidity rose. Steam from the red clay trail lifted and swirled around my boots. The trail snaked up a steep hill, large rocks now replaced the smaller roots. I was limp with exhaustion after four hours.

"Are we close?" I asked Ernesto.

"Close? No, we're less than halfway there."

I dropped to a flat rock, let my knapsack fall and looked up to the top of the hill towering above us. Searching I found my now-empty water bottle shook it and turned it upside down and started to cry.

"I'm just kidding, it's over this rise," Ernesto said.

Too tired to be angry, I stood up, glared and then turned slowly in the direction of Mayalan, swung my knapsack over my shoulder and took a step.

Only four weeks before I had been gardening in temperate California. My enthusiasm dissolved. I was not acclimated to the jungle and wondered how I would ever acclimate and if I wanted to. I could only think that Ernesto had no idea of how spent I was and thought teasing would spur me on. I felt like giving up, but there was no way to escape the remoteness and the heat. I could not be magically transported. The only way was forward, one step at a time.

We finally reached the summit, and I looked out to see more rainforest and some areas of a lower, dense tangle of cane and dark green leaves. There was no evidence of civilization and no Mayalan in sight.

"Really, Mayalan is just beyond here," Ernesto said. I had no reason to believe him now and felt tricked into coming with him on this trek. Didn't he know it would take me time to adjust? I was a hiking virgin, and this was not even hiking, but a slow slog, pulling my boots up from the thick, steaming mud with each laborious step. All I knew was that I definitely did not want to be in the jungle when darkness dropped; we didn't even have flashlights.

I continued to move cautiously, slowly, weighed down by not knowing where I was on the trail. This feeling of forced movement and needing to push myself would stay with me for the two years we lived here, pressed in on by the anxiety of the lurking unknown.

As we climbed another rocky ridge, I gasped as a wide-open valley and the panorama of Mayalan finally came into view—a swath of open grass pista and a few larger buildings with lamina roofs. There was the co-op bodega, with the two-way radio, an open church and school building, a thatched clinic and maybe 100 tiny thatched cane dwellings. The sky was a deep, darkening blue, transitioning toward navy, and small, green-tinged clouds portended an afternoon rain to the south. A stream of sunlight hit the metal roof of the bodega, highlighting the size and illuminating the relatively populous settlement, quite a change from tiny Centro Uno.

Larry, tall and dirty blond, was easy to pick out. Even from high up on the trail we could see him way below us digging in the demonstration garden at the back of the padre's house by the pista. He saw us as we stumbled down the hill toward him, waved and let out a whoop. "Ernesto!"

I was so relieved to have arrived that I sobbed, "Larry!"

I had only talked with Larry in passing when I visited the Mesa Garden in Santa Barbara before he and Ernesto left to go to Ixcán and then a brief goodbye when he climbed into the plane to leave as I arrived in Centro Uno. I knew that he and Ernesto had little in common. Their relationship was strained by the time he pulled himself up into the plane destined for Huehue. But now, just to see another volunteer and someone who spoke English, was a cause for celebration. We took off our muddy boots and shuffled into the two-story wood plank house. It was much like our house in Centro Uno but a bit larger and had a working bathroom, all in all it was more "luxurious."

A group of children descended on the house as soon as they saw us. We went through introductions. "¿Somos Don Ernesto y Doña Lucinda y vivimos en Centro Uno, cómo se llama?" "¡José!" "¡David!" "¡Lazaro!" In a short time, we were no longer interesting and they dashed off. Larry asked a little girl who was peeking from behind a bush, "¿Tu mamá puede traer la cena?" Having not expected visitors, he asked the if the girl's mother at the local comedor could bring us beans and tortillas for dinner, and we settled in to talk. I sat on a cot by the door, massaging my feet, and now that I was a bit rested, I wondered why I had fallen apart on the hike.

We talked and talked about the challenges that the Ixcán co-ops were facing. As we did so, my shoulders dropped, my mind eased, and our conversation turned to the immediate concerns following the plane crash.

"How do we get in and out if there's an emergency?" I asked.

"I'm not sure since there are no other volunteers coming down," Larry said. "I didn't want to be alone, that was never my interest and now without Ann…the garden is growing well and people are very interested in learning to garden, but I may need to leave sooner. There's no way that I can be here by myself for two years. Also, I heard that the army is looking to set up a camp here because guerrilla activity has picked up."

What would Larry's return to the U.S. hold? Cold water, hot showers, something to eat other than beans, no mosquitoes? I had been in Ixcán for a bit over a month, and the U.S and California were already fading. Larry's leaving, though still months off, meant Ernesto and I would be the only volunteers. I hadn't realized how important having someone to share our thoughts and concerns was until we "dropped by."

We spent a hot, sleepless, mosquito-ridden night in the single wall plank house with ripped screen windows. The house was built for a short overnight stay, similar to ours. No one had ever lived there for a long period of time. I understood Larry's need to return; the loneliness must have been so depressing. At least Ernesto and I had each other.

In the morning, putting off the minimum six-hour return hike, we drank a cup of hot boiled coffee with sugar and cinnamon and bandied about the absurdity of what we were doing.

"I mean it's one thing being an evangelist for Christ but being evangelists for French Intensive/Biodynamic family gardens in the middle of the jungle where the entire population spends every waking minute struggling to survive is just exhausting," I said with a laugh.

Then, before I could really take in that thought, Ernesto joked, "Who came up with the idea of applying for a grant to bring hippie gardening to Ixcán jungle dwellers?"

"Ha...someone who has never lived in a jungle," I said. We all laughed. We were true believers in organic farming and not just organic farming, but French Intensive/Biodynamic gardening, and believed it would change the world by creating tightly packed small organic vegetable gardens with healthy food for families worldwide.

Larry said, "I haven't seen any guerrillas, but apparently, they are out there. The army is growing concerned about their increasing presence. What do you think the increase of army troops will look like here?"

"Probably just a few big tents and not much more since there isn't electricity or a road." Ernesto said. "I wouldn't worry about it."

We said goodbye to Larry a bit reluctantly the next day. The hike home went a bit faster as I recognized important milestones along the trek. A three-foot bright green iguana doing push-ups watched us from the large rock outcropping where I had sat down and burst into tears. Parrot flocks and toucans squawked loudly as they flew over us on their daily transit from the east side of the valley through the rainforest back to the ceiba by the Río Ixcán.

We stepped aside for about ten minutes while an entire herd of large-horned white cattle meandered down the single track. The vaquero wore a Led Zeppelin T-shirt that he must have gotten in the market in Huehuetenango, giving us a good laugh. I had just seen Led Zeppelin in concert in Santa Barbara a few months back and almost asked if he'd liked the concert. We then stepped to the side to let a string of men wearing two-inch thick leather mecopals, headbands with sisal ropes looped to support 100-pound bultas of corn, coffee and beans loaded on their backs pass us as they were walking more briskly than we were. We passed a few vendors walking in the other direction, one a hat vendor with 15 hats balanced on his head and another dangling 10 or 20 machetes from his waist.

Once the long string of people and animals passed, we looked at each other and Ernesto said, "That was quite the parade!"

"Well at least we didn't see any guerrillas or soldiers."

"Yes, but who knows anyone who passed us could be a guerrilla or a soldier how would we know?"

We turned toward Centro Uno and methodically followed the trail, slipping and sliding on our trip back home. But now, the danger wasn't just the snakes, red ants and caterpillars—after talking with Larry we knew that we had the army to contend with, and maybe the guerrillas as well. Two Americans, alone on the trail, were vulnerable. Either side could find fault with our presence. Surviving the trail, placing one foot in front of the other through the jungle, was foremost in my mind.

# CHAPTER 10

Our concerns about the military abated as the days developed a peaceful regularity. We'd get up before dawn, cook for the day, work in the garden, and then rest during the heat of the day, studying potential crop ideas and planning the garden or reading. We returned to the garden in the afternoon. The lack of distractions—of car motors running, honking, TV's and even radios—made our time together so much quieter and focused. Working together, brainstorming ideas on what we could do to improve our work and the garden and sharing our thoughts about the books that we read became our life. I hadn't realized how those continual distractions took so much of my attention. I also hadn't realized that I had been searching for community.

Never having gone to church or been part of a group had seemed just fine back in the U.S. But here, I came to look forward to the children arriving at the front door filled with questions and daily events to share. Waking up I could hardly wait to hear the sweet sound of, "¿Doña Lucinda, con permiso?" "May I come in?" I walked through the village visiting my neighbors and talking about the weather, the upcoming fiesta, how the corn was doing and more. A big part of the day was also devoted to laundry and bathing, and that was my best opportunity to connect with the women.

The Todo Santos women's hand-woven huipiles were much more durable than store-bought clothes and held up well to washing on the flat, slightly corrugated boards and rocks of the small creek below our house. Every day the women and girls would saunter by in full traje with bare feet or rubber flats, carrying large bundles wrapped in older and slightly frayed hand-woven manteles, tied tightly and balanced on their heads. They never failed to say, "Buenos días," in a long-drawn-out sing-song, so soft and friendly as they made their way down the rocky trail to the creek. As they reached the top of the trail, there was always the trailing, polite, "Adiós ..."

I purchased a washboard slab with the thought of joining in and learning how to wash our clothes in the creek. Time together washing clothes, washing our hair, bathing and relaxing and chatting sounded perfect—just what I needed, friends!

One morning as the daily group passed, I waved and said, "¡Voy a venir!" in a happy and confident tone. They all smiled, and Elena said, "Qué bueno, vamos a ensenarte." Elena said that she would teach me how to wash clothes. Teaching me proved to be much harder than any of us thought. It quickly became apparent that I lacked the coordination and strength required to slam the sopping wet clothes on the board rhythmically and wring at the same time. Laughing at me, they mimicked my pathetic attempt with warmth and humor, including me in the joke. We all cracked up. Clearly this was not something I would ever master. Given that Spanish, our mutual second language, was rudimentary at best, it was a hilarious discussion. I quickly exited with my own, "Adiós...."

After my washing debacle, I noticed that my washboard was frequently missing from its location to the right side of the front door. At first, I thought someone had taken it, but then it would return. One day I looked out to see Faustino's daughter, Chaya, swinging by and grabbing it as she trotted down to the creek.

I opened the door and she said, "Ayyy Doña Lucinda, I left my washboard at the creek, and it washed away. Now I am in trouble, so I have been borrowing yours since you are no good at washing clothes and don't need it."

I laughed because she was right. We worked out a deal and arranged a time for her to come by our house twice a week to pick up our clothes. She was just 13 and very excited about earning a little money, so she could buy ribbons and candy at Viviano's storefront.

She sang out, "¡Doña Lucinda, Buenos Diás! Aquí estoy!" laughing as she passed by and grabbed the clothes. She and her best friend Luisa, our neighbor Pabla's daughter, raced to see who could get down the rocky and muddy hill to the creek faster while balancing the ropa on their heads.

Chaya never just walked anywhere—she bounded. Her long braids were tied together with a big floppy bow at the bottom that bounced and swung with her energy. She was one of the oldest girls in the village and curious, asking me about the U.S. and just about everything else. Her younger sister, Francesca, at four years old, worshipped her and followed her around with her friend, Pepe.

At three and a half, Pepe was never without his baby brother Diego on his back, hanging in a sling of old hand-woven striped fabric. Diego was almost as big as Pepe and peeked around his brother's head, wanting to be part of whatever was happening. There was no such thing as babysitting; everyone in the family worked together in every task required to sustain their family and their lives.

Chaya's oldest sister had died of a snake bite when she was very little, so she was very cautious and worried about snakes, but that was about the only thing that she feared. Faustino didn't have much help working his parcela. His wife was busy all-day cooking and caring for the house and family, so Chaya, his eldest, helped him in the fields, fetched water and did laundry.

For the children, never having lived in Todos Santos, the cold, mist-covered peaks were just the stuff of stories their parents told them, reliving the lives of their ancestors in the frigid highlands. In Centro Uno, the day-to-day worries of snake bite, malaria, jungle rot and infection were balanced by the beauty of the jungle and the tranquility of isolation. Even with such differences, the traditions continued and all young girls learned how to weave. Chaya, Luisa and Julia, Elena's step daughter who was a bit older and didn't go to school, were all learning, and I would soon join them.

# CHAPTER 11

Excerpt from the Hortaliza Anna Garden Journal-May 1977

As the days passed, we became a greater part of the routines of the village. I had become an unexciting community member by the duration of time and experience. I had also finally acclimated to the heat and humidity.

Isolated in Centro Uno there was little news or visitors. So, when we heard that the President of Guatemala, Kjell Eugenio Laugerud Garcia, would come to Mayalan in mid-May 1977 we were intrigued—a presidential visit was a big deal.

Our neighbor Tomás told us that the Mayalan co-op was hoping the president's visit would bring more assistance to the farmers selling their crops. The bodegas in the five co-ops were bursting with unsold bultas of coffee and cardamom. Although it was approaching the dry season, the narrow trail and the cayuco passage not an option to move large quantities of agricultural products and it was hard to send out so much weight in Guy's small plane

We decided to hike to Mayalan for the festivities and visit Larry. The President didn't fly in everyday, so it was bound to be a fiesta.

Just as we were getting ready to go to Mayalan, the children arrived at the door and sang out, "Doña Lucinda ya viene un maestro para nuestra escuela." Doña Lucinda, a teacher will be coming soon for our school! Their anticipation was infectious—a teacher was coming to teach at the school and the ideas about what they were going to learn ranged from rockets to math to, "¿Talvez vamos a estudíar inglés?" "We will study English!"

I laughed. "And I will eventually understand Mam!"

The hike was easy, almost second nature this time, and I wondered why I had cried that first time just two months before. The towering trees afforded much welcome shade. The mud and rocks were still the same slippery mess, but my balance was better. My eyes adjusted to the darkness and colors, showing me nuances in subtle shades of dark green and browns that had been a blur before. The leaf litter sparkled with purple and orange petals showered from flowers above. I inhaled deeply, enjoying the rich scent of decomposition and taking the time to jump over leaves floating in the root basket pools and watch the hand sized bright blue butterflies' flit over tiny sweet-smelling flowers.

We caught a glimpse of the iguana basking on the flat rock at the halfway point. All of these main points on the trail gave me a sense of familiarity and progress. When we crested that last hill and saw

Mayalan, I expected to see the open field of the small pista, the lamina roof of the bodega, and the small ranchos, tiny houses, and a view for miles of thick deep green jungle.

Instead, a small military installation crowded the valley floor. I paused, shocked, and brought my hand up to wipe my forehead and clean my glasses. The rumble of a generator rose even above the buzzing of the cicadas. The formerly small grass pista had doubled in size and was ringed with fencing and barbed wire. The mowed green field held huge troop helicopters and a few smaller helicopters. Military troops parading army and air force personnel were mowing the pista with hand-push lawn mowers, and Todos Santeros, in their red and white striped pants, were leaning low to clear with machetes and hooked sticks.

Larry met us at the gate to the garden again, anticipating our arrival for the event since everyone in the Ixcán co-ops had shown up—Mayalan, Los Ángeles, Cuarto Pueblo, Xalbal, and La Unión. This time, even before we reached the bodega, he called out, "Hey, welcome, I knew you would come, long time no see! Can you believe this? This is crazy," gesturing to all of the people, co-op members and the army. In a lower voice he added, "This has all happened in the last two months. It's terrifying. I feel like I'm living in a military encampment."

We entered the gate and admired the garden's profusion. The tidy beds were bursting with mustard and other greens. He even had a few very large cucumbers.

Stepping through the doorway we pulled off our muddy rubber boots and set them outside and then padded in on the cool concrete to sit with our feet up on the homemade chairs. Larry said quietly, "They say that the Ejército Guerrillero de los Pobres (EGP) is stepping up activity and killed a soldier on the other side of the Ixcán in retaliation for Father Bill Woods' death. There's also a rumor of a gringa traveling with the EGP." My relaxation quickly shifted to shock. The only women in Ixcán were Maya women other than me and Christina. I was so much taller and although not fair clearly a gringa; there was no place to hide or blend in. How would the army know that I wasn't a guerrilla?

"We have to stay apolitical if we're going to be able to help here and survive," I said in an effort to not show my fear.

"A young Ladino finquero came by the garden on his way out of Ixcán for good last week. He'd gone to the city for a week and when he returned his house had been torched by the EGP," Ernesto added.

"I don't know what to do," Larry whispered. "Every day the number of troops and the flights in and out increase. They now have generators going at night—sometimes you can see them over there by the big army tents. You should see the masses of insects; light at night in the virgin jungle is ridiculous. The lights are almost obscured by those giant flying cockroaches."

Outside, everyone milled around, a sea of red and white traje and concerned conversations. The President was an hour late. Finally, we heard the engines of the plane in the distance before we could see the President's plane flying low over the southern mountains.

"That's an Arava," Ernesto said. "An Israeli-made plane designed for short landings and take off."

It dropped into the valley and flew toward us circling low and quickly landing. The props bellowing reversed and it slowed, taxiing to the far side of the pista by the military tents and barracks on the east side. President Laugerud and his entourage climbed down from the camouflaged guppy plane and marched across the field, pausing to shake hands as he walked. A platform had been set up by the bodega in the huge covered church space with hi-fi speakers and a microphone.

He started his speech with, "Somos amigos! We are your friends and the soldiers are your friends. We are here to help. Since there are fewer private planes, we will help you to fly all of your crops out temporarily on the Aravas. The Franja Transversal del Norte needs to be constructed with in the co-op boundaries so that the trucks can come through and you can sell your crops. That will allow for development and make sure that there is access."

"I don't think the intent of the road is to help them," I whispered to Ernesto. We knew by now that road was destined to help U.S. and

Canadian companies access oil reserves, lumber and minerals deep in Ixcán at the edge of the Mayan Biosphere, far from oversight.

A concerned rumbling rose from the crowd about this road being forced upon them. The main focus of the President's speech, that "the soldiers are our friends" was also unnerving, and we doubted anyone trusted it. It was a new spin. The co-ops were now required to check in with the army on all movement in and out, where they had previously been autonomous.

"Why are the soldiers growing in numbers?" I asked Ernest. "What was the focus on the soldiers being our friends?"

He shook his head. "I don't know, but it's going to force an increased dependence on the army and air force."

We were surprised to see our neighbor, Tomás, stand up on the podium with the President. Instead of demanding that the co-ops should be allowed to bring in more transportation on their own if they chose to and develop better avenues for communication with vendors, Tomás, who was the co-op president, and the other governing members, rallied support for the army.

"At least the army or air force could help transport people and crops in the short run," Tomás said.

"What choice do they have?" I said to Ernesto, "Given the incredible force and presence of the army."

With a flourish and a sonic boom, a squadron of fighter jets appeared in the sky, shooting over the ridge and the mountains, dropping down menacingly as if to strafe the pista. Back home, I'd felt a delighted kind of fear when the Blue Angels flew in formation on the Fourth of July at home, but that was for fun. This was terrifying; clearly the intent was to terrorize the community. Ernesto and I clutched each other closely.

Following this show of force, we were greeted personally by the President, "Gracias a ustedes por su trabajo ayudando la gente aquí." He thanked us for helping the people in Ixcán, shaking our hands as the La Nation reporter and photographer took a photo of us...Peritos agrónomos trabajando en Ixcán. Young American agronomists working in Ixcán. Walking back through the crowd, he crossed the pista and boarded the Arava, pausing to look back and wave.

Coronel Castillo, of the Guatemala air force, had also flown in with the President but stayed behind after the President left.

"Please join me for lunch at the local comedor," he said.

We couldn't say no, so we walked slowly to a tiny cane restaurant that Larry knew for black beans and tortillas. Coronel Castillo was excited about speaking English and told us, "I learned to fly and train at the School of the Americas, (a U.S. Department of Defense school at Fort Moore in Columbus, Georgia). We were taught in Spanish, but I had English classes too."

I was surprised to hear that the U.S. provided training for Latin American troops on U.S. soil. I hadn't heard of it at the time. "Most of the instructors were Americans and had Vietnam combat experience," he told us through mouthfuls of food.

I had to take this in—the Vietnam War had just ended and yet the tactics learned and practiced in such similar conditions were already being transferred to the steamy lowlands of northwestern Guatemala. Eventually army and air force officers were sent to Israel for additional training. But the U.S. base was initially the main training ground.

We talked about the U.S. and what he liked as well as a bit about the buildup and his interest in helping move the crops out to market. He was particularly interested in the co-op and shared, "I am working throughout Ixcán, not just in Ixcán Grande, but also in a new area that is being developed on the eastern side of the Ixcán valley, the Israelis are doing a lot with co-ops they are going to helps us."

As we said our goodbyes and walked back to Larry's house, we were both steeped in troubled thoughts. A black and white film of the war in Vietnam on the evening news ran a loop in my brain. The majestic jungle denuded, the tall trees scorched and bare, all the plants and animals incinerated, and the people fleeing while white bombs exploded in their wake.

"Vietnam couldn't happen here, could it?" I asked Ernesto. And then I thought of what we'd heard about "the guerrillas and the gringa" and the Melville's book and involuntarily ducked my head as if to avoid something falling.

Not long after this, Larry would also pack up and leave Mayalan, not just from loneliness but to escape the threatening military presence.

# CHAPTER 12

The children had told me about a teacher coming but given all of the military buildup and our lunch with Col. Castillo, I had forgotten. When we walked the trail from the village to our house at the end of the plateau, a young handsome man with a guitar sat on the stoop of the co-op house with a group of children clustered around his feet. Chaya and Luisa were the first to call out to us, "¡Mira aquí está el nuevo maestro!"—"Our new teacher is here!" Juan was not just the teacher, but our new neighbor too. In return for a government scholarship and loan, if teachers worked in the campo for a short period of time, their education was free, and here was Juan, fresh from his teacher training. As if by magic, the cooperative meeting house was transformed into the teachers' house, and he moved in next door with his guitar and lots of enthusiasm.

There had been no teacher for almost three years. The older children had been hiking for more than an hour each way to Segundo Centro to attend classes. Now they could stay in the village. Their parents were committed to making sure the children could go to school, as education was an opportunity for their children to succeed. Now even children who didn't make the trek to Segundo could study.

The community came together and cleaned the old school/church overhang, knocking down the cobwebs and a couple of birds' nests, removing a snake, raking the dirt floor and then compacting it with sprinkled water before brushing it with a broom made from bundled weeds. Under this open canopy, the children sat attentively in rows on the rough-hewn mahogany benches. The slate blackboard was mounted on a portable stand that Juan moved with the lesson turning it around to teach the older children on one side, the younger on the other.

The children's ages ranged from the oldest, 14-year-old Luisa, the daughter of our neighbors Tomás and Pabla, to the youngest, Pepe and Francesca, Chaya's sister. It was a challenge for Juan, but he was up for it and quickly became not just the teacher but an integral part of the community. He was from the village of Ixtahuacán and spoke a very similar dialect to the Mam spoken in Todos Santos, so he fit right in and could communicate easily with the families.

One day I mentioned something in Mam about the fire burning in the hearth at Elena's. "¡Hay Aacchg!" I pointed to the fire, "Look, fire!"

He replied, "That means bridge, or if you pronounce it this way, water." I realized that I was literally playing with fire, since minor changes in the guttural sounds could mean dangerously conflicting scenarios.

Juan had studied in Huehuetenango, a town of thousands rather than a village of fifteen families. Centro Uno lacked everything other than black beans, tortillas and enthusiastic children. In the late afternoon he would sit on the porch, break out his guitar and strum and sing the plaintive songs of the campo, of hardship and want. Having Juan live and teach next door enlivened our end of the village and made me feel more connected to the overall town. I also felt safer knowing he was nearby when Ernesto was on one of his many treks out to the city or across Ixcán teaching or bringing in new plants and seeds.

I soon realized that for a young single man, there wasn't much to hold him in the village on weekends or vacations. I knew when he put on his knapsack and slung his guitar over his shoulder that he was off on an adventure.

But when school was in session, there was nothing more beautiful than the sound of the children next door laughing and singing as we toiled in the garden. Chaya's voice was high above the others as she sang, bouncing on the balls of her feet while Juan played the guitar.

Juan was also a great teacher, I learned as I crouched over a vegetable bed, listening to his lessons. "Vamos a estudíar los verbos." I learned how to conjugate verbs with the littlest of children. "Vamos a probarlo otra vez, repitan después de mí." I would find myself repeating a sentence with the second graders. Then he would break out the guitar, and we would all join in.

Juan and the children decided to make their own garden one day as part of the curriculum, and they excitedly farmed two beds and learned how to make compost. The children's joy at learning everything new was inspiring given the simple classroom set up. Different from my compulsory elementary school, the lack of regular school pushed the students to want to learn. The oldest children taught the youngest. Luisa and Chaya, having studied before in Centro Dos were willing to help out. Juan thought that they would have mastered some skills, but Chaya said, "¡Ay Don Juan solo jugamos como Tarzan en los arboles!" Apparently, they did a lot of playing and swinging on the aerial roots dropping down from the trees, and not much learning.

Physical education was also a part of the curriculum, and both the boys and girls played games at recess, throwing the ball and running across the deep grass that stretched from our house to the market stall. The soccer field was down below the village on the alluvial plain by the river, too far to venture for recess, so they played a version of dodgeball outside our house.

One afternoon after a particularly rising game of keep away, Chaya was hit in the chest with a soccer ball. She seemed fine initially, just a bruise on her breast bone. She came by the front of the house and called, holding her side, "Doña Lucinda, no puedo lavar hoy pero tal vez mañana no lo siento bien—maybe I can come and wash tomorrow? I don't feel well today."

The next day the pain in her chest worsened. A few days later she was having a hard time breathing and began coughing up blood. Faustino ran to the house and called out, "¿Doña Lucinda, que vamos hacer? La niña está vomitando sangre." Ernest and I were shocked at how this seemingly small accident could lead to anything dangerous. I told him, "She needs to get to the hospital immediately."

We looked out to the pista deep with grass at least three feet tall and then at the sky clouding up. There would be no passage of the Río Ixcán, which was raging. The cayuco might have been able to cross with passengers but certainly not a horse. All communication had to go through Mayalan, a minimum five-hour minimum hike away. No one would fly in because the pista was so high anyway. This was the best option. Faustino wrapped her in a blanket and mounted his horse, holding her light body tightly and rode to Mayalan.

Tomás later reported to us that he had seen Faustino and Chaya waiting in Mayalan for two days for a plane to the hospital. Without money to stay he was only able to drop her off and return to Centro Uno, leaving Chaya in the hospital by herself. No one knew what was wrong but they believed that since she was in the hospital, she would be fine.

Several days later I heard a high-pitched scream of agony. It was Chaya's mother. Chaya's sister, Francesca, ran fast on her tiny three-year-old legs by my house, sobbing and choking as she called out, "Chaya, Chaya, Chaya."

Chaya died in the hospital all alone. My own chest ached as I imagined her lying there so far from her family. They always slept together in the same broad bed. Did she reach out in the night believing that her mother or sister would be there but find only emptiness instead? The hospital sounds so cold and mechanical, and the buzz of fluorescent lights continually lighting the rooms and hallways. I wondered if she thought about the deep darkness of her home, a place with no lights or noise other than nature, comforting and enveloping her. Could she imagine it and feel comforted? Her first huipil, half finished, her back-strap loom hanging next to her mother's?

It happened so quickly, none of us could accept it. She was so vivacious and silly. I had never experienced the death of someone close to me other than grandparents, and sadness enveloped me every day of her absence. My chest clenched with sorrow, and a sob rose to my throat every time I noticed the unused washboard by the door. Her joy and bounce were missing, and the whole tightly knit community was shocked how a simple game could result in tragedy. Death slithered by us on a daily basis…but a soccer ball? No one could believe it. Market Day was solemn, women whispered to each other softly in Mam, which I couldn't understand, but I knew that the sadness reminded so many of them of their own losses.

The fact that Chaya would not be buried in the small village grave-yard made her death even harder. It was as though she was not just gone but completely lost. There was no grave to visit on Día de los Muertos, no place to pray for her. Her father drank and screamed, sounds that came from a place deep within him. I remembered that first scream I made when I thought that Ernesto was dead and felt that loss and fear. Now Faustino was wracked with agony; he alternately screamed or wandered, unseeing of anyone or anything around him, ghostlike. Overcome with guilt and sadness all through the day, he drank into the night for at least a week. The strict alcohol abstinence policy of the community, part of the original agreement for the families to emigrate to Ixcán, was not enforced in his case. I had never heard the sound of such grief. To have lost two joyful children left an indelible mark on him, his sadness and loss palpable.

Chaya's absence in the small cane house left it empty and raw. Living and sleeping together in such close proximity seemed to meld families into a safe single unit, so different from the lone bedroom I'd grown up in. It was hard to imagine her warm and bouncing presence gone from that family bed. Worse, there was no way to survive in Ixcán without children to help out in the day-to-day act of survival.

Chaya's death prompted other mothers and family members to share with me how few of their children had survived. Elena told me, "Yo también perdí muchos niños, así es. Es triste." She too had lost children and only Julia and José, her stepchildren, and her son Manuel were alive. Every woman in Centro Uno had lost at least one child, but usually babies or very young children. Chaya's death meant that in the eleven years of having lived in Centro Uno, there was no magic age when a parent could sigh, "¡Ya está grande, gracias a Dios!"—"Thanks to God, my child has grown up." Those words meant nothing with so much danger and isolation.

# CHAPTER 13

Strong men's voices rising and falling in guttural Mam tones from the open church reminded me that the consensus-based cooperative meeting was in process. Meeting weekly, the village men addressed problems with crops and sales of cardamom and coffee as well as municipal issues. Following Chaya's death the men had given Faustino a pass since his grief was so extreme but at the weekly meeting it was decided that it was time for him to stop and follow the Community rule of no alcohol..

Sometimes the meetings would stretch for hours, late into the night. Consensus-building is very time intensive and requires listening to each person respectfully before mutually agreeing on a decision. The five co-ops all had large group meetings and the small villages and aldeas met but Tomás, was not just the Centro Uno President but the Mayalan Co-op President so he brought information from Mayalan and the other four co-ops to the meetings. He was not shy about using his power to influence decision making and frequently proceeded without conferring with the co-op members. It took him further and further away from the original shared focus that was the centerpiece of the weekly local co-op meetings and the integrity of co-operative thinking but, it was hard to know the true undercurrents; what the government was saying to him and how he could help move the co-ops goals for selling their products.

The villagers in Centro Uno had been extremely successful—their original plantings of coffee and cardamom were well established and productive. Tomás and Viviano raised beef cattle, and everyone had a milpa and grew their own black beans. The earliest landowners had received land on the banks of the Río Ixcán, and when the water receded, soft alluvial soil was deposited bearing nutrients and minerals perfect for multiple years of growing the sustenance of their lives corn, or the milpa.

Others, like Santiago, had found a niche managing the cayuco crossing from one side of the trail to the other, profiting from the only entrance to and from the Ixcán trail when the water was too high to ford. Viviano, Tomás and Nicholas had small storefront tiendas at the front of their houses. Viviano's tienda stood in the middle of the town right on the main trail and also offered tailoring (with a treadle sewing machine) and his son offered letter writing. Nicholas' tienda was far outside of town, the last of the Centro Uno homes before the trail meandered down to Centro Dos. His wife and young daughter sold bottled sodas and cookies and skeins of colorful hilo for weaving to those passing by from the open window with a small ledge.

Centro Uno also was the first place to stop and eat if coming from the highlands and the last place to rest and eat if leaving Ixcán. Elena's and Demetria's small comedores were continually busy with the co-op families and residents as well as new settlers and sellers, like the hat vendor, carrying all of his wares on his head. I loved sitting on the worn smooth mahogany bench at the table, holding a blue speckled metal cup of sweet coffee and listening to the talk of the trail.

Given the opportunity to farm their own land and create a community, "Todos Santos in Ixcán," they had done just that and so much more, given the challenges of taming the virgin landscape.

But life was precarious. Just before our first DID group had arrived in 1975, the El Tigre de Ixcán, owner of the Finca La Perla, was executed by the EGP, the Ejército Guerrillero de los Pobres, for his "crimes against the people." Left-wing guerrillas had risen in the early 1970's to provide "the landless poor," as they were called in the 1970's, with viable land. In this case, they'd risen to combat the blatant land grab of over 10,000 acres of land from indigenous Maya native lands by El Tigre, José Luis Arenas. The EGP held tribunals and asked people in the local pueblos on the east side of Ixcán how they were being treated. The people testified that they were not paid for their work and that the finquero had stolen their land, forcing them off it. Arenas's execution passed into history but was not forgotten by his sons nor the U.S.

But now in 1977, the new landowners had developed their linked tracts of land into thriving towns and pueblos, planting cash crops and creating a surprising vision of possibility with their ability to penetrate the vast rainforest and jungle with the simplest of tools. This was not lost on those who understood the underlying richness of the region. As time passed, more questions arose among wealthy landowners about why the Guatemalan government was involved with the original Ixcán project, Proyecto Ixcán. Others who were focused on land for the families who had migrated from the highlands, wondered what the army was protecting. Beneath the surface, community members whispered questions like: Why was Padre Guillermo killed? Will they steal our land? Do we have title?

The middle ground was shrinking. The army feared the villagers were assisting the guerrillas, and the guerrillas feared that the villagers were assisting the army, and no one actually cared about the Maya villagers. This was, sadly, nothing new—the indigenous Maya had been mistreated for centuries.

With Padre Guillermo gone, there was no consistent intermediary to navigate the new changes happening in Ixcán and help the co-ops stand up for their rights. It's only years later that I can see how the rising number of international companies and Guatemalan investors were speculating and buying up tracts of land along the periphery of Ixcán during that time were beginning their shift toward economic exploitation and removal of the co-op members' land. The Maya families were considered expendable.

The Guatemalan army's deployment to Mayalan and the cessation of any private flights effectively isolated the communities. Centro Uno was 20 miles from Barillas via the trail, so the use of mules to move crops to the highlands to sell was workable when the river was passable.

However, the central sales area for the co-op, Mayalan, and the towns deeper in Ixcán down the sinuous trail, were now held hostage by the army and air force as air transport in and out was curtailed.

In Centro Uno, however, still unaware of all that was unfolding, we took pleasure in the garden expanding. The dry season had given us some hope for tomatoes and other vegetables that would bring some variety and familiarity to the community and those who passed by. Vegetables that were from other countries, like Taiwan, weren't very popular even though they were high in nutrition. The mid-day sun was so hot that on a day in late July 1977 I decided to work in the late afternoon when the shadow from the vigorous rubber tree blanketed the top half of the garden. The play of light and darkness was enchanting as the last rays hit the flowers of the last blooming radishes that we were saving for seed.

I was at the edge of the garden madly hoeing the twining Kudzu that grew vigorously in the garden when I paused to watch the light purple flowers dance with light.

Out of the corner of my eye I thought I saw movement at the edge of the forest. I called, "Hey Ernesto, something big is moving in the trees!" Before I could call again, a platoon of Guatemalan army soldiers materialized on the trail by the house. In full camouflage with green and black face paint, eyes vacant and cold, and carrying machine guns, they silently surrounded the village, walking through quickly, searching ... and just as quickly and quietly they vanished into the jungle. I froze, clenching my hoe tightly, my breath so shallow it was almost non-existent.

Ernesto had been in the house sitting at the seed sorting and selling desk writing up the daily journal when he heard me call out. He quickly came out of the house to join me, I whispered, "It's as though they aren't human. The blankness of their stares and the silence ..."

"Where are they going?"

"I don't know, but by the look of their uniforms and camouflage, they are the Kaibiles, not just the regular army. Kaibiles were trained like the Green Berets. Elite and deadly. The book we'd gotten at the Penguin store talked about their brutality and how they were required to raise a puppy only to kill and eat it. I didn't think that could possibly be true but after seeing their blank stares, I revised my thoughts. "They must be following the guerrillas, the EGP."

We left all of our tools in the garden and tried to walk purposefully back to the safety of the screen house, pretending that it would somehow keep us free from danger. Any feeling of safety and ease I had been cultivating evaporated that day.

# CHAPTER 14

## June – September 1977

El Infrascrito Teniente Coronel de Aviacion DEMA,P.A.————
FERNANDO ALFONSO CASTILLO RAMIREZ, hace constar que los ————
Señores Ingenieros Agronomos ERNEST LE GRANDE COLE, JR.,————
LARRY MICHAEL SAWYER y la Señorita LESLEY LUCINDA MILES,————
———— estan prestando sus servicios como ASESORES AGRICOLAS, a ————
las Cooperativas de la Zona Reina "IXCAN", brindando sus conocimientos
en beneficio del desarrollo agricola y technico de dichas Cooperativas, el cual redunda en beneficio directo de nuestra Patria.————

Y para los efectos legales que a los interesados convengan, se ex-
tiende sella y firma la presente CERTIFICACION, en la Ciudad de ————
Guatemala a los veintiun dias del mes de Septiembre de mil nove-————
cientos setenta y siete.—————————————————————————————

CERTIFICA:

El Teniente Coronel de Av. DEMA,P.A.

FERNANDO ALFONSO CASTILLO R.

REGISTRO

Nº 189579

QUINQUENIO
de 1973 a 1977

Access to Proyecto Ixcán

Suspicion was intensifying among the community members and us. We all grew increasingly distrustful of the army and with no clear idea of the intent of the EGP it was hard to know which way to turn. For us there was an even greater lack of support from DID. Ernesto and Larry had been told that they would be getting a radio at Centro Uno in December of 1976. That had not materialized, and initially we thought it was just delayed due to the accident. Now, however, our letters to the DID head gardener Warren went unanswered and we still didn't have a response about the radio. We wrote, "What are we doing here? Why is no one responding to our questions?"

Our bi-weekly reports were met with odd comments, "It sounds like things are going well. And by the way there are no funds for a radio," or we received no response at all. We were especially vulnerable, as our house sat at the edge of the jungle far from the rest of the village, isolated and completely open to the elements and whoever wanted to hide in the darkness. Unable to even strike a match because the humidity had dissolved all the matches into a gooey mass, there was no option for light of any kind unless we lit the cooktop with a striker..

I lay awake as Ernesto slept, listening, always waiting, my heart racing, straining to see out of the screened window into the dark, and ready to flee. But there was nowhere to run. We were alone. As the day broke, the terror dissipated in the streams of sunlight that pierced the darkness and illuminated the valley.

In early summer we went to the city to get our visas renewed and Sr. Oriano told us, "I can't help you. DID is not paying my bills." Not paying the immigration attorney was a problem; it was near impossible to get a longer-term visa without the attorney's help.

Steve, the director, and Joe, the new program manager, denied our request for a horse to provide both emergency access (since we didn't have a radio) as well as a compost machine. In June of 1977 we started to question why we were still there at the inception of a military operation and not receiving any support for our fledgling home garden and health projects. After some reflection, we decided that given the overall lack of interest and support from DID, we would simply focus on helping the people and the co-ops in whatever way was needed to further agricultural and health sustainability. If that meant deviating from our specific direction to research and teach only French Intensive organic vegetable gardening, then that is what we would do. We had already dropped the Biodynamics since it was difficult to explain and practice so this was just another piece. It never occurred for us to leave and instead it opened up a new way of thinking that was central to both our curiosity and underlined our ability to move more freely in and out of Ixcán being relatively close to Barillas. We researched cash crops and reforestation and analyzed how in some cases small amounts of pesticides made the difference between losing an entire crop versus having food to eat. I was glad I had an understanding of pesticide use and toxicity from classes at Cal Poly.

Although we didn't personally subscribe to chemical use, it was hard to be overly critical to risk of losing a family garden convert when a new gardener wanted to use some chemicals. We focused on teaching about levels of pesticide toxicity and how to select those that were the least toxic for the environment and humans. However, we stressed that complete reliance on composting vs. chemical fertilizers was the only way to develop and maintain the soil fertility, with the intense rainfall and subsequent leaching of nutrients.

Ernesto took the lead in researching new ideas by traveling to the hot humid Costa to get new vegetable varieties initially from a Taiwanese based program, learning how to graft fruit trees, and eventually setting up a hardwood tree nursery. Traveling for days and often weeks due to the inability to easily return often left me alone in the house at the edge of the plateau.

Just as the rain came thundering in a defined curtain in the late afternoon, the night dropped in one piece. Softly and gradually candles and gas lamps illuminated the village. Far from the center, we were engulfed in thick moist darkness. Lighting the Aladdin lamp from the propane cooktop was the first step of night. It cast a soft glow, and then the avionetas would descend, banging into walls and the sides of the lamp. Candles were iffy as the avionetas driven to the light lit up and fried.

Flashlights and batteries rusted and failed within a few days. Years before, the padres had used a generator and ferried in gas by plane, but that was all in the past. Navigating the narrow trail to the village at night was a walk of trust. A feeble light created a trail through the weeds, enough to scan that it would be clear of snakes. At dark, hopefully they would be asleep in the weeds.

The sounds of insects and animals changed at night and became deeper and more all-enveloping but no less insistent. I was a tiny island surrounded by a sea of darkness amid the continual waves of night noises.

I lay awake listening. Without windows, just screens, no lock on the door and no one around, I lay thinking about how vulnerable I was and how the army or the guerrillas could just walk in and kill me. Exhausted, I eventually fell asleep in the early morning hours.

Isolated in the village, the women who spoke only Mam had kept to themselves when I first arrived but they gradually opened up over six months and now they wanted to chat. Even so, it was hard to have a more in-depth conversation since I still didn't speak Mam. I finally got a Mam dictionary, but the pronunciation was a challenge and invariably someone would teach me an inappropriate word to say and then everyone would laugh. I was frequently the butt of good-humored jokes, but I knew English and they didn't, so I told my friends, "Just wait, I'll teach you English, then you won't know what I'm teaching you to say!"

After numerous futile attempts asking the women if they wanted to plant a family garden, I finally realized that I was not going to be able to convince any of them. Instead, they said, "Doña Lucinda, you grow the vegetables, and I will buy them." I had somehow become a sharecropper.

The men were in the fields all day, cultivating black beans and corn or their cash crops for export, coffee and cardamom, so they had little time or interest. There were also animals to care for—cattle, pigs and chickens—and their care fell on the entire family. Even so there were a few men and a younger boy very interested in vegetable gardening. In most families a small family garden was considered women's work, but the women were busy everyday cooking for survival, taking care of the children, and weaving the family's clothing. There was very little time to garden. With Ernesto gone so much, I spent more time visiting and "eating out."

Elena and Santiago Cruz lived right in the middle of the village on the trail. I first saw Elena balancing a magenta and white striped olla filled with water from the pozo on her head as she elegantly floated above the mud and bunchgrass. Completely put together, her expertly woven huipil was creative with a nuanced design that was out of the ordinary, and her navy blue corte, with the thin white stripe tightly wrapped around her hips, was held in place with the wide red wool belt of Todos Santos. A bit taller and slimmer than most of my neighbors, initially I thought she was reserved, maybe even a bit standoffish. Unlike the other women in the village, Elena spoke Spanish although not fluently.

Elena not only cooked for her family but also ran a comedor, an extension of her home kitchen, taking advantage of the increasing number of campesinos passing through, some days seventy-five people on the trail. The large kitchen table seated up to eight with roughhewn benches on the long sides and two handmade wooden chairs at the ends. The floor was swept compacted dirt, each day sprinkled with water, brushed and re-compacted to a firm non-dusty surface.

I gravitated to her small comedor in hopes of meeting the women in the village since I didn't speak Mam, and gradually we became friends.

Santiago's business, taking people and their belongings across the Río Ixcán in his cayuco, was not only very lucrative by Ixcán standards but also provided the first contact with the Ixcán region from the highland town of Barillas. It also gave him the opportunity to say, "Mi esposa es la dueña del comedor allí en el pueblo."—"My wife owns the comedor in the village."

When I was alone, Elena's kitchen was a place where I could relax and chat. Hers was the only comedor after Demetria and her family moved to another village so it was also the only place to get tortillas and beans. It was so comfortable to sit on the worn bench holding a cup of sweet coffee and be among friends. When Ernesto came home, the comedor was the first stop where we shared ideas and thoughts about future crops that he had brought in and what was happening in the overall Ixcán.

Travelers stopped by briefly for lunch or dinner on the long trail. The stories at the table were of hardship in leaving highland pueblos with no hope of survival. The Ixcán co-ops provided a new frontier and the families in Centro Uno provided proof that migrants too could leave their village in the highlands with only what they carried on their backs, to start over and carve a new life for their family. But there was a significant difference—the people in Centro Uno had been vetted as part of the co-op. They were landowners not just migrants.

Families trudged by in the mud, the fathers leading, mothers and children following, sometimes stopping to rest for a day or two in Centro Uno before they forged on to unoccupied properties outside the confines of Ixcán Grande. The heat and the humidity were a shock to those from the highlands and exhausting, but for many, all too familiar, as they had worked on the Costa at a finca cutting cane. I had seen the one-ton trucks on the highway in Huehuetenango. The trucks had high sides enclosed with planks. Workers were packed in standing vertically, no benches, no place to sit down on the 18-hour trip from their highland village to the lowland cane and coffee farms to work for fifty cents a day. Leaving their families for months at a time, they often returned with nothing saved.

Though Ixcán was hot and humid, the families' hope of having their own parcela was contagious and even though families had no idea where they would end up, they kept coming.

One day when Ernesto hiked to Cuarto Centro, a six to ten hour walk away, to teach a group of men from the co-op how to grow vegetables, create a compost pile, and build garden beds, I asked Elena about learning how to weave. Our talk turned the vegetable garden tide. We were sitting in the comedor just chatting and I was eating a bowl of frijol negro when I asked, "Puedes ensenarme a tejer?"

She said, "Si voy a enseñarte y tú puedes enseñarme como crecer las verduras." Okay, I will teach you how to weave, and you will teach me how to grow vegetables. We had a deal. I think more than anything she felt sorry for me as I wasn't able to convince any of the women to start a garden. Friendship and pity go a long way.

Once we made our deal, we started work immediately. Together we built two raised garden beds using asadons, heavy hoes, and enclosed them with a small cane fence, a practice that we had perfected in our own garden following a loose horse attack, the pig subterfuge and the even worse an agouti attack, the large rodent was interested in our seed flats and wiped out two weeks of seedlings. We topped the beds with a woven lid to keep out the free running chickens and also mitigate the intense sun and heat. We planted radish and mustard seeds that we had had luck with and then some crops that were from the highlands that Elena wanted to grow but proved to be unsuccessful: beets, heading cabbage, and tomatoes. The family bathroom area was relocated to the other side of the house away from the garden to make sure we had no contamination. I hoped for the best.

My weaving education began following the completion of the construction of the garden. All the women settled into weaving after lunch, when it was too hot to do much else. We interpreted the ancient designs and patterns originating from before the conquest, using the backstrap loom with just sticks and hilo. The red and white threads and designs held the history of Todos Santos.

I started as any young Todo Santera girl would by weaving a narrow belt on a small simple version of the backstrap loom. Keeping the tension needed for the loom required kneeling and keeping pressure on the wide raffia belt around my hips so that the threads were always tight. Kneeling was hard on the packed dirt surface. My knees were bony, and my ankles had never been bent backward and stretched flat other than a few minutes in a yoga class. Every so often the pain would become unbearable, and I would jump up mid-lesson, and stagger around Elena's outside overhang where she had tied the loom to the post. The women in the neighboring ranchos burst into laughter as I lurched to my feet. My lesson was much more difficult than Elena's and longer.

Elena's stepdaughter, Julia, was engaged at fourteen to the young man who worked for Santiago on the cayuco. She had been weaving with Elena since she was a child and now was an intermedíate weaver. Since we were both learning, we helped each other. She and I would compare our work. Laughingly I teased her, "You just want to get it done," as I was much slower and more methodical.

She teased me back saying, "Doña Lucinda, you are so slow!"

When we started a new project we worked together, first measuring and winding the red and white weft. The fine deep rich red color thread came from Germany. Loose skeins were brought by traders to the village by mule. After winding we soaked the very thin and breakable thread in a combination of cornstarch and water and then stretched out the strands to dry in the sun until it was crisp. Once the stretched-out threads were dry, we broke them apart, rolling the thin weft in our fingers. Gently stretching the threads, we then began inserting the sticks that became the structure for the backstrap loom. I learned some Mam while weaving. "I am going to wind the thread," and then "Bach y ole n chi," "See you tomorrow," spoken with a deep guttural tone.

As time passed, I finished a belt, a colorful moral, or bag, another moral with dibujos or designs, and then I was ready to work on larger pieces.

Elena was both an artist and a very good teacher. All the women in the village wove daily, but close to special holidays it was very serious business, and they would weave for large blocks of time to get their family ready for El Día de los Santos or Semana Santa. All Saints Day was the most important holiday, but Christmas and Easter were close behind. While I was learning to weave, Elena and I would talk. I asked,

"Has the main color pattern always been red and white striped with different designs?"

"No, it used to be wider white stripes, we used to spin our own cotton thread and then dye just a bit of red thread, so it was more white than red. If we go up to Todos Santos together for a visit, you will see," Elena said.

"This is so cute," I told her, noting that she had added ducks along with geometric symbols into the bodice of the huipil that she had woven and was wearing that day.

She laughed. "A mi me gustan los patos!"

I found that I enjoyed the relaxing and timeless rhythm—the passing of the thread and the heavy thump of the weighty wood beater of the loom. When I became competent enough on my own, I moved the loom to our house and used the wooden platform bed post support to hold the top harness of the loom and knelt on a blanket on the concrete floor. Once or twice a week I carried my work over to be critiqued and to spend time chatting working in the cane overhang of Elena's rancho.

We often talked about her gift as a weaver and her interest in interpreting what was around her, whether it was the ducks in a row on the bodice of a huipil or alternating yellow and pink triangles and squares incorporated into a collar. Her art was important to her; it was what she felt made her special and different. She told me, "El trabajo se hace uno muy cansado." The demands of the day made her tired and overwhelmed her ability to be truly creative. This awareness was something that I too found difficult to take in—so much of our creativity was sacrificed to the mundane work of survival. There was no mental space to consider anything but what was happening right now. For her that was an inescapable fact of life, and there was no way to break free of it.

To have such a friend made it impossible for me to even imagine that I would leave in the future. This was the first time that I had felt useful and a part of anything. I now understood what Ernesto had meant about how good it felt to be able to help and be part of the cultural and physical transformation of Ixcán Grande. Our impact was becoming evident daily as more and more people came by the garden to ask about seeds, trees, compost, and anything agricultural or health related. If we didn't know the answer to a question, we would research it.

Gradually Elena's garden started to grow in spite of ranging pigs and her young son Manuel's distracted tending. Her garden beds, situated right by the comedor, had the unintended but welcome effect of encouraging travelers to visit the main garden, the Hortaliza Anna, and learn about vegetable gardening in tierra caliente.

My life became a steady flow, from waking to cooking to gardening and writing or researching to weaving. And in the background, the tension of survival remained constant. I had no choice but to truly live in the present moment.

Ernesto and I both liked to read and when he returned from a trip, he would bring books from the well-stocked English bookstore that we visited when I had arrived in Guatemala City. Our first focus was Europe at the beginning of the 20th Century, including the Frenchman Emile Zola and the Czech, Franz Kafka. Reading offered a bizarre juxtaposition of time and space, transporting us from the jungle to Paris in our minds. I failed at an attempt to read *100 Years of Solitude* by Gabriel Garcia Marquez in the original Spanish, so I read it in English, feeling the magical realism in both the prose and my life. Ernesto read out loud while I wove indoors during the rest period of incinerating midday heat.

We were developing quite a library. Occasionally he would bring back another non-fiction book about Guatemala, too, which we would place in the non-fiction area next to Guatemala. *Another Vietnam* was tucked on the third shelf of the built-in shelves by the bathroom door. Little did we know then that book would put us in danger.

# CHAPTER 15

In all communities, leaders rise. In Centro Uno, one man rose immediately, Tomás, our neighbor. He was not just the leader in the small
village but quickly became a decision maker and power broker for the
entire Ixcán.

Tomás started out working directly with Padre Eduardo to set up
Centro Uno. Tomás's office, a small shed, was the gateway to Ixcán land
ownership. He vetted new co-op members and assisted in administering
land titles. Ixcán Grande was a highly regulated, planned community,
and only those who had the ability and gumption to succeed were given
the opportunity to purchase land. Sometimes families would wait up
to five months in limbo in Centro Uno, waiting to receive approval to
become part of the cooperative and be able to move to their parcela.

After Padre Eduardos death just a few years into the project, Tomás
stepped up and continued the process, working with Padre Guillermo
when he replaced Padre Eduardo as the priest managing the Proyecto
Ixcán project.

First to the virgin jungle, Tomás had not only secured the best
and most productive land but received cattle along with a few other
co-op members, and a beautiful speckled Appaloosa stallion from Padre
Guillermo. A striking horse in contrast to the scrawny small roans and
bays that were the typical horse of the campo.

Every year the people of Todos Santos Cuchumatanes celebrated
their Saints Day, the Día de los Santos, with a horse race the day after

the Día de los Muertos or the Day of the Dead. In Todos Santos, riders on horseback race through the center of town and reach up to rip a live flapping chicken from a rope strung across the road.

When the pueblo first arrived to build Centro Uno, they celebrated the Día de los Santos in the same way as they had for centuries in the frigid highlands. Although there was no road, the race was still the main event. Riders galloped their horses through the Sunday market stalls to finish by the church. Just as in Todos Santos it became the highlight of the fiesta. A tall and strong horse gave clear advantage and was invaluable and prestigious. Once Tomás had Padre Guillermo's stallion he was the sure winner.

In addition to land and his horse, his house was located next to the church and the padres' houses. An excellent businessman, he could afford a solid concrete-floored mahogany board and batten home with a small store at the front with a large open window and counter. He and his family, usually Luisa and Pabla, sold short white candles, cookies, candy, some thread for weaving, cooking oil, and alcohol for lanterns. When a pack train was spotted crossing the Río Ixcán, the children ran down to intercept it and see what was being delivered to Don Tomás's store.

About five months in, I had reached a point where the black beans, thick corn tortillas and boiled platanos had become incredibly boring. I started supplementing my meals with candy. The only candy was a small oval-shaped multi-colored hard-shell candy called a huevito, little egg. I lined up with the children and had twenty-five cents to their five cents, so I was prepared to stock up! Tomás happened to be manning the store one day as the huevito supply was replenished and admonished me, "Lucinda, estos están para los niños, puedes tener uno or dos pero no más." It was all I could do to utter, "Claro que sí." Properly chastised I clarified, "Of course the candy should be for the children. I understand just one or two is fine."

Although his patronizing was a bit tough to deal with, he was right. I had previously tried to buy a dozen eggs at the market, but they were sold individually, and I was told I could only buy two.

Eventually, to drive even more business to the store, Tomás bought a two-foot wide by five-foot tall refrigerator/freezer that ran on propane. It arrived strapped across the back of the pack mule from Barillas and was a huge hit. The anticipation alone drove the first day of slightly cold slush to an event that bordered on a holiday. Pabla, and the children had a production line making hielos, brightly colored flavored slushy water in tiny plastic bags. I savored the sweet, incredibly cold, bright pink slush, huevitos driven temporarily from my mind.

As travelers walked from the highlands, the welcome cold slushy was their first stop. Tomás was a very strategic and focused businessman. This was just a small part of his financial portfolio: his 28-acre tierra was planted with coffee and cardamom in the slightly mountainous portion and then, in the flat land next to the Río Ixcán, his milpa. In addition to the co-op property, he was also able to buy additional property elsewhere, like that of the young finquero we had met early on leaving the Ixcán after his house had been burned to the ground by the guerrillas. He sold his land to Tomás.

The co-op's focus on both subsistence farming of maize and frijol negro and cash crops were exemplified in Tomás's plantings of coffee and cardamom, both understory plants that encouraged maintaining the large rainforest trees. The trees attracted and held clouds of moisture needed to naturally irrigate the crops. Planted ten years before, the plants were well established and produced a viable crop of beans and pods. Other portions of the 28 acres were clear cut for cattle and other stock, not as sustainable an approach.

During harvest season Pabla and Luisa spread the cleaned coffee beans and cardamom pods out evenly on the large broken concrete slab overlooking the Río Ixcán and the soccer field. When the daily deluge of rain came like clockwork, they would hurry over from next door and sweep everything up into white woven bultas and park the bags in our house by the front counter. The drying cardamom pods scented the house with a potent fragrance. It was a treat to fall asleep to the sweet herbaceous aroma.

Pabla or Luisa typically took care of the store as Tomás's oldest son, Roberto, was being trained in his father's other business, as well as learning to negotiate a rapidly changing political landscape. Pabla, as the wife of a powerful and wealthy man, could have kept herself even more separate, but her kindness and thoughtfulness made her a joyful neighbor. My lack of the Mam language didn't allow me to really understand the nuances of the women's relationships since I couldn't understand the gossip, but I felt that she experienced some separation as a wealthy elder in the village. It was hard to really understand the complexities of the relationships. All Centro Uno Ixcán villagers were originally from Todos Santos Cuchumatanes. Todos Santos and the aldeas surrounding the town center had been there for centuries, and like any small insular town, there were long-standing relationships.

Here in Ixcán I wondered how they figured me into the community. Was it good to befriend me, or did it create envy or enmity? Initially I wasn't sure and I always thought the worst, that they didn't like me. Yet in many cases I'd learn that I was just different and, of course, the language barrier made things difficult.

Women and girls didn't have the same advantages as men. Tomás, focused on the success of his family, made sure that all of his boys were well educated at boarding school while Luisa, who was whip-smart, was relegated to classes in the village.

Walking a very fine line as the co-op representative, but always concerned about his own businesses, it was hard to tell Tomás's game plan. It had been such a short period of time between the inception of the Ixcán co-ops with Padre Eduardo to his death, and his replacement with Padre Guillermo. After Padre Guillermo's suspicious death and the lack of anyone to replace him, Tomás stepped up. The difference between having direct American missionary involvement in the governance and securing land entitlements and local Maya representation was significant. Prejudice against the Maya trivialized the co-ops' concerns.

The local co-op meetings in Centro Uno took a turn for the worse. Gone were the balanced discussions rising up over the garden regarding crops and who was drinking too much. Instead, voices grew heated. I didn't understand the growing separations and discord across the Ixcán co-ops even though they argued just steps away from my house. There were growing resentments with Centro Dos regarding land titles. Centro Dos members didn't want the security of the co-op as a title holder. This was an added dimension. The dynamic between the army and the guerrillas continually impacted the decision making in the background and I did understand that Tomás threw his support toward whoever could help with the co-ops' business.

It was becoming impossible to exist in the middle—you had to take a side. Which side would survive?

Four years before, Padre Guillermo met with the Alcalde of Barillas, Sr. Reyes, requesting municipal service to the Ixcán, so that the inhabitants didn't have to walk for days for simple municipal functions. He requested an office location in Ixcán to document the residents' land titles. Given that Ixcán was in the Barillas jurisdiction it made sense. But as before, the Mayor of Barillas called it "Little Cuba," casting the entire Ixcán Grande development in an unfair Communist light. This title was used repeatedly and soon as an excuse for the buildup of army forces, and to this day it is still used to justify the scorched-earth campaign that commenced less than three years later. Even untrue words repeated over and over have power.

Tomás's apparent decision to throw his support and the future of the co-op to the army since it was the only option to fly in and out was met with suspicion from the EGP, or so we gleaned by their increasing presence in the community. At the same time, it was hard to say just how many EGP we actually saw. The jungle was so dense and their ability to disappear quickly made the logistics hard to understand. The isolation of

Ixcán, exacerbated by only army planes flying in and increasing patrols, moved Ixcán Grande into a clear military zone. Entering without proper documentation had been prohibited since I had first arrived, but the restrictions increased to absolutely no admittance.

When I started researching Father Bill's death and the crash online years later, the only story that I had ever heard from the community was that helicopters had forced the plane down into the jungle. We had believed it at the time. Based on numerous additional accounts I found in my research, that was not the truth, however. Without communication of any kind other than word of mouth, all truth lay in the teller. Person to person sharing across the Ixcán about the happenings of that tragic day was like the child's game of telephone where, with each retelling, the story evolves. Now, doubts about everything began to fill our minds. The confusion haunted each and every person in Ixcán as we wondered what was true, and what was really happening?

# CHAPTER 16

My parents, in spite of their separation over my father's self-absorbed obsession with EST and his slew of girlfriends, managed to come to visit together in late May 1977. Somehow my ever-tolerant mother ignored his clear infidelity. They traveled by train down through Southern Mexico and by bus to Huehuetenango where I hiked out and took the bus from Barillas to meet them. I made arrangements to stay in a great place for $3 a night. They were both adventurers in their own right, but the quality of the $3 hotel just didn't cut it, particularly the straw mattress with bed bugs. Their fragile relationship was challenging, too, as I learned when we took a bus to Quetzaltenango along the highland passes. My father rolled his eyes and made snide comments about my mother's admittedly poor Spanish accent and tendency to add a Spanish sounding ending to any and all English words. His travel style involved talking with everyone except us, so that gave us a brief respite from each other.

I didn't have a map, and my father, disoriented, pronounced, "Where the hell are we?"

A family of map readers, we'd take trips by car with folded maps picked up at the local AAA. With ball point pens we'd circle points of interest, unfolding and refolding the ungainly maps. Unfortunately, I had forgotten a map and the AAA in Santa Rosa didn't have one of Guatemala, so we wandered untethered to geography through the highlands.

"Oops, there goes Lake Atitlán, referred to by Huxley as the most beautiful lake in the world."

My father exhaled, "Good god! Can't we stop and look at it?"

I explained, more patiently than I felt, "No, we've reached Los Encuentros the turnoff for Chichicastenango and Quiche. We'll stop soon. We need to get a flight to the Ixcán if we are going to make sure that you get back out on time for your plane back to the U.S. We have a place to stop up ahead."

"It would be good to know where we are!" Mom complained.

The contrast of having been in the lowland jungle to the now crisp highland mountain air as the bus rolled up the highway toward Quiche was a great relief. I could breathe, and my energy returned. I hadn't realized the extent of my lethargy in the heat of Ixcán. I laughed to myself, finding patience with the bickering and focusing on my amazement that my parents had come all this way together.

We stopped in Chichicastenango for two nights, the Maya and colonial town that we had passed through on our way to our first flight into Ixcán. Even though it was touristy, it was a good stopping point and lovely too. The narrow cobbled streets clung to the top of a ridge and the hotel was atmospheric, with antique dark wood furniture and handwoven colorful bedspreads and huipils on the walls.

The indigenous Mayan market was in full swing when we awakened the next morning. The women's huipiles in Chichicastenango were so different from the Todos Santos huipils. These had an almost needle-point-like appearance, depicting flowers or layered diamond shapes and angles in pink, red, green, blue and yellow blocks at the top of the bodice and sleeves. The vibrancy stood out against the elegant ancient white stone of the 16th Century Santo Tomas Apostol Church. Men wearing tzute, large woven and folded scarves on their heads, primarily red, but with beautiful and intricate designs, dibujos, of flowers or geometric shapes, paced the wide crumbling stone steps swinging ancient thuribles scenting the air with intoxicating piñon and sacred copal incense as they chanted.

The market extended for blocks and included sections of tourist crafts and antiquities as well as the necessities for life: vegetables, meat, shoes, bright pink and blue plastic tubs and bowls, everything needed by the community.

On our second day we explored the outskirts of Chichicastenango and visited Momostenango. Perched at 7,500 feet on a small, almost alpine mountain range, it was populated mainly by sheep. The village was known for beautiful naturally colored spun wool and woven wool blankets. I reveled in the brisk air, breathing in deeply, knowing that the next day I would be flying back to the suffocating humid lowlands of Ixcán.

We checked in the next morning with Fabiano and my parents showed him their passports. I guess family was ok to travel with. I hadn't even thought about them not being able to enter Ixcán. It was a clear cloudless day as we took off from Quiche. My father was just learning how to fly a small plane, so he was delighted to chat up Guy. The flight was uneventful, and the miles of virgin verdant jungle stretching below us entranced my mother who exclaimed, "Como naturaleza," "How natural."

There were no grandparents in the village and the children had heard that my parents were coming so they were excitedly waiting on the recently cut pista as the plane landed. As we climbed out of the plane the children burst out in unison, "¡Buenos tardes abuelos!"

Francisca, the tiny four-year-old with an infectious laugh, became my mother's buddy, following her through the garden and the village. My father, an elementary school teacher, squatted on the front patio and charmed the boys with silly stories in broken Spanish.

Though life was difficult here, both my parents were in their early fifties and pretty physically fit, so I wasn't too worried about them when we flew into Centro Uno. But soon my mother refused to eat any more of the small, thick and slightly gooey tortillas and black beans. I tried boiling platanos for her breakfast, but that didn't appeal either. She grew weak from lack of food, and more emotional with each day.

A dog lover, she became teary when she heard that Demetria's dog, Pinga, had disappeared.

By the second week of their stay, my parents were coming apart. They had "scheduled" their flight back out with Guy for a week from their arrival, and that week had passed.

One day, we walked the narrow muddy trail to the comedor where we pulled out a bench, and sat at the uneven hand planed mahogany table. Chickens flapped and scattered as we settled. Demetria passed out a chipped enamel plate with a hunk of meat floating in an oil slick of soup. She joked, "Es Pinga, muy deliciosa!"

It was not Pinga the dog for lunch; it was actually agouti, a giant rodent with a stocky body and a blunt turned up nose. When alive, it foraged in the milpa on tiny rat feet, climbing the corn, its weight bent the stalks to the ground while it devoured the fresh sweet corn kernels, cobs and all, with razor sharp rat teeth. Lunch, vermin eradication, and meat. That was it for my mother, normally polite and accommodating, now flustered, she pronounced an ultimatum, "I refuse to eat any more 'meat' or black beans, and I can't stand those thick tortillas."

Rapidly succumbing to the "all white men fall apart in the tropics" syndrome, after my father's initial week of fun playing with the children, he largely confined himself to his mildew-scented cot with a bottle of alcohol, the local illegal cusha. Given my father's chatty ways, even with limited Spanish, he was able to buy the blinding moonshine from a campesino who fell for his enthusiasm and thirst. Filthy and disheveled with the cusha bottle clutched in one hand, he leaned back against the wall as he read and then re-read his one book, a Raymond Chandler detective novel, five times, during what turned out to be three weeks marooned in Ixcán.

Tomás expressed concern. "Estan triste," he said, worrying that they were looking pathetic and haggard.

Not knowing what would become of this great experiment, these young families were especially concerned for their elders and my parents were no exception. We all watched with horror as my still youngish parents grew stoic and mute, slowly sliding into torpor.

The next morning, just as the sun was rising, I reached for what I thought was my batik skirt wadded in a pile on my side of the bed, and it stirred.

"Snake!"

Black, bright green and yellow, my alleged bunched-up batik skirt unwound slowly to stretch seven feet along the edge where the sleeping platform hit the wall. My father, rising from his cot with renewed vigor, and Ernesto quickly mobilized, working as a team. Ernesto ran outside and cut a rubber tree branch to end in a short, tight Y and handed it to my father. The snake raised its head and started to slither up the wall, head moving from side to side. My father, holding the end of the stick, reached over the bed to pin the snake's head against the wall. Ernesto cleanly decapitated it with one blow of the machete, the head sailing up to hit the ceiling only to ricochet off and land on the concrete floor by my screaming mother's foot while the length of snake contracted, still writhing in the sheets.

We didn't have any idea what kind of snake it was, and 50% of the village said it was, "venenoso," and the other 50% said, "No es problema." I am still not sure to this day, though I believe it was a non-venomous rat snake. Without the internet or an encyclopedia, it was hard to know.

That same day my father almost died during the hike down to the Río Ixcán while testing the first leg of my parents' potential departure. The heat and the humidity were unbearable, 105 degrees in the shade and I had forgotten that it had taken me months to somewhat acclimate to the weather. As we sat beside the river on the cobble and gravel, my father suddenly slurred, "I can't breathe." His face turned ashen and then took on a clammy grey-green hue.

My mother was momentarily distracted by a bird as she splashed in the shallows following it with her binoculars, ignoring him. She waded a bit further away and called back, "I've never seen a Trogon, even in Costa Rica!"

I was left alone to imagine my father's death in Ixcán. The large smooth white rocks just beyond the shallows shone with water, but at the river's edge it was still and smelled of algae and rot. The buzzards started to circle. Ernesto and I doused him with the lukewarm river water, cupping it in our hands and dumping it over his head, cooling him down a bit as he continued to mumble.

We sat there until the sun moved down toward setting and a slight cool breeze lifted off of the river's surface, and he felt he could manage the trek back to the house. I suspected that the unfiltered, highly alcoholic cusha was exacerbating his addled mental state and contributing to dehydration.

Eventually my parents were able to leave Centro Uno when, one day, the grey clouds parted, the sky cleared briefly, and Guy flew in. They ran down the trail, leaving most of their belongings behind, leapt into the plane to Quiche, waving as the plane lifted off. The children ran behind, the cool breeze blowing the girls' braids straight back and swirling their skirts. "¡Adiós abuelitos! Adiós ..."

Not much later my parents started writing letters to me from separate addresses.

My parents weren't our only visitors. Right after my parents left, Ann Kerndt's brothers and sister hiked in to see where Ann had lived before her death in the plane crash. We had named the garden Hortaliza Anna. They had traveled from Minnesota to Guatemala and hiked down from Barillas, crossing the Río Ixcán in the cayuco. Legally at this point there were no tourists allowed in Ixcán, so it was quite surprising to see them, as we had no way to get a heads up. Ann's siblings saw their visit as a way to try to understand what had pulled her to this remote place. Her brother, a volunteer doctor in a small village in the highlands, not as remote as the Ixcán, was very familiar with Guatemala but had not been to Ixcán.

They also saw the Ixcán landscape as a park, which was utterly at odds with the way I saw the Ixcán. Although the beauty around us was spectacular, organic gardening was incredibly difficult, and it was hard to take time to do anything other than work. The heat, illness and responsibility of working to make the garden viable took every ounce of mental and physical energy.

When they suggested floating down the rapids of the Río Ixcán, I was cautiously enthusiastic. We walked down the pista and over the forested top of the bank into blinding light and heat reflecting off the white rocks at the river's edge. Lacking inner tubes, we waded in and lay back into the water, suspended in a deep pool, floating. With no idea what lay ahead, we pushed off. The clear aquamarine blue water was lukewarm but felt cool and refreshing. The rapids picked up, splashing over rocks, cooling the surface. The current gently dragged us over rounded slightly submerged rocks. Pushing off boulders we found quiet eddies as we drifted, surrounded by hundreds of fluorescent lime green and turquoise dragon flies and iridescent blue butterflies the size of salad plates. The river, untamed and unexplored, meandered as we pushed forward. Then, all of a sudden, the current picked up and the soft playfulness changed. We navigated to the river's edge after hearing the rapids roaring ahead.

A group of children watching us ran along the top of the rocky bank calling, wanting to join us, dodging the tall trees arching over the river and jumping the tangled roots to follow along. Never having seen their parents be so playful, they were delighted and laughing with us. The day was beautiful and fun ... for just a moment.

Not long after Ann's family left, I spotted a hiker coming down the trail and said to Ernesto, "Wow, we are becoming a tourist stop."

The hiker was a French-speaking man who claimed to be just out for a hike. As the Ixcán was not in any European guidebook for traveling in Guatemala, we were immediately suspicious. But when he asked in broken Spanish, "Puedo quedarme al noche?" we said, "Of course you can spend the night with us."

The timing of this visit was even stranger as we could now hear and see the flash of bombing at night in the mountainous rainforest to the west of the Río Ixcán. It was highly doubtful that anyone without proper papers could enter via the trail or by plane, but Ann's family had so it was hard to know. Also, it was nice to have a visitor even though he could not speak English. He introduced himself as Jean.

We invited him into our home, speaking Spanish together when suddenly his face hardened and his jaw clenched as he stared fixedly at the bookcase on the wall. Our collection was comprised mostly of novels, gardening books, medical books, and the few books of non-fiction about Guatemala that we'd purchased in the Capital. With a swift grab, he pulled down *Guatemala—Another Vietnam*, whirled around, and shook it violently, saying in English, "This book is against the government."

Shocked both at the anger in his voice, and his sudden use of English, I froze, not sure what language to respond in. I said in English, "We got it in Guatemala City at the bookstore; it's an approved book."

"It was just something I grabbed off the front table," Ernesto added.

"Why do you have it?"

"We want to understand all sides of the politics here in Guatemala," Ernesto said.

Following a long pause while he looked from one to the other of us, he just shrugged and said, "OK."

When he left the next day, we waved goodbye from the stoop more cheerfully than we felt, and then stepped back into the house to shut the door. "I wish I could lock it," I said, as we slid down to sit on the cool floor.

"What are we going to do? Who was Jean?" We tried to piece together his origin.

"I think he has to be Israeli, possibly from their secret service, Mossad, but it's hard to know," Ernesto ventured. The Israelis were working with the Guatemalan government and that seemed the likeliest option.

Just trying to do our job and keep a low, non-political profile was hard when a mere book could get us into trouble.

Months later, we were on a bus leaving the hangar to go back to the U.S. for a brief visit when we saw our "French" visitor leave the Guatemalan air force hangar at the Aurora airport wearing a Guatemalan air force T-shirt waving enthusiastically to the cadets. He was definitely not a tourist, but we never learned his true identity.

# CHAPTER 17

I was consistently nauseous with a low-grade fever and not much interest in eating anything in Ixcán. When I did eat something, it was followed by intense explosive diarrhea. Ironic, given that we were proselytizing about new ways of managing matters of health and nutrition. As my arms and legs shrank and became skinnier, my stomach bloated. I stopped having my period, so I thought that I might be pregnant but had been taking the birth control pill. Over half the children in the village also had distended bellies and skinny arms and legs and most had intestinal worms. I didn't think that it was worms because I wasn't feeling any wiggling movement in my stomach, but I knew I should probably seek medical attention.

Rapidly losing energy as well as weight, the arduous hike to Barillas was out of the question and even the hike to Mayalan was rapidly becoming untenable. I needed to begin soon, or I wouldn't make it. With no communication I wasn't sure that there would be a plane available when I got there. By then the Centro Uno pista was never cut. We had heard that the army was increasing its presence in Ixcán and that there was construction work being done on the runway to make it larger so that the Israeli-made Arava paratrooper planes, and larger planes, could land.

Even a few days without watering during the brief annual dry spell was likely to result in the loss of much, if not all, of our crops, so Ernesto stayed behind to care for the hortaliza and I went alone. The garden was now much larger and producing more for the Ixcán community all the time; it warranted our complete dedication and maintenance. The importance of providing seeds and education on an on-going basis superseded personal safety. Only on reflection can I see that we had reached a place where we had completely separated from rational thought.

Leaving Centro Uno, the first segment of the trail wound directly up and over boulders into the rainforest. I was surprised how weak I felt. I looked down and realized that I had not only lost fat but all of my muscle—my legs were like sticks. My confidence as a competent hiker tanked as I panted up the second hill. The cooler darkness was welcome, but as I hiked further along, my mind began to wander. The changes that were happening quickly in Ixcán were confusing. The increase in the army presence was hard to understand.

The trail was now more crowded; I saw someone every 15 to 30 minutes. The newspaper in Huehuetenango had stories on the Ixcán expansion and the organized development process was apparently in the past; it was now a free for all. Families I didn't recognize carried all of their belongings as they passed me along the muddy trail.

People I didn't know recognized me as Doña Lucinda, the gringa "nurse" and vegetable gardener who lived in Centro Uno. There was even a catchy tune on the radio that occasionally came on that was called "Doña Lulu"—my nickname. We would exchange a brief, "Buenos Días," followed up with, "Adiós" as we passed.

I needed to pick up my pace if I was to get to Mayalan before dark. There was a brief moment when the heat of the day cooled slightly and the cacophony of the jungle changed almost imperceptibly to the roaring insect machine of early evening. In that dip the malarial mosquitoes swarmed. No amount of Deet, even if I'd been able to obtain it, could stop the dusk feeding frenzy, so I wanted to get to the padres' house before dusk.

Pressing harder, exhausted, I crested that final hill and I could hear the sound of equipment and generators. In the gathering darkness

Mayalan had been transformed; the short green grass pista, now more than tripled in size, was bordered by a concertina wire fence. The airstrip, no longer the small runway for the private planes and the initial military installation, was completely replaced. A fleet of helicopters perched at the side. Just as we had heard, the pista had been "improved" yet again by the military.

Larry's house was empty when I arrived. He had been gone now for over five months. Before it had been quiet and isolated, and now it was in the middle of the construction project. Kudzu vine tendrils breached the roof, and the garden was overrun with thick cane grasses and a low growing shrub with little white flowers and bright red berries. The house and garden were returning to the jungle.

The door, latched with a hook and rusted handle, turned easily. The musty mold smell indicated that it was probably opened last when we had walked to Mayalan months ago. The Padres had not been there. The town children met me at the house, but I was not much fun. Usually, I was cheered by their curiosity, but I was just hungry and tired. Grateful for the recent rains, the toilet could flush, important since even though I was famished, I knew I would return to the house and probably vomit and have diarrhea both, my stomach slightly reducing only to re-fill with more noxious gas.

I left my knapsack in the house and made my way through the cut grass and mud pathway to the local comedor for dinner, frijol negro y tortillas, como siempre. My distended stomach was hard to hide and painfully gurgling. I wondered if this was how the children felt. Was it as painful, and how would they be able to go to a doctor? I went to bed on the metal cot and a thin mattress in a room off the main living space, wondering what was wrong with me, relieved to be lying down. I did not know what it was and when I would get transport out.

I checked in with the cooperativa early the next morning to see if I could get a seat when the next plane flew in. It wasn't raining, so there was hope. The airstrip had no tower or lights, no ability to communicate with a plane, so it was dependent on the weather as usual. I was told that a visitor was being flown in and that I could leave right away, as soon as the plane touched down briefly and was ready to take off again.

The Arava landed with a burst of engine noise and came abruptly to a stop. Large compared to Guy's 185, but small for a military plane, it taxied to the opening in the barbed wire fence near the bodega. The Arava cracked open in half like a giant egg. The co-op manager said, "Se puede salir con el avión." I could fly out. I jumped at the chance.

Before boarding, I peered into the wide-open halves of the plane and saw canvas-strap hammock-seats lining both sides of the interior of the plane and a shadow that looked like a person. Climbing up and into one half of the plane, I sat gingerly in the sling. The shadow materialized into a non-military person, a visitor I didn't recognize. He was wearing city clothes, slacks, polished black shoes and a clean white shirt. He said in English, "Hello, who are you? What are you doing out here in the jungle?"

Colonel Castillo and several other army officers climbed in after me saying, "Buenos Días" and I realized that the Colonel had flown in the visitor.

In English, the stranger introduced himself and said, "I'm from Israel, from the Defense Department. Who are you and what are you doing out here?"

English was a shock; even Ernesto and I spoke Spanish some of the time when alone together. I wasn't up to a conversation.

"I'm a U.S. agricultural volunteer here working with the community. My name is Lesley Miles," I said.

Then, as if not hearing me, he added, "We just sold more of these Aravas and helicopters, Uzi and Galil guns, boots. We sell them anything that the government needs."

I was just trying to get to the city and find a doctor. Shocked, I looked around the new plane and at the arms dealer speaking English. I tried to pull all of the pieces together. Wracking my brain—the U.S. and Israel had very close ties. Were they connected to our likely Mossad visitor? The Carter administration had placed an embargo on aid and weapons to Guatemala due to the developing humanitarian crisis and what looked like the beginning of a civil war. I puzzled over what the Israelis were doing here in such force? All information about current affairs was relegated to newspapers, radio and TV. In my addled state I wasn't able to understand the nuances, the juxtaposition of Israel and the U.S. and the preponderance of not just Israeli army gear and weapons but also U.S. helicopters and even boots.

The plane halves swung closed and locked. The engine revved up and the pilot taxied down the grass strip and lifted surprisingly quickly given the size of the plane. The engines growled as we circled slowly around Mayalan. I looked down at the rusted lamina roofs that dotted the deep, verdant jungle. The beautiful reds and whites of the Todos Santos men's pantalones and camisas moved through the town, providing a contrast to the dark jungle-green and orange-red of lateritic soil. Peering down from the small rounded windows, the arms dealer asked, "Did the army give those people those outfits, so that they could keep track of them, like jail uniforms?"

Incensed and determined to speak for the community, I said, "No, the men's wives and mothers wove them on a backstrap loom as they have for centuries. Also, they speak a unique language called Mam. Throughout Guatemala there are twenty-two language groups and many different communities of Mayas, each with their own clothing or traje."

He snorted, "Are they really human like you and me, or are they more like animals?"

I didn't know how to respond. My body went cold with a shock beyond anger, just incredulity. I sat mutely for the duration of the flight while he continued to talk about his business of selling weapons and military equipment. "I sell all over the world, but here in Guatemala, this is a big sale. The army is buying helicopters of course, Aravas, and lots of different weapons."

He also talked about Israeli military training as an export. "We are here to help Guatemala in any way that we can now that they have the weapons. We will have training programs here in Guatemala and maybe even send a group to Israel. Since the U.S. can't provide weapons directly, we are stepping in."

As we were taxiing into the military side of the Guatemala City Aurora airport, he asked, "How about lunch with me? I am staying at the El Camino Real Hotel."

Our individual monthly stipends of $100 didn't go far. Of that, we had to pay the rent for our house in Ixcán, all of our food, and any travel. We had been told by our DID team that the average Guatemalan made $1 a day, so we were making roughly three times that and should be happy. Having an opportunity to change his mind about the people I knew and loved, eat a real lunch, and find out a bit more about how someone could possibly think that the people that I was living with were less than human, I decided to have lunch with him. My health could wait, as usual. I stopped at the El Camino bathroom, the first real bathroom in months, looked at my reflection and was shocked at the change. I knew that I had lost weight but had not seen how dull and stringy my hair was and how gaunt my face had become. Later I would find out that I had lost 40 lbs., down from 135 to 95 lbs.

The central patio in the hotel was elegant—round tables with white tablecloths and crisp green folded linen napkins, umbrellas and comfortable heavy white iron furniture with colorful cushions. The space was warm without being too hot, as the tall walls of the hotel provided just enough shade and a sense of safety and enclosure, the contrast so different from the jungle. In just a few hours I had gone from survival to opulence. It was so easy for those with power and money.

The conversation, over a lunch of salad niçoise and fresh crispy rolls and butter, focused mainly on the additional arms deals that he was making with the Guatemalan army.

"Guatemala is ripe for weapons purchases they need everything. We even have a training program in Israel for officers. Thinking we will have around 100 officers attending in the next few years."

"Are you also working with farming projects too like you have in Israel with the kibbutz?"

"I don't know. I'm not interested in that. What did you think about the Arava? It's a great plane that can take a squad of soldiers in to the jungle. By the way where do they find those soldiers? They look pretty young."

I thought for a moment. I had heard from my neighbors that their relatives and friends in the highlands were grabbed while walking along a village road and thrown into an open truck with other young Maya men. "Well, the regular army troops are made of typically indigenous Maya boys and young men not interested in becoming soldiers who are often conscripted straight from the streets." I bit into a fresh roll, savoring the rare experience after months of beans. "They are often unable to return home for months or years. The Kaibiles, the Guatemalan rangers, carry themselves differently, as though they have no fear, just focused hunting and killing machines. I have seen them occasionally when they materialized from the jungle only to disappear seconds later."

Horrified by his complete lack of care or interest in the people that he had seen, I tried to open his eyes. "The people from Todos Santos in Mayalan have a long and rich history that includes being the first people to not only make their homes in Ixcán jungle, but to successfully transform large tracts of rainforest and jungle into productive land. They've also developed a very successful governing cooperative body, which you saw in Mayalan."

My words did not seem to make an impact; he just shrugged and laughed. As lunch ended, the real reason for the invitation finally materialized. He looked me up and down and said, "Now that you have had lunch, come up to my room."

My safety as a woman came rushing to the forefront of my mind. Until then I hadn't considered myself a vulnerable woman. I had thought about my gender only in connection with the other women in the village and my intimate relationship with Ernesto, but had little reason to fear for my safety. For the first time, I felt how vulnerable it was to be a woman, alone. At the same time, I was dumbfounded to think of myself as attractive, having had no hot shower in months, with my distended stomach and my dirty linen yoga pants, T-shirt and boots. It hadn't even occurred to me that this was the expected outcome of our lunch. Additionally, I had not viewed my safety as a woman as different in the jungle and along the trail from that of a man. I now added the fear of being sexually assaulted to my existing fears of snake bite, caterpillars, and murder

This didn't stop me from speaking my mind. "I somehow thought that you, of all people, as an Israeli, would understand and fight for the equality and dignity of all human beings. Thank you for lunch." I slung my knapsack over my shoulder and left to go to the hangar to spend the night, stopping at the pristine restroom again as my stomach cramped.

Leaving the El Camino Real I walked in a daze and completely missed the bus stop down the street and ended up walking around the block in search of a stop. I was shaken by not just his business-like approach to the Ixcán but afraid of what would happen next. Was this all just another opportunity to sell weapons?

I made it to the hangar without incident and used the phone there to make an appointment with a doctor first thing the next morning so I could find out what was wrong with me.

The doctor's office was not unlike Sr. Oriano, the attorney's office, vintage 1940's noir. After a series of tests, it was determined that I had excessive amounts of e-coli bacteria and needed to take a pill to kill and/or reduce the amount of e-coli. The complete lack of sanitation in Centro Uno had hit me with a vengeance. I was lucky though; I could leave and see a doctor.

Ernesto surprised me by showing up three days later; he too had been sick and had finally found someone to water the garden while he was gone. His diagnosis: lombrices, worms the size of large earthworms swimming in his stomach. We were walking advertisements of unhealthiness in the village. But even so, after a few beers and trips to Auto Mariscos, I was longing to return to my village and garden.

Little by little the challenges of the hot and humid environment had become more manageable. I was now keenly aware of how fragile we were but unsure how to stay healthy. More pressing was my laser focus was to help the community and the co-op grow.

Recounting my lunch with the Israeli, I told Ernesto about how I had shared that the Proyecto Ixcán Grande development was a vision of social, agricultural and financial success, planned and administered democratically. A testament to the early efforts to engage all co-op members, and how exciting it was to be a part of it. I also shared the Israeli's incomprehensible derision. Yet I didn't share my new awareness that as a woman alone, the fear of being raped had just entered my mind.

"It makes no sense to me why the Israelis are here selling weapons, and who knows what else," I told him. "Surely the Israelis didn't act alone."

"It's all so confusing," he agreed. "But there's no place to research or understand what's happening, no information."

The relatively benign army regulars would soon have even more weapons, but why? What was the plan? Why was that necessary, and where did the money come from to buy all of these weapons? I suspected the U.S. played a role but how would we find out? Santiago and Elena had the only radio in the village, a transistor radio that played ranchero songs and offered a bit of news and weather, so there was no way to check on anything. Anyway, I had no mental space to be able to even think about what was changing around me.

I flew back in with the army to Mayalan and Ernesto continued to the coast, for more research and new ideas for cash crops.

# CHAPTER 18

After about eight months in Ixcán, my friend Marjorie visited me. We spent several days traveling around the capital and visited the beautiful colonial town of Antigua before flying into Centro Uno with Guy. She was particularly fixated on her boyfriend, Michael, and was very sad to be away from him for even a moment. Marjorie was brilliant, an engaging conversationalist and usually up for anything. We had a very good gay friend in the early 70's we would go dancing with. Once, a couple of homophobic guys started harassing him. She beat them off with her purse, all the while shrieking, "We are peaceful people." The irony was not lost on her, and it became our tagline.

Once again, since she was my friend, Fabiano checked her passport and waved her into the tiny plane to sit on a bulta of sugar. She looked squeamish and then terrified as the flimsy door closed tightly. We intended to stay together in Centro Uno while Ernesto went for two weeks to the coast to take a class. I hopped out of the plane and unloaded her suitcase along with all our boxes of provisions. She climbed slowly out of the plane, hesitating on the last rung. On the ground for maybe two minutes, she took a look around and said, "I can't do this!" Climbing back into the plane she yelled above the sound of the engine, "I'm sorry, I want to go home now!"

Shaky with surprise and shock, I watched them fly away until I could no longer see the speck in the sky, and I could just barely hear the plane increase in velocity over the Southern mountains. I trudged up to the house, stunned and alone once again.

I was always alone when something momentous happened. For months Sergio, who lived at the edge of the village with his family had begged me to take him to the U.S. to get his cancer treated. He had been ill for a long time and all of a sudden declined rapidly.

Francisco, his son, was my garden helper. At age 10 he was strong and very helpful, working with me daily. He was really interested in developing the garden, and had a real knack for understanding the overall garden process from planting seeds in seed flats to transplanting into the raised beds.

Working in the garden provided a respite from worry about his father, but one day when we were weeding a garden bed together, squatting on each side and reaching across plucking out grass and shaking off ants, Francisco told me, "Mí papa quiere hablar con usted."

I wasn't sure if Sergio's illness was why he wanted to speak with me, but I went to visit to see what he wanted. He was propped on his side under the front overhang and looked gaunt, wasted by the illness. Face distorted in pain, he was very direct: "Doña Lucinda, yo tengo cáncer y no hay tratamiento aquí en Guatemala, yo necesito ir a Los Estados Unidos para la cura." Everyone in the village and, it seemed, in all of Guatemala viewed going to the U.S. as the magic panacea. In Sergio's case, his cancer diagnosis and the few weeks or months that he had to live, would not have given him enough time for a cure even if he had been able to travel. There was no possible way to be able to get a passport and paperwork for a visa, and the cost alone with no health insurance would have been prohibitive. As it was, we couldn't even have a radio, much less medical help. At one point we had asked DID to help us bring a doctor down to visit the community, but the nun in Jacaltenango who trained the local health clinic operators nixed it, saying it was unnecessary.

With tears in my eyes, I told him, "I am so very sorry, but I don't have the power to help. There is no way that I can get you the paperwork needed to be able to go to the U.S." That first time I had spoken with Sergio I had contained my helplessness until I returned to the house where my tears spilled over as I told Ernesto, "I can't do anything. I can't help?"

Now two days after Marjorie left with Ernesto in the plane, the day was hotter than normal and I was weeding the radish bed when Francisco's little brother, David, came running toward me. Tears streaming down his muddy cheeks, wearing his usual ripped dirty white T-shirt and loose shorts cinched at the waist by a frayed and flapping piece of rope, he choked out, "Venga a mi casa ahorita por favor, mi papa se murió."

Not knowing what lay ahead or what was expected of me, I quickly rinsed my hands and washed my face with water I poured from the yellow plastic bucket next to the front door. A green tree frog watched me from the edge, hopping off as I lifted the bucket. Time stood still as I focused on the colors and contrasts of daily life, the lemon yellow of the bucket, the lime green of the frog, knowing something terrible awaited me.

I brushed my long hair back and tied it in a ponytail, changed into a cleaner version of my yoga pants and T-shirt, took a deep breath, and set off slowly for Sergio's rancho on the other side of the village. Following the narrow mud track, struggling through the razor-sharp grass that steamed after the recent rain, my canvas tennis shoes were sucked off with every other step, and I was quickly covered with sweat and mud again.

Uncertainty, along with the thick suffocating heat and saturating humidity of the jungle further paused my sluggish steps. Deafening shrill calls of the birds and cicadas were no longer an external background noise; they lived inside me. My community of 15 families—parents, adolescents, children and babies, devoid of grandparents or older people—stood ahead with the body preparing the funeral. I had no idea what it would entail. This was not a good time for Ernesto to be on the coast getting seeds yet again. Although we shared our work, and I encouraged him to go out and bring back seeds and plants, at times like this I felt so alone. I was terrified of seeing Sergio's dead body.

The guilt of having been unable to help Sergio weighed heavily. I dreaded meeting my neighbors and was sure that they didn't understand that it had been impossible for me to have prevented his death. I couldn't help him go to the U.S. I was not a doctor, nurse nor savior, I was a 22-year-old gardener, hardly more than a girl, in the jungle by myself, now going to see a dead body for the first time in my life.

I came around a bend in the trail and 20 yards ahead the community was gathering in front of Sergio's rancho. The bright reds, pinks and blues of the women's huipiles and the men's red and white striped pants shifted about as they moved toward the door. These alternating colors were framed by the deep, forest greens, a kaleidoscope moving and turning as it was on my first day brilliant against the deep blue sky

Arriving, I paused for a cue, waiting to see if someone else would arrive so that I could follow them in, but I was apparently the last. Everyone there was at least six inches to a foot shorter than me. Their faces turned up toward me with expectation. I crossed the clean-swept dirt threshold as I made my way into the single-walled cane room, asking, "¿Con permiso?"

"Pase adelante."

Sergio's body lay on a cane and rough mahogany litter in the middle of the room. A large turquoise plastic olla filled with well water sat to the side of the body and Santa made a gesture, indicating I was to wash my hands. I dipped my hands in the olla only to realize, seconds later, that I had made my first mistake; I should have used the blue speckled enameled cup to take the water from the jug and pour it over my hands. The precious well was a long walk away, and I had now fouled the water and forgotten my manners in my anxiety of being so close to the body.

The women and children gathered around Sergio's body, dressed in his finest traje. Laid out on the platform, his swollen body was bursting at the seams as though an incredibly fat man had been shoved into a child's clothes. The strained buttons left gaps revealing the skin beneath the red and white striped shirt. His face, puffy and blackening, was covered with flies. The women took turns fanning them away enveloping the room in the sweet stench of death. The mid-day heat pressed in through the cracks in the cane and rough hand-planed boards. In the thick and confined air, I gagged and nearly vomited.

Searching for relief, I looked at the faces surrounding the cane cot. Francisco was there at the head looking ashen. His older brother Julio, now the head of the family, stood stiff in shock. The women, dressed in their finest huipiles, were keening high pitched cries and screams as they touched the body and dropped to their knees. I hadn't heard the grief from afar; the jungle noises left no room for the small presence of human sounds. My neighbors, red-eyed, had left money at the foot of the corpse. The men were clustered by the door now. I didn't know that I was supposed to bring money. In fact, I hadn't brought anything to donate. I was two for two on what not to do. Always conscientious about doing things correctly the first time, I looked around for judgmental eyes directed at me, but there were none.

Elena made an ox soup. Grease floated thick on the top with two-inch chunks of ox meat, mostly gristle and a small bit of cabbage from the mountains brought down on mules from the highlands. Everyone passed white enameled bowls with a ring of small blue and yellow flowers from one person to the next around the room. I needed something to focus on. Always good at conforming to the current social situation, I slurped from the bowls, saying, "Gracias."

Once the visitation was complete, we moved to the graveyard with the body. Because of the heat and the body's decomposition, the grave had been dug immediately. The window of time was about six hours before the body fluids made the body messy to move. Sergio's body was lifted, wrapped with muslin, and carried to the grave. The men, already fairly drunk on cusha, staggered under his weight as they maneuvered his body into the hole. The bright red soil contrasted with the ivory of the muslin shroud and the luminescent green grass. The heat of the day increased as the sun bore down on the small open graveyard.

We stood around the grave, the men swaying, passing the shovel and a bottle of cusha and a large shot glass—one trago for me, one for Sergio tossed to him in the hole in the ground, and so on, circling around the group until the bottle was empty. There had been no Padre, no last rites. We were alone and isolated as a community. The veil between life and death was much thinner here. The graveyard of mostly young was far too full for a village of 15 families in the space of only 11 years.

There was no one to talk to about what I had just witnessed. The children in Centro Uno were more accustomed to death than I was and even played graveyard, "Muertos." Just as I had played Barbies. Their dolls did normal things but then also died and were interned in the graveyard.

Choking, I said to Elena, "I hope he knew that there was no way to help." I really couldn't express the feelings that were inside—the fear, the sadness, the loneliness that I was so far away from everything that I knew. Elena responded, "Es la voluntad de Dios." It is the will of God.

Alone that night, I lit a candle by the screened opening at the head of the bed and thought back to my response to Elena's comment. I said how worried I was that I had let Sergio down and then I had put it from my mind and stepped over the freshly turned dirt.

I watched the flame dance in the evening breeze until it extinguished. Everyone and everything would return to the mud, or in the brief dry season, dust.

# CHAPTER 19

8/4  Hot & Humid  rain
Helped the school kids with
their compost pile. They
are using weeds - soft
manure (lots), a few dry leaves
and soil. It looks really good
   The Herb Garden is looking
kind of cheesy 2 rue plants
died and some penny royal too
   There are Horse footprints
in bed # 16 a.

Excerpt from the Hortaliza Anna Garden Journal-August 1977

Ernesto and I were family garden evangelists with few other skills. The Health Resource Center concept at Centro Uno only met the goals of family gardens and included minor tidbits of public health education. We answered any and all agricultural and environmental questions, but since neither of us had medical skills, we relied on *Donde no hay doctor* and luck.

Our research into different varieties of vegetables that could flourish in the lowland tropics was developing into a resource for education about growing vegetable gardens, tracking weather and overall horticultural research with an "organic" focus. My initial fears of the absurdity of organic vegetable gardens in the jungle had been largely dispelled as we gradually gained more and more success with new crops appropriate for the conditions. The amount of work that we put in on a daily basis to make the garden successful was daunting to everyone in the village. Being young without family responsibilities and a small stipend made it easier for us to devote so much time and energy to the continual caretaking required.

Even with all of our time devoted to gardening, the Hortaliza would not have flourished without the help of Diego, a short, stocky man whose quiet nature masked an intense care for his family. He threw himself into learning how to grow vegetables and make compost. Many mornings we awoke to the soft swishing sound of the tall grasses and weeds being gathered with a hooked stick and cut with a machete. The morning sun glinted off of Diego's two-foot blade as he threshed the yard, clearing the area around the garden, and in the pathways creating mounds of compostable material. He then would check on the several beds that he had planted with radishes and mustard greens before he left to work his milpa.

Nestled between the back and side of the house and the open lamina-roofed school, the mounded raised beds of the garden were limited in size. With both community gardeners like Diego and the need for more beds for testing these new varieties, we built beds in areas that we hadn't anticipated. Using a wide triangle made from two thick straight branches and a hanging rock, our crude level made sure the garden beds were perpendicular to the slope of the hill and laid out straight and level. Diego became an expert at bed development and spent days when he wasn't tending his milpa digging and weeding to get the tenacious wiry vines and running grasses under control.

Garden tools including the elegant Bulldog spade that was central to the French Intensive approach were unavailable anywhere in Guatemala, so we worked the beds with an asadon, a heavy thick steel hoe-head mounted on a tree branch. Turning the soil with the asadon and then lifting tangled roots out with a forked stick, the garden gradually cascaded down the hillside toward the pista, eventually to over a quarter acre.

In only a couple of days without weeding the beds and pathways, the jungle would take them back, making Diego's help invaluable. The Kudzu was the most voracious, rapidly overtaking the garden beds and the narrow 12-inch pathways between the beds in less than a week. The prolific stringy vines were a continual nuisance and not even viable for compost.

The compost piles were located in the center of the garden under an umbrella of shade. Protected by the large, thick-leafed rubber tree, they were not as productive as we needed to ensure that the plants would grow. Compost was critical to the success of the garden, the secret sauce for plant growth. Building the pile was a continuous, time-consuming process; we collected soft leaves that composted easily as well as dry grasses, garden weeds, occasional manure from local horses, and food scraps. It wasn't the ideal pile, as the level of nitrogen was low, and the amount of moisture high, but it gave the garden a boost. At any point in time, we had three piles in process.

The almost constant rain leached out nutrients and minerals so quickly that we had to add compost on a weekly basis. Adding chemical fertilizers was becoming more common across Ixcán even though they were expensive and carried in by mule. By not providing the needed humus, the soil rapidly lost fertility and became dark red and rock hard.

The fertility of the soil and the success of the crops was completely dependent on keeping the compost pile steaming. In order to get it hot enough, we needed a more consistent manure source. With the increase in the army troops and guerrilla activity (and a childhood dream), I proposed to Ernesto, "It's time to get a horse. It may be our only option out if we need to leave quickly. Maybe we can convince DID that the manure can be considered a necessary tool."

A horse was well beyond our means, so we wrote a letter to DID again asking for assistance with the purchase. We had given up on asking for a radio and though our first horse request had not proved fruitful perhaps this new horse strategy would work. It took us several letters back and forth with DID from our first attempt months before via the Guatemalan post to get them to spring $250 for a horse. The need for safer transport hadn't resonated, but the purchase of a horse to supply manure for the compost pile was considered a worthy cause and expenditure. The funds were deposited in the bank in Guatemala City.

We heard that livestock auctions were held in Huehuetenango every couple of months, so we planned to buy the horse there. The community garden had expanded beyond just Diego, and now three men had beds of their own and volunteered to take care of the rest of the garden for our brief trip to town.

Ernesto and I set out for the auction, hiking up the trail to Barillas. We crossed the Río Ixcán with Santiago in the cayuco and then climbed the almost 4,000 feet to the cool highlands. The combination of the width of the trail, the mud and the number of mules, horses and people that we passed with a cheery "Buenos Días!" resulted in an almost 12-hour slog. We finally arrived just as the last bus left where the trail intersected the road construction that would eventually become the Franja Transversal del Norte Highway. Small bulldozers and a couple of trucks were mired in the deep mud and a group of men were working to try to extricate them, but the trucks were digging deeper into the muck as their tires spun.

It was a ten-hour trip over the Cuchumatanes Mountains down to Huehuetenango and Chiantla with random stops to drop off a child with a chicken or pick up a family alongside the road with their belongings. The fabric-wrapped balls balancing on the women's heads changed in texture and color from San Mateo—bright graphic embroidery, to Todos Santos—red and white stripes, to San Pedro Necta—thin horizontal stripes on a white background. Patience was a necessity and became easier over time as I settled into the bus, rumbling down the hairpin turns.

Arriving in Chiantla, we found a $3 a night hotel and headed to a restaurant close to the horse sale grounds for cold beer and wood fired grilled chicken. My vegetarian diet with the occasional piece of ox meat was not enough to sustain me. I was ready for some meat. I had regained some of the weight I had lost but was still quite a bit below my normal weight. At least my stomach wasn't gurgling and distended anymore since I'd gotten the e-coli infection under control. The open-air restaurant overlooked a large rutted dirt field filled with horses, a great view of the sales prospects. Most were small and rangy looking with wild eyes and manes that had never seen a brush.

There didn't seem to be any organization to the sales process, so after lunch, we wandered through the milling herds of horses and sellers, shielding our faces from gusts of dust as the horses' hooves scuffed the hard packed dirt. We initially intended to get one horse, but when we returned to the restaurant, I suggested, "Do you think that we could get two with our $250 … we each could have a horse? It would be so fun! We could gallop along that section of trail near the river." I visualized my hair blowing in the wind at a stiff gallop.

Ernesto chuckled. "Sure. Just think, you'll have an even larger manure machine with two horses."

My job was manure-hunting and Ernesto's was to bring up water from the stream in the dry season. The idea of faster manure collection sounded like a great idea and maybe the horse could also help hauling water.

I had ridden a bit and had some experience grooming, riding in a ring, a bit of trail riding and overall horsemanship, and Ernesto had gone on a few trail rides. We were green, and the sellers saw us coming. After an hour or so of checking out the horses "picking up hooves," sort of like "kicking tires," we laughed and settled on a beautiful big bay mare and a smaller scrappy-looking roan stallion. We paid to have two wranglers bring the horses by trail, over the Cuchumatanes Mountains and down into Ixcán.

The two-week trek over the mountains soon became three weeks and then four weeks. We asked everyone that passed through Centro Uno if they had heard anything about the horses or seen anything and initially there were reports about them coming and then nothing. The last we heard was that only one horse had made it over the ridge and that the beautiful big bay mare had pulled back on her rope and strangled in Polop. That was doubtful, but neither of us were able to hike to Polop to find out what had really happened.

Apparently, the roan was at the Finca Felicidad. I was in Mayalan when Ernesto took off on a six-hour round trip hike to go and get him.

I got back before they finally arrived, both of them exhausted. The small scrappy roan gave a halfhearted neigh.

After a thorough health check, we discovered that the roan had only one testicle, thus he was christened Lugnut. I don't know if it was due to a lack of testosterone, but he was the sweetest and most willing horse I had ever known. Given our complete lack of horsemanship, we were very lucky.

Every morning the damp garden's earthy, rotten leaf smell welcomed another day. Overnight there might have been a change and the red ants from the day before with their cigarette burn stings had moved on, or the small tangle of coral snakes had moved away from the compost pile below the Ficus. The day after Lugnut arrived, I did not hesitate, it was time to feed the compost pile. I slipped on the heavy turquoise rubber gloves after breakfast and picked up a white plastic five-gallon bucket in each hand to harvest fresh horse poop. The salty barnyard stench gagged me as the mid-morning sun baked the manure, and moisture from the nightly rain and humidity created a cloud around each steaming pile. The next day I started at dawn.

The jungle never slept and was never quiet, but the rhythm changed at first light. The sounds were softer, the cicadas started cranking up slowly first thing...a slow click, click that became a chaotic whir. The loros called and soared above me, bright spots of green, vermillion and yellow in the deep blue sky on their morning trip from the stately ceiba tree crossing the Ixcán basin, searching for exotic fruit and seeds that I could not see.

I followed Lugnut's footsteps meandering through the thick razor-sharp grass methodically walking across the pista with white buckets swinging as that first light of day flooded the valley.

The grass was 20 inches high and thick, a wild overgrown Saint Augustine. Lugnut had a rope looped around his neck, wandering on the far side of the "runway" now. Some days finding his manure was like searching for eggs on Easter. I laughed to myself and petted his flank.

Both buckets were two-thirds of the way full, just heavy enough to make for a bit of a struggle up the slippery lateritic red rock and mud path to the garden on the plateau. I slid to the edge of the narrow path, my rubber boots lacking purchase. I righted myself, grabbing a fleshy colocasia leaf, yet another house plant gone wild.

Dumping the manure on the compost pile, I was relieved to see that the tiny coral snakes had moved on. The steaming pile garnered so much interest from the community that the daily collection was unrelenting in preparation for classes on composting.

But then, one night, I dreamt of eating horse poop, salty and tangy. I woke up and said to Ernesto, "I can taste it!"

"What are you talking about?"

"The manure ... all night long I could smell fresh manure and taste the salt...but the texture is the worst!"

Lugnut proved his weight in gold not just as a manure factory but also a wonderful pet and a reasonably good mount. Every day I walked down to the pista and he neighed, welcoming me. My dream as a young girl of owning a pony, or in this case a horse, was finally fulfilled.

# CHAPTER 20

October 1977 and February 1978

I had been alone at our house at the end of the village path for several weeks when Ernesto and Pamela Crombie from DID finally flew in to prepare some additional health workshops. My role expanded from agronomy and family gardening to health education, just by the fact of my sex.

In the year that I'd been there, I had identified areas that would benefit from some additional help and sent a request to DID. Pamela wanted to develop a baseline of health so we could determine if there was malnutrition and then if so, figure out how to document our work to help solve it. She brought a tape to measure height and arm circumference, and we measured all of the school children. My relationship with the women in the village gave everyone a level of comfort in proceeding with this process of evaluation and being open to some simple ideas like daily teeth brushing.

Many of the children had rotted teeth, so Pamela and I gave two classes in dental care, the first to a group of eight women, and then, with the parents' okay, to the children during school as a health class. We were all very excited about toothbrushes coming, but when the toothbrushes didn't arrive in time for the class—the river was quite swollen from the rain—we improvised with lemon tree branches that we carved into sticks and tied pieces of ripped towel to with weaving thread. Only a quarter of the children had brushed their teeth before, so for many it was a new experience. Everyone thoroughly enjoyed making the tool and brushing their teeth.

One of the things that came out of our discussion with the women at the dental class was that they were interested in learning more about hygiene. This led to a request to have bi-weekly classes on a wide range of topics from basic sanitation and nutrition to the single most requested topic: family planning.

Over the past year, I had been asked by both men and women alike if we were "maridos," and if so, why Ernesto and I didn't have children since we were clearly a couple. Some asked, "Do you sleep together?"

I said, "Yes, we are a couple but aren't married, and we sleep together and have sex, but I take a pill, so I won't get pregnant."

The women asked, "¿Como puedo conseguir la pastilla?" How can I get the pill?

I suggested that we should do a class in one of my Women's Groups, now called La Cocina, and one woman, speaking for the others, said, "We have to do a class with the men or they won't pay any attention to us." That was how we ended up giving a class for seven couples on sex, reproduction, and birth control. I was hesitant to talk about birth control since the Catholic clinic in Jacaltenango had voiced that the whole Health Resource Center concept was unnecessary due to their clinics. The competition of NGOs and the church occasionally resulted in a lack of coordination and care for those who needed help.

Given the interest, however, we decided to risk it and give the class. However, we realized that we had no visual aids to explain the reproductive process and had to wing it. We held the class at our house since we had the only place large enough with a door to keep the children out. We pushed the cot and the chair back against the wall and all the women knelt on the concrete floor, blue cortes wrapped tightly around their knees, in a ragged semi-circle. The men sat behind on the cot and chair and a couple of the men leaned against the board and batten wall with their arms crossed. Their annoyed faces suggested they were there against their will, but their wives were fixed on their attendance. Outside, curiosity overcame the children, and they pressed their faces against the screen and the big brothers and sisters lifted up the little ones, so they could eavesdrop on their parents' class.

All the families were Catholic, and birth control was against the teachings of the church. Even the rhythm method was suspect. Josépha said, "The padres don't understand how hard it is to have children and to raise them when you are poor." One of the men chimed in, "Los padres no saben cómo está para nosotros." He wondered if the padres could understand how hard it was for them, too. He explained that unplanned pregnancies were tough on everyone.

Medical attention was days away by horseback and giving birth was very dangerous, as I had seen with one mother's death following her breech birth. All the women in the room had lost at least one child, and it was hard for them to accept that as "God's will." I realized that I didn't need to sell anyone on birth control; the group assembled was focused on taking charge of their reproductive rights regardless of the church's teachings.

Our lack of drawing tools and artistic ability resulted in a piece of lined binder-paper where Ernesto drew a man and a woman with a blue ballpoint pen and then zoomed in on close ups of the vagina, uterus and penis. I explained that the period was a time when the uterus was cleaning or clearing out, and there was no baby inside then. He added drops of blood.

The women conferred, then shared that the sign of their period, was thought to be a sign that they *were* pregnant. Clearly backwards from fertility science. But in this case, their period signaled their fertility and there was rarely time between their first period and the next pregnancy. In other words, they were almost continually pregnant.

Next, he drew on our simple flip chart an egg forming and falling into the uterus followed by the man's penis moving toward the vagina, with the little sperm as fish swimming to the egg up through the vagina and into the uterus.

Raucous jokes in Mam that we couldn't understand issued forth accompanied by lots of laughing.

When we were discussing the egg getting fertilized, Lucia asked seriously, "¿Aye dios mio se puede comerlos?" "Can you eat the eggs?"

"No, están muy chiquito…" I explained that they are way too small. Any opportunity for additional nutrition was welcome and that drew another round of collective hysteria.

Once we went through the descriptions of graphic sex, someone asked, "No queremos mas niños como no podemos a tener mas?" "We don't want to have more children; how do we not have more?"

I explained, "The first method is the rhythm method, sort of approved by the church, where you identify the time that you are fertile during the month and avoid sex during that time."

That got another round of laughter with both men and women saying at the same time, "No serve!" That is not going to work. "Hay otro ideas?" "Any other great ideas?"

On to the condom, but condoms were a solid, "No!" from the group. The idea of placing a condom on for sex in the family bed was messy and complicated at best and curtailed any spontaneity.

My dilemma was how to introduce the birth control pill, which clearly seemed like the easiest approach but required a doctor. The small clinics run by the nuns from Jacaltenango were not an option, and there really weren't any other clinics.

The entire group assembled on our concrete floor said in unison, "¡Quéremos las pastillas!" We had our marching orders: figure out where to get birth control pills. Should we bring a doctor in? We had suggested that once with the measles epidemic to a resounding no from the clinic.

One man spoke up, "¿Se puede quitar el pescado de una vez?" He brought up the possibility of a vasectomy. This was beyond what we had planned for, and we didn't know if and where you could get one and at what price. "We will need to research this too."

Ernesto added it to his list for his next trip to the city. The list was long, first the bank then hilo, thread for weaving, film, Digesa (the Department of Agriculture), the seed store, the mercado, the bookstore, and now the Clinica Central…how much for a vasectomy?

After the class, I realized that the community knew that the way out of poverty was not just through owning land but the ability to make decisions based on education and reproductive rights. They were ready for any help getting there, and we became yet another conduit.

It wasn't until after we left Ixcán that I received a letter from one of our "students" in 1979, saying that the "Clinica en Mayalan" finally had the pills.

# CHAPTER 21

From the platform-bed raised high in the corner of the house, I could see clearly into the garden and jungle, and it called to me all day and throughout the night. Every morning was a surprise. I anticipated what the night brought—would it be the beauty of a sunflower budding to full bloom, tiny radish sprouts filling the bed overnight with a fresh bright green mat, or the shock of our tiny corn field, tall and ripe with young elotes, flattened in a circle as though extraterrestrials had landed?

Our work began at daybreak when we could just make out the silhouettes of the trees. Thin rays of light spread over the rough green mountains to the south and through the tops of the trees, gradually filtering down to encompass the wide Ixcán valley. To the west, the Río Ixcán rippled, with sparkling peaks and frothy rapids. After manure harvesting it was still cool in the early morning. Soaking in the beauty and peace, I made coffee, toasting the raw dried beans in an aluminum frying pan on the two-burner propane stove. Grinding the toasted beans in the molino with a bit of sugar and cinnamon released a sweet scent. The water heated, the coffee ground and boiled and its rich aroma, slightly burned with cinnamon, hung heavily in the humidity.

Sitting out on the concrete stoop, I gingerly balanced the enameled cup and sipped. Those first hours of the day in the garden though were the time of assessment. Had the ants taken over? Had the neighbor's horses gotten loose and run through the garden again? That would determine the day's work, from daybreak until 10:30 a.m., then resting until 3:00 p.m., and resuming work when the rain and cooling breeze returned.

In addition to tiny ants, the garden soil was alive with invasive nematodes, a soil borne microscopic worm-like creature that attacked plant roots and caused stunting and death of non-native plants throughout the Ixcán. The nematodes in the garden varied in location and some beds were more impacted than others. Harsh chemicals were often used to mitigate the problem elsewhere, but that was not an option here. Growth was so quick that just a bit of stunting often meant nematodes. We played a kind of roulette, determining which plants would survive and thrive unaffected by them, and which would succumb. No need to try planting again if we pulled up an affected plant and the fine roots were brittle and dry with oozing nodules. It was not a problem that organic compost alone could solve.

Figuring out which seeds to plant required testing, testing, and more testing. Try this seed and see how it does against the intense heat, the rain, the lack of rain, the tiny black ants rushing to see if it was palatable. It was a continual process of discovery, elation, and then disappointment. Every day, we documented the successes and failures.

New vegetable varieties, particularly those from countries with a similar climate, including wing bean, okra and different Asian greens that Ernesto had brought in, were successful. But it was hard to introduce different flavors and textures beyond the basics of black beans, corn, squash and cabbage, because they were not always well received. Mustard and radish greens continued to be a hit; however, okra was too slippery, and wing beans too oddly shaped, compared with the standard beans that our neighbors had grown up with. Both grew well, strong and fast, so it was unfortunate that they weren't popular. Although many hybrid varieties were more resistant to disease and fungus than heritage varieties, we focused on plants that would be easy to propagate and set seed, so that farmers could continually grow their own.

Planting seeds was a challenge. The seeds rotted or tiny ants ate them before they sprouted in the garden beds. The impact of the scorching

100-degree sun and then torrential rains decreased the germination rate and washed the seeds away. At the center of the French Intensive process was planting seeds in seed flats rather than directly in the ground in order to maintain continual use of the garden beds and ensure better germination.

Early on we had built the lath house, a covered open cane structure with high cane benches for the flats with openings to allow for drainage, and it worked well. Insects, for some reason, weren't very interested in climbing up the cane posts to the bench, so we had a bit of a chance to get the seeds to sprout. We built seed flats from mahogany boards that were 18" x 24", durable and beautiful, and we used those to seed the crops. Campesinos came by to see the garden and were impressed with the lath house's functionality. Soon we started to see it replicated.

We attempted to grow tomatoes, including varieties from more humid areas, but were continually disappointed. We had success once and harvested over 25 lbs. of tomatoes! Our next planting of 30 tomato plants was three-feet high with small green tomatoes on the vines that looked promising until, overnight, a white wilt crept in. The following morning, we went out to the garden, and there were just piles of mushy stalks and stems covered with a fine white powder mold.

We could not grow the tomatoes consistently, and the lowland tropical weather was just too hot and humid to grow the potatoes and cabbages that the community was used to in the highlands. Centuries of a diet that included potatoes and cabbage in addition to corn and beans, made these foods not just sorely missed but a requirement that was impossible to fulfill.

Amaranth, the original Aztec grain, thrived in the tropical moisture and generated more local interest. Growing almost eight feet tall, it had large heavy heads of seeds high in protein. A short, wild version called "bledo" grew along the trail and was a nutritious green with a mild spinach taste.

After numerous plants succumbed to the relentless heat, we built little cane corrals around each bed and used cut palm fronds that we moved strategically all day long to allow for more or less exposure to the sun. This helped to shield the plants from the overbearing sun that burned the seedlings as well as minimizing water loss through evaporation. Many days there was an afternoon rain and we waited, vigilant and ran to move the fronds before the first drops hit.

We stood on the broad concrete space that had been a clinic the late afternoon, watching as rain clouds gather. They started in the south and came thundering toward us like a giant curtain, the individual droplets visible beads. I wondered how quickly the building that was there had succumbed to the environment, where did it go in just 12 years? Did it dissolve? I stepped back and then looked at the garden in the misty rain and thought about the Maya civilization that had been here for centuries and then just disappeared. I had a small collection of arrowheads, pot feet and then a big chunk of obsidian in a bowl in the house that I had found in the garden. Why had no one had inhabited this jungle in 600 years? I felt a chill and saw what I thought was the army moving in the bushes and trees and then I shook myself and saw the red and white of Luisa's huipil, not camouflage.

Pabla and Luisa used the concrete surface for drying their coffee and cardamom. Usually, they were very organized and the daily drying went smoothly, but every once in a while, they misjudged the timing. Luisa had darted out of the orchard and ran down the path toward the concrete slab screaming, "¡Ya viene!"-"It's coming!" The rain would pound toward Centro Uno from across the valley and Luisa and Pabla would sweep up all the coffee and cardamom pods and stuff the sweet pods and coffee berries into the white woven bultas, dragging them into our house right before the deluge hit.

The next morning, once the sun baked the concrete dry, Luisa arrived with a cheerful, "Buenos días," and dragged the bags back to the concrete slab, spreading out the light green beans and pods for another day of drying.

When the rain stopped during the dry season, the lack of running water was a constant problem. The padres had a pump that carried water up from the stream below the house. But given our continual lack of basic support from DID, we toyed with asking for one but realized that if we weren't going to get a radio, it was doubtful we could get a pump. Ernesto made up to ten trips a day carrying two five-gallon buckets up to the garden from the creek. He balanced the buckets on each side of a yolk he had made from a heavy branch—the water sloshed with the buckets swinging, precious water splashing out as he trudged up the hill.

In the late morning, we retired inside away from the blistering heat and documented the amount of rain from the day before and the temperature with a high/low thermometer. Nothing scientific but it offered an estimate of the anticipated rain and dry period for planning the next year of garden crops. The journal became a running dialog of all that happened in the garden, crops seeded, dying, happy and harvested as well as composting. In addition, we wrote notes about what was happening in the community and kept track of the transformations that we were seeing, not realizing then how those notes would help tell the story of what would become a genocide.

What had started as an idea just to develop family gardens had transformed to meet the needs of both Centro Uno and the extended Ixcán. As campesinos walked through Centro Uno, they had questions as well as ideas about how we could help. Families and men and women by themselves came by the garden, and we listened and tried to determine if there was something we could do, either by bringing in different seeds or plants or even medications. Cardamom bleached out with sun decreased its value substantially, so we spent many months trying unsuccessfully to get a solar drier that would keep the pods green and increase the sales price. As much help as we offered, DID and any other organizations' support was waning.

We kept looking for ways to spread our research and share our successes, so we wrote a small booklet in Spanish with illustrations, titled "How to Grow Your Hortaliza." Working with a Catholic Charity in Guatemala City, Ernesto was able to make copies. It was so successful that whenever one of us went out we would get more copies. We gave them away with seeds. We also brought in other books on growing cash crops and multiple copies of *Donde no hay doctor* to sell or give away.

Francisco had been my right-hand helper working several hours daily, digging, moving the trellises, turning the compost and planting, but his family needed him full time after his father died. He and his elder brother, Julio, assumed the role of heads of household, and the other kids were not as interested in doing the work he'd done with such gusto. I missed his energy and help, but gradually the garden became more manageable as we cleared and manicured.

José, Diego and Mariano's other brother in the village, told me one particularly hot mid-day, "You are working way too hard. With the milpa at least we have a rest occasionally." Clearly there was no way to maintain a garden at the same level that we were doing as well as complete all the work they were already doing. Everyone knew from watching our travails that complete annihilation of the garden was an ever-present possibility. Even so the community garden, maintained by several families, was gradually expanding following Diego's first beds. In addition, he and his brother Mariano Jerez had built garden beds at their homes. Mariano was also interested in the community garden approach, so word and interest spread. Diego's wife loved zinnias, so she planted a bed of zinnias at the front of their house while he grew the vegetables.

A constant threat to our garden were loose horses, pigs, and even cows running through. To keep the neighbors' horses out of the garden we planted a hedge of Rosa de Jamaica, a small shrub with a beautiful pink flower that, when dried, makes delicious hibiscus tea. Soon after planting I looked out of the house to admire it just starting to bloom only to find it had been completely stripped of leaves and buds. Taking a closer look, a long line of leafcutter ants made their way in a caravan from our garden to a large hole, each carrying a bright green leaf sail above its head. Referring to one of our reference books, we learned that they made their own compost and grew their own food—a kind of mold in a large underground chamber. It was pretty impressive, just not with my favorite Rosa de Jamaica.

Diego suggested moving the entire ant colony since we didn't have any poison to eradicate them. I didn't really want to kill them, so we dug up the ants and some of their compost and moved them deep in the jungle and far from the garden. We judiciously doused the few remaining ants with a kerosene and water mixture.

The garden was now large and flourishing. It was a destination for people who wanted to know how to grow vegetables in the humid lowlands. We were surprised and encouraged by the interest and excitement about family gardens and even had some community members planning "truck gardens" with vegetables to sell at the weekly markets.

With that, we felt a renewed sense of purpose and urgency to help. It was hard to think of being anywhere else. Sometimes, sitting on the stoop, we imagined that San Francisco was just over the ridge and yet I still felt no attraction. We lived in Centro Uno now, without a thought of returning to the U.S. In spite of being very sick at times, I felt that I had a reason to be there, and that I was making a significant difference. I was deeply connected to the Centro Uno community, something that had been missing from my life back in the U.S. The day-to-day rhythm was so familiar that it became as natural as breathing. But when we least expected it, that tranquil rhythm was breached.

The co-op required community abstinence from alcohol, except for the occasional fiesta, which helped ensure that everyone pulled their weight. But that did not apply to anyone who wasn't a co-op member. One morning a small bright orange helicopter dropped off an older Ladino man carrying a bag of tools, a surveyor hired by the co-op to survey property lines and parcels. We thought that it would be entertaining to have a visitor from the city.

A couple of days into his surveying he managed to secure some cusha from the local bootlegger. Intoxicated, he wandered from our house throughout the village howling, and when the cusha ran out he started looking for anything that had alcohol in it.

One night I heard the front door slam open as he barged in, yelling, "Hay alcohol?" Before I could respond, he had gone into the bathroom and grabbed my bottle of Muguet de Bois, perfume that I had brought with me for some bizarre reason and downed it as I stood by dumbfounded. He then staggered next door to Pabla's kitchen area and took the bottle of alcohol that she used for her lamp and chugged that, too.

Without a police force, the co-op met and determined that the surveyor had to go. They decided to take him out into the wilderness the next morning, tie him up to a tree and leave him. There weren't many options since there was no secure building in the village. To pass the night, they tied him to a support post on the school overhang next to our house where he screamed profanities all night long, wrestling with the ropes and urinating on himself.

Before being left in the jungle, his nephew showed up on horseback with a large bottle of aguardiente, a pre-rum liquor, in the saddle bag. Unbeknownst to me, one of the co-op members had gone to Mayalan and called the company he worked for who called his nephew in the city. The nephew had flown into Mayalan on a private plane and ridden by horseback to Centro Uno to collect his uncle, arriving just in time.

Standing in the kitchen of our house with the front door open and the surveyor vertical but listing, the nephew handed me the large bottle and said, "Let him have a drink."

I hadn't realized that I was supposed to pour a small amount into a cup for him. The surveyor grabbed the bottle from my hand and polished off the entire thing, then dropped to the concrete a few minutes later, passed out cold on the stoop in front of the house. The co-op members lifted him up and slung him over the saddle. Tied across the back of the horse, head and arms hanging loosely on one side and legs draped over the other, his nephew set off on the long trip back to Mayalan, leading the horse, intent on returning to the city as quickly as possible.

I wasn't sure what the outcome would have been if the nephew had not arrived when he did. Would they have left him in the jungle? I didn't ask. I didn't want to know. There was no place in the day-to-day survival for the derelict.

# CHAPTER 22

Word of success in Ixcán spread via the newspaper and radio and soon the number of families trekking to Ixcán in search of a better life had increased by a factor of 10. This was not an organized process, more of a homesteading approach where people had been told by someone that there was land available, and they came with all their belongings. They moved into new virgin rainforest areas and felled the huge first-story ramon, mahogany, and ceiba trees. Slash and burn increased throughout the Ixcán valley, smoke mingling with the humidity, created smog-like conditions.

The verdant jungle and rainforest had been untouched by human hands for at least 600 years since the Maya civilization had crumbled. One of the volunteers from my class, Sylvia, who had been scheduled originally to go to Ixcán, learned that the native breadfruit or ramon trees, which produced a rich healthy nut, had been the mainstay of the Maya diet until conditions gradually declined due to what some assume was a massive drought, perhaps brought on by the clear cutting of the forests.

To watch this complex ecosystem's swift destruction was particularly concerning, given that theory. Would this be a disastrous repeat? As the trees were cut down, the climate began changing. In just 11 years the people in Centro Uno had seen a significant reduction in rainfall. Our two years of documentation from 1976 to 1978 provided a snapshot of rainfall. Current rainfall shows a shocking 40% decrease in annual rainfall.

Animals had been impacted by human intervention—jaguars had been eradicated, killed early on by scared villagers and the monkeys had all died of yellow fever in the first five years. A delectable soup made from parrot and toucan led to the slow-moving birds being dispatched quickly by boys armed with slingshots. My first experience with parrot soup was at Demetria's—a parrot leg, floating in broth, just a tiny bit of dark meat morsel on a petite bone. It was cute but creepy and sad given the beauty of the birds.

The hippy-gringo tendency that even I had ascribed to initially assumed that all indigenous peoples somehow had a cosmic connection with the plants and animals and acted as informed protectors of the land. As in any community, there were some who understood and revered nature and maintained a relationship to the spirit of it, but not everyone. The campesinos did not appear to understand the human impact on the climate as they continued to slash and burn.

Under virgin conditions, the tall, high canopied trees were alive with epiphytes, bird nests, and vines that were constantly changing, dropping both soft and hard leaves, creating leaf litter and humus. When large swaths of the jungle and rainforest were felled, exposing the red lateritic soil, heavy rains quickly leached minerals and humus resulting in a soil so depleted that it could not maintain plant growth. Tropical soil is very different from temperate soil and I was glad to have the two Purseglove books since it gave us a bit of tropical soil information. My daily chore of picking up horse poop was one of the few things that kept the compost pile actively transforming and generating humus and fertile soil for the garden and one of the only ways to slow the rapid soil leaching and depletion. We soon realized that for the continued health of the rainforest and jungle, the slash and burn needed to stop. Educating about the importance of the tree canopy and replanting the native trees became an important part of our work.

Out of the blue one-day Tomás announced that the President was to fly in and visit the Centro Uno community. In preparation for the fly in, the pista was filled with men by 6 a.m. from the surrounding co-op pueblos with machetes and axes. Trees at the edge of the pista were felled and the three-foot high grass was macheted to three inches. As the group moved toward the parrot tree, and I heard the first whack of an axe, I immediately ran screaming, "¡No, alto!" Frozen, axes in midair, they looked at me askance as I explained, "Este árbol es al lado de la pista y es la casa de los loros." I shared how important the tree was for the ecosystem as well as the home for the parrots and how it was not in the way of the runway, in fact, not even close. They stopped and backed off from my screaming as though thinking, "Let's not upset the crazy gringa." As it turned out the President did not fly in, so the clear cutting of the trees around the pista was for naught.

The men met at the school that night to discuss the President's no-show. They were concerned because co-op members had come together from across Ixcán to make this visit happen. Was the government becoming even less interested in helping the co-ops? The visit was to have been an opportunity to show the fecundity of Ixcán and the birthplace of Proyecto Ixcán and now the pervading concern and question was, "¿Por qué no vinieron?" "Why didn't the President come?"

Given this most recent unconscious felling of the trees, Ernesto took on the task of learning more about forestry, so we could teach about the important functions of the rainforest that campesinos from the highlands didn't realize they relied upon. He connected with INAFOR, the Guatemalan forestry department, and traveled to Guatemala's West Coast to learn about reforestation and discover new crops that might be grown in the shade beneath the tree canopy in addition to the main export crops of cardamom and coffee.

Now, whenever Ernesto left the village and I was alone, the children came over and offered to sleep with me. They couldn't understand how I could be alone in the house. They wanted to make my day alegre and couldn't imagine sleeping alone without their parents and siblings in bed with them and didn't want me to be sad. Their parents would tell me too, bringing the children by, "The children are here to sleep with you." At the time I couldn't imagine why I would have them stay. As an only child, I had always had my own room and never slept with anyone other than Ernesto, so I really didn't know what to make of it. I didn't realize what a gift I had missed out on and how much they cared about me until I returned home.

Staying alone in the half-screened house surrounded by the jungle pressing in at night was never restful. I was vigilant from the moment that the sun went down, waiting for the unknown and unexpected to happen. Listening to the night noises I waited for the cessation of sound that indicated an intruder, person, army or guerrilla, sneaking into the house where I was exposed and defenseless. I lay alone only knowing my own terror. Even with Ernesto there, I never experienced shared safety and didn't even know how to think about it. I read, trying to immerse myself in another life somewhere safe, as the candle wavered in the breeze on the windowsill of the screened opening.

When Ernesto returned from the first forestry trip to the coast, he brought renewed energy about beginning the reforestation project as well two large bags of ramon and mahogany seeds. INAFOR was helpful and interested in working with the co-op to understand the importance of the forest and retain the large ancient structural trees for timber rather than simply burning them. The lath house now worked as a tree nursery in addition to housing the vegetable flats. We nicked the thick coated seeds to encourage sprouting and planted them in black plastic bags filled with soil and compost. As the sprouts broke out of their hard shells with two fleshy cotyledons, they rapidly grew into twelve-inch saplings in three months.

One day, a group of 13 men gathered on the front stoop of the house for a workshop on the importance of maintaining the rainforest. Ernesto shared, "The native trees are protecting the soils, which are very different from those in the highlands."

Several members of the class were concerned and expressed an interest in understanding the forest cycle. Having come from the mountains that had been over-farmed for centuries, the Ixcán was a lush never-ending expanse of green, and it was hard to imagine that it could change. We showed the class the rain and temperature information that we had gathered. Those who had lived there the longest had seen a significant reduction in rainfall with the ongoing clearing of large swaths of the jungle and rainforest and noticed an extended dry period that used to be just in the month of May and now encompassed some of April and June as well.

"¿Cómo cultivamos los árboles grandes y explicar al gente?" The class wanted to know how to grow the trees and how to explain to others the importance if they were asked. Their interest in understanding the science of the natural lifecycle was exciting, and we felt a growing interest in reforestation and maintaining the large first story trees to help the entire Ixcán.

"Gracias para enseñándonos de esto," "¿Hay más?" They asked when there would be more saplings. That request and the polite, "Adiós," was so rewarding.

The opportunity for all of us to learn about the transitioning forest and how to properly manage that transition by saving large trees and replanting also reengaged the co-op landowners in understanding best practices for developing their farms. It was a glimpse into a future, and we were excited about how we could help with INAFOR to ensure that soaring ancient trees would survive and live on.

I became so lost in my excitement to connect with the trees and the jungle, immersing myself in the garden and weaving, I missed the changing political climate, and I blocked my anger about being left alone terrified at the edge of the village.

# CHAPTER 23

Even without the direct influence and assistance from the Maryknolls or other outside organizations, the five main Ixcán cooperatives were prospering. The cooperative structure had been set up in a way that encouraged consensus in all decision-making processes, and it was working well, not just in our village but across the Ixcán Grande Proyecto. Land ownership, with homes at the village centers, created a feeling of community. The safety of being part of the larger co-op organization encouraged entrepreneurism and production. Our small village of Centro Uno was a forerunner and a microcosm for what was happening across the Ixcán.

Passing through Centro Uno, the conversation in Elena's comedor was guarded. When the residents of Centro Uno arrived 11 years before with their lives on their backs, they were part of the organized Maryknoll project. Now new homesteaders arrived and the settlers asked, "Aquí estamos…¿Adónde vamos para el terreno?" The response was, "Muy retriado y lejos de aquí." "You cannot stay here; you need to go further down the trail to the other side of the Ixcán."

It was a long trip and far from easy. Land was not available in Ixcán Grande.

For centuries, campesinos and their families had toiled on the fincas of large landowners, making pennies a day, with not even enough to eat. Now, clearing and planting their own land, the campesinos gave vision to what this land could be. This was not lost on wealthy Guatemalans and international corporations from Canada and the U.S. who coveted Ixcán and its huge tracts of land with valuable trees, minerals and agricultural potential. Oil companies and the Guatemalan government's request to build the Franja Transversal del Norte, a road through Ixcán Grande, was temporarily quashed by the co-op.

Rumors ran rampant that the Ixcán co-ops were supporting the rising tide of guerrilla warfare and the EGP. The comment by the alcalde, the mayor of Barillas, two years before Bill Woods' death describing the Ixcán as "little Cuba" stuck.

An occasional sighting of the EGP had shifted to their more significant presence. When we returned to Centro Uno from a volunteer conference in Honduras in early 1978, Santiago told us, "Un grupo del EGP, vinieron aquí buscando por Tomás." We knew that Tomás, as the co-op president, was working with the Guatemalan military. It was hard to find fault given that there really were no other options for entering and leaving the Ixcán as private flights had been limited to just Guy flying from Quiche and Tonino and Christina flying their tiny personal plane. That the guerrillas had come looking for Tomás showed a new boldness and awareness. It was a tenuous situation and the co-op's success was based on the ability to transport their agricultural products in and out of Ixcán. One thing we now realized was that tiny Centro Uno was well known to both the EGP and the army.

The decision to starve the co-ops financially by not allowing independent air transport and then limiting army flights was strategic and ruinous. The Ixcán Grande co-ops were completely dependent on moving their main cash crops out by plane. Cardamom, a valuable crop, was just reaching maturity and a level of viable production. The pods weren't perfect, but the campesinos were learning the culture. It was a tedious and dangerous job picking the small green pods at the base of the plant. Tomás told me, "La Barba Amarilla, se mata uno entre tres minutos."—"Yellow Beard, a viper that kills in three minutes, nestles in among the tangled roots and challenges the harvesters." Fungi and insect pests were rampant in the virgin jungle. At night, as I savored the rich aroma of Tomás and Pabla's drying cardamom filling our house during the rain, I thought about the dangerous work it took to harvest.

Coffee plants produced well but did not provide the high value of highland coffee or the price of the cardamom. With 28 acres and one-third of that in cardamom or coffee planted beneath the tree canopy, there was an opportunity to make enough to buy cattle and expand into other opportunities. But cattle required pasture and that meant cutting down the trees.

Over frijoles and huevos at Elena 's comedor, I talked to the travelers straggling through Cento Uno. A Todo Santero from Mayalan said, "Cuatrocientos de las EGP entraron La Resurrección, cantarán canciones y dío una lectura de cómo le chocaron un helicóptero." He described in detail how 400 guerrillas entered La Resurrección singing and talking about how they downed an army helicopter.

Another traveler at the comedor said, "Ellos lo matarán un capitán en Los Ángeles," telling the small group at the table that an officer, a captain he thought, was killed by the EGP in the large Ixcán co-op town of Los Ángeles.

I was shocked that all this had happened in the two weeks we had been gone to Honduras. As Ernesto and I walked back to the house I said, "This is nuts; how could all this happen in two weeks?"

"Don't worry, we're far away, over a day's walk from there… it shouldn't be a big deal."

"Yeah, easily maybe two days' walk." As if that somehow meant safety.

The enclosed jungle didn't allow an open view of our surroundings, and everyone was on edge. There was fear of reprisals by the army searching for guerrillas, and then of the guerrillas entering pueblos and the army following them. Fear had come to Centro Uno. The conversation in the comedor was just the start of the talk. Army escalation increased and included the construction of a huge army and air force encampment in Playa Grande. There was also a rumor that there were now *two* gringa women traveling with the guerrillas making my existence less safe. How would anyone know that I wasn't a guerrilla?

Our village was obscured visually by the dense tree canopy and thick sharp cane and audibly by the raucous calls of the parrots and cicadas. Helicopters and planes flew over the mountains at night, dropping bombs on hills to the west of Centro Uno. We could see bright sulfur flashes and feel the thunder of bombing startling the forest on February 1, 1978. Our monthly report to DID laid out the increasing presence of both the EGP and the army and the perilous balance of the community and our work. Who would think that making people more self-sufficient would be political and how did we all tread the line between supporting the army so that there was transport and supporting the guerrillas whose rhetoric supported the land-poor.

These larger terrors were offset by smaller gifts, like Marta from Centro Dos saying, "We are tired of radishes, everyone is growing them now." My joy at "too many radishes" was simple. Each moment was precious may sound trite, but we lived very much in the moment, be that fear or joy.

One day walking down the trail to Nicholas' house, I was stopped by an army platoon and shoved by a terrified private who, seeing my jungle boots, screamed, "¿Dónde consigio estos?" His gaze fixed on my green canvas and "leather" jungle boots.

Heart racing, throat suddenly dry, I looked at my boots: red mud stained the scuffed black plastic-leather and khaki canvas. A lieutenant hiked up the narrow trail, quickly moving to the front of the group, pushing aside those in the way. The steel blue snout of his rifle swung skyward as he knelt to check. I watched the muzzle shift and catch the sun streaming through the trees, only aware of the sound of my loudly thudding heart. Scraping away the lodo, he said, "¿Estas botas las que llevaba el capitán que lo asesinado?" Are these the boots of the dead captain?"

"¿Usted tiene papeles? ¿Qué está haciendo aquí si no es guerrillera, unas mujeres gringas lo mataron el capitán?" Your paperwork now. Why are you here? What are you doing here if you are not a guerrilla? I didn't understand why he was asking me these questions. Then a rough voice said that some gringa women had been with the group that killed the captain.

"Tiene suerte estas botas son baratas de plastico," The lieutenant said. Leaning closer and scraping with his knife he finally shook his head. "These are cheap boots, not the real thing," he decided.

My hand shaking, I said, "Momento por favor," while I reached into my backpack and brought out the letter from Coronel Castillo allowing me to work in Ixcán.

"Llevaron sus botes, hay que quitarlos no se permite." The captain is dead and they took his boots. U.S. issued Vietnam boots are only for military officers in Guatemala. You need to get rid of them now!

They let me go. I was lucky that time.

Back at Centro Uno I dug a hole and buried the boots immediately, my hands still trembling. I racked my brain for other items that might provoke them.

Later that night, when the darkness stretched forever, I tried to wrap my mind around that moment and why I immediately decided to just bury the boots and not ask, "Ernesto, should we leave?" But I didn't ask. Neither one of us spoke our fears, we just moved forward. It wasn't until many years later that I realized the true depth of our survival mode. We too had become soldiers, yet without the awareness to connect the dots of the coming conflict.

# CHAPTER 24

One day, Pamela Crombie flew in to follow-up on the community health issues that we had discussed at the DID meeting we had attended in Honduras with the other volunteers. Her visit intended for a week in Centro Uno extended to several more while we waited for Guy to fly in. Thank goodness the grass on the pista was still low enough for landing after the community-wide machete-cutting took down the tough grass to a few inches for the President of Guatemala's visit that never happened. Even with the pista cut, however, Guy did not come.

Leaden skies and rain had settled in for the past week, curtailing small planes and drenching the trail, which was muddier than normal.

Two nights of concussive bombing on the east facing slopes of the Sierra Madres just outside of Centro Uno left our nerves jangled. "Do you think we're in danger?" Pamela asked, and I couldn't reassure her one way or another. I didn't know what to expect next after the reports of the guerrillas at La Resurrección and the boots incident. A passing campesino getting seeds at the garden told us that the killing of the captain and the stealing of his boots was in response to a massacre in Ixcán Chiquita. "Muy peligroso por todo," he said. Clearly it was getting very dangerous for everyone and then torrential rains came, sealing off any opportunity to leave.

Finally, two and a half weeks into Pamela's stay, we heard the larger military helicopters and Aravas flying in and a plane or helicopter dropping bombs. They only bombed at night but we waited to see if we could learn more during the day before we set off on the isolated trail to Mayalan. Once again, with no radio, there was no way to know when we arrived in Mayalan if we could leave. Just setting out on the trail was an act of faith and peril.

Pamela, pale and shaking, told us the night before we left, "We're going to have to leave tomorrow! I can't stay here. I'm going to die." I thought that she was being overly dramatic, but by the next day, I too realized that we were in serious danger, not just of bombs but of blood poisoning. Rubber boots and the humidity had led both Ernesto and I to come down with granos, a severe case of jungle rot.

I discovered it one morning when I reached down and scratched a pimple about the size of a mosquito bite on my ankle. Ernesto had a grano first; his small innocuous pimple grew to a four-inch, slightly swollen red patch, but his infection stayed fairly small and wasn't changing quickly. Mine, on the other hand, quickly blossomed out of control, leaving my leg itchy and red and so swollen that I couldn't fit my foot and ankle into the neck of my rubber boot. Probably just as well given the moist rubber inside, but there was no way to even cram it into my rotten but still serviceable tennis shoe.

There was no immediate cure for it in the village. In fact, in Segundo Centro, a mother had used a remedio called Aldrin to cure her child's granos. Aldrin is one of the world's most toxic pesticides. Fear of the granos infection had pushed her to try this toxin on her little boy when she felt there was no hope, and it had killed him.

"You need to get that treated and I need to leave," Pamela insisted.

We set out the next morning right before daybreak on the trail to Mayalan. Ernesto saddled up Lugnut with a pack saddle and strapped on Pamela's American Tourister luggage as well as her briefcase with documents on the testing we had done and her analysis of the health of the community. My mochila was strapped to the very top. Lugnut was not a pack animal—in retrospect it would have made more sense to have gotten a sturdy small mule rather than a horse, but good-hearted Lugnut lumbered along behind us, trying to keep his balance in the deep mud and rocks. We were quite the Health Resource Center team, trudging and hobbling, infected and sick. I was in such pain it was hard to feel anything but a pulsing throb in my foot. Every time I slipped and hit a rock or a root, I thought I would scream. I started the hike with my rubber boot on my good foot and a piece of nylo wrapped around my swollen foot. The cheery yellow piece of plastic stripped off in the third deep muddy root pool as we entered the trail. I blocked out imagining mud crawling with microbes and hookworms as we pushed through the eight-and-a-half-kilometer hike.

Pamela kept repeating, "I am going to die, I need to get out of here now."

"It's just over the next hill, keep going we can't slow down." As I heard the words coming out of my mouth, I stifled a laugh thinking back to my first hike and how I'd felt like just giving up and lying there in the mud. It was hard to fault her, but I had become hardened to the environment and pain, and I rapidly lost patience and had just repeated Ernesto's words.

After six-and-a-half hours of fighting the slippery mud and rocks, my leg a throb of agony, we finally arrived at the hill above Mayalan. Just focusing on the hike had taken so much energy that we had stopped worrying about who or what was beyond the tree line. Pamela had never seen the militarization of Mayalan, having only flown into Centro Uno, and now, she turned to me, shocked. "What is going on?"

Descending into the village from the rocky ridge, an Arava circled in for a landing. We sped up. I hopped faster, slipping and sliding over the rocks and slimy roots. My leg and foot had swollen to two to three times larger than normal. Just pausing briefly at the top of the hill had caused the blood to pool.

We arrived at the bodega right as the Arava on the pista opened up, and Tomás and another Todo Santero climbed down the metal stairs. I asked the cooperativista in charge, "Estamos muy enfermo podemos salir hoy?" He told us that no; the plane was there in Mayalan for at least a night, if not longer. Even though I was sick, there would be no leaving that day. I asked, "Can you please check and see if there is anyone else flying?"

Just then, static from the radio broke our depressed silence, and he said, "Guy ya viene y hay espacio para una persona." Guy had been at La Resurrección and had heard that someone needed to fly out but only had space for two people. One was a sick child and the other person ended up being Pamela.

Within 30 minutes she was gone.

Lugnut and I started back to Larry's abandoned house. Alone and unable to do anything but drag my leg, I wondered how I was going to get back to Centro Uno.

Lines of red were creeping up past my knee onto my thigh. In my addled state they seemed to be writhing and twisting like tiny snakes running up from the dark red grano. I staggered and then veered over to the clinica, a small 10 x 10 board and batten wooden building with a metal roof and a dispensing window.

Melicio, the prometor, asked me, "¿Ha tomado Penicilina?"

"I've never had any antibiotics of any kind," I responded. He replied, "Aye Dios mío hay veces es peligroso pero vamos a ver." I remembered … there is a potentially life-threatening reaction that some people have to penicillin. Not much of a choice, I would either lose my leg or die.

By then the children had found me and helped me hop to Larry's house and un-saddle Lugnut. Finally able to sit, I lifted my leg and propped it up and then realized I was unable to bend or lower my leg, the pain too excruciating. The children enthusiastically brought me dinner from the local comedor. At least I wasn't alone.

I spent a sleepless night with my swollen foot propped on a small stool I'd placed on top of the cot. Maybe it was the penicillin or maybe the infection, but I was plagued by paranoid dreams of being left in the house unable to move. Why had Pamela just left me? In the dark, my foot stood out high above the mattress balanced on the stool. It was eerily light out with the night lights high above the coiled barbed wire line powered by generators that overwhelmed the jungle sounds. It had been so long since I had heard unnatural sounds and saw unnatural light it was disorienting and menacing. I wanted to retreat back into the jungle.

The next day my leg seemed a bit better but was still very swollen, and the red lines of blood poisoning were running further up my leg but looked thinner and less serpentine. To my surprise, I heard a shout and saw the children running to the house escorting Ernesto, who hobbled my way, one hand on a hefty branch that he was using as a cane. He too had gotten worse and decided to seek medical help. We were able to fly out the next day on an Arava to Guatemala City.

When we arrived in the city, we found a clinic immediately and a doctor who knew about granos and jungle rot. He looked me in the eye and said, "If you had delayed a day longer, the streptococcus infection and blood poisoning spreading up your leg would rapidly have become gangrenous, and it would have been necessary to amputate your leg." He suggested that we relocate our work to the capital. "The Ixcán is killing you."

Despite the doctor's warnings, my own personal safety and health were less important than returning and doing the work. As I now look back at the letters I wrote during this period when death was at hand—whether by disease, or the army or the guerrillas—I see how disconnected I had become from myself and unconscious of my own mortality.

A week later, having soaked it in an anti-bacterial bath all week at the hangar, my leg was partially healed and the swelling greatly reduced. We discussed our next steps.

"Should we return via an Arava, or are we going to try to go up to Quiche and get a flight with Guy?" I asked Ernesto.

He considered and said, "Let's go with the air force; we can get back sooner. In a week a lot can happen, and we've been away from the garden for over a week now." Not once did we discuss or even consider leaving Guatemala or staying to work in the city.

We returned on the next Arava flight. The Arava circled Mayalan in preparation for landing on the runway where even more camouflaged tents hugged the concertina wire at the edge of the field. The handful of soldiers that were typically checking the planes in and out had increased to about 20 and they all held machine guns.

I said to Ernesto, "I don't think I have anything dangerous with me this time." I was glad my jungle boots were well buried back in Centro Uno.

I climbed down the ladder and saw the gauntlet: army regulars with Galil rifles hanging across their chests, muzzles pointing down, checking the passengers with routine dispassion. The jaunty, almost joking, way we had discussed not having anything dangerous with us rapidly dissipated and was replaced with a growing cold despite the heat when I dumped my pack, and paperback books fell out. The closest soldier picked up *100 Years of Solitude* and fanned it, perhaps looking for illicit messages of who knows what ... coordinates to a guerrilla camp? Then, one they called José grabbed my kit, poking through the small flowered bag with toiletries, with the frosted zippered compartments, and fumbled as he unzipped one by one: toothpaste, toothbrush, pills, dental floss, and several tampons, the kind that doesn't have a tube, just a string. In his hand with the tail hanging down it looked like a firecracker or maybe a small bomb with a fuse cord.

He jumped back, releasing the safety as he swung the blue-black muzzle of the Galil up to my face and held up my tampon, screaming, "¿Qué es esto? Es una bomba!"

Reading the terror in his eyes, his shaking hands and the gun moving from across my chest to my head, I froze; this time I realized that I was one false step away from being killed. Ironically, I hadn't had my period in months due to malnutrition and disease, and now I was going to die for something that I didn't even use?

I started to laugh hysterically. He pushed me to the ground, knocking my glasses off. Time stopped, the thick grass damp with humidity, drops of water beading up, magnifying the sun and heat, my cheek pressed to the rain-soaked grass. It was a scent I remembered from childhood, in my mother's friend's backyard, the lawn, where I'd once done somersaults on the rough thick grass. My thinking jumped from one indescribable scenario to the next. Was this my life passing before my eyes? I spotted Ernesto behind the rifleman and being held by another soldier.

I had no explanation. How to describe the use of something so foreign? Their wives and mothers just used rags. With sweat dripping into my eyes and down the back of my shirt, my leg still aching, and my things strewn on the ground around me, I sat up, too overwhelmed to explain their incomprehensible use.

By sheer luck, the private's superior wearing aviators happened to hear the terrified yelling, saw the commotion and strode over. He wrenched the tampon out of the private's hand and smacked him across the face yelling, "Cayate."

The private continued yelling, "¡Es una bomba!"

And then I heard a thud as he hit the private on the side of the head with the butt of his gun. "Idioto."

A hand was extended toward me and I grasped it. He helped me up and returned the tampon to the flowered kit.

And then in English, he said, "I am so sorry, they know nothing."

Having studied in the U.S. at the war college as so many Guatemalan officers had, and speaking fluent English, he clearly knew the function of a tampon. Shaken, I bent down and scooped up my books and the rest of my toiletries and stuffed them into the pack, focusing on the trail head back to Centro Uno.

Before we could leave, he wanted to talk, to practice his English. He asked us an obtuse question, "Was that unalloyed banter?" Ernesto and I tried to figure out what he was saying without being rude.

We asked, "Unalloyed?" and he responded, "It was in the dictionary. Cómo puro en español." And then we put it together.

"Was that pure as in a pure metal?" Which made a bit more sense but still was nonsensical.

He smiled and said, "Yes!"

And then we wrestled with banter.

"Banter?" Ernesto asked.

Yes, he said, "Like talking."

Ah, it was coming together.

I asked, "Pure chatter?" And he said yes!"

Clearly running out of dictionary words he knew, he trailed off. We moved toward the trail and waved goodbye, immediately starting the long walk to Centro Uno, scared to even look back as we started up the winding trail. How bizarre to be faced with death and then a nonsensical conversation.

Just three years later, this officer would lead the genocide, but not that day.

With so much changed every time we left, I wondered aloud, "What will we find in Centro Uno after all of this?"

"Who knows?" Ernesto said.

I was right to wonder. The atmosphere had changed in the two and a half weeks we were gone; the children ran up to greet us when we made the rocky descent into the village, but their parents looked more somber. The dense green jungle and the rainforest now provided shelter for both the guerrillas and the army. The lack of clear site lines and the general unknown bred fear that materialized as doubt about their neighbors on all sides. Before, the sound of a bird or an agouti bounding through the underbrush would have elicited a shrug or curiosity. Now, as terror of guerrillas and soldiers seeped in and gradually infected everyone, people jumped or screamed at the commonplace sounds of the jungle. With fear so widespread, just leaving the village and going to the milpa daily to work was worrisome, but there were no options. The villagers were all unarmed, their only defense machetes.

At this time, a letter that had traveled via mule train reached us with the news that we needed to return to give the new class of volunteers in the U.S. a report from the field. Opening it, I said, "I can't believe this! I thought we had more time before we had to go back to report on what we are doing. It's in only five weeks!"

Ernesto sighed and said, "Well, it might be good for us to be apart for a while." But before that would happen, we were summoned.

# CHAPTER 25

Early spring 1978, Guatemala City

Memories are not always so clear, hanging like spirits or wraiths waiting to be dispatched. I knew that day in the urban jungle of Guatemala City that the U.S. might be involved in the escalation. It had been just a question mark before. Burying my U.S. army look-alike boots, I was aware that the U.S. must be providing some type of military assistance, and then there was the Israeli arms dealer.

Before it was time to return to the U.S., we were surprised when two USAID workers showed up in Ixcán and told us that we had to report in the USAID Mission Director. Though we were nearly as remote as another planet, their reach was long—all the way out to the deep green rainforest, raucous jungle, and our house on the edge of the plateau, sitting on Maya ruins.

We explained that we had an agreement with the DID, not with USAID, but they said, "Well, they get their funding from USAID, so you have no choice but to check in, in Guatemala City."

With human rights a thing of the past in Guatemala, we were now precariously situated between the EGP, the Guatemalan army and this new specter of USAID. The opportunity provided by a uniquely progressive partnership of the Catholic Church and the Guatemalan government just eleven years before was now suspect. That pure motive was about to be further tainted.

Ernesto and I took the bus from the hangar downtown, both of us quiet in our nervousness. My batik T-shirt and voluminous linen pants, tied with a string belt, were stained and abraded from rock beating in the creek, clearly not office attire, but clean. The mid-rise building was a beige box with small windows puncturing the rough stucco for five or more stories. What could they want to know?

Pulling open the aluminum and glass storefront door, a blast of cold air hit us, pushing me back. The air conditioning was a tangible force, the cold weighted air smothering.

Checking in with the receptionist, we waited, whispering.

"Let's just listen,"

"Share nothing,"

We waited, anxiety tightening in my chest, shivering in the too-cool space, wondering if we were going to be on the receiving end of more trouble. Finally, after twenty minutes, we were ushered upstairs by an assistant into the office. We sat awkwardly across the wide expanse of desk from the director or some man presuming importance. We never knew his title, but his crisp white button-down shirt clearly said bureaucrat.

He launched into a series of friendly, simple questions: "Good morning, how are you? How is your project in Ixcán? Are you teaching gardening, and have you gotten to know the people? How are the cooperatives doing?"

We answered honestly. "We are doing well the people are really gravitating to our garden and the testing that we are doing and yes, Ernesto has even hiked to Cuarto Pueblo to teach. The co-ops are doing well but are challenged to get crops out."

Then he asked, "Are you aware of a new area just outside Ixcán Grande? Are there people living there? There is a road being constructed close to there."

"Yes, we have seen some homesteaders, and they have developed similar cooperative arrangements. They came from the highlands too and are learning how to govern using the co-operative principles practiced in Ixcán Grande."

He frowned. "Well, that is a problem. We have a plan to develop the area, moving people from this village and that village in the highlands. We have already selected those who are to emigrate down to this new un-inhabited area in the east of Ixcán next year."

The clammy cold air pressed in. I held my breath. My heart raced. "There are people who have done that and are successfully building co-ops already living in Ixcán Chiquita."

"They will have to go; they are not part of the project. I have spoken to the general and the colonel, and they will be taken care of. The intent is for this new area that is currently unoccupied, to be a model village, starting fresh. The villages will hold people from different areas. We have been working with the Israelis for some time on this project."

The cool efficiency of the words "taken care of" hit me hard, though I still had no idea what was really coming.

As I wrote these memories in 2023, I paused and kept circling back. I know that what Ernesto and I had heard that day in the bureaucrat's office had chilled us to the bone. Now I researched.

A USAID agricultural analysis in the early 1980's of the Franja Transversal del Norte triangle and Ixcán, "Land and Labor in Guatemala" by USAID, mentioned a $7.3-million project to develop that and the surrounding areas. The data mentioned in passing that there had been cooperatives in Ixcán Grande but by late 1982 they had "ceased to exist."

The USAID project including model villages in the report evaluated large-scale farming of palm oil and other agricultural crops in addition to oil exploration and mining. In the final analysis, there was a brief mention of some minor military issues as a reason for why the initial concept was not successful, noting that two towns in the USAID area of

Ixcán were "evacuated and burned" by the townspeople in the home-stead area. There was no mention of the army. Was USAID, or was it the CIA, in spite of the humanitarian embargo, actively involved in the calculated and planned removal of the people?

"Taken care of," the bureaucrat had said. I knew now, with great grief for all who were lost, what that meant.

# CHAPTER 26

Spring 1978, California

When we were asked by DID to return to the U.S. for a month and share our work with the next class, we didn't really understand what it was going to be like. It was not so much a request as a requirement and it was a surprise that it came without much time to organize, particularly given the "USAID" meeting in the city. We had to move quickly to get everything set up for a month out of the garden.

When we'd both left for a week to go to the Capital to see the doctor and were stranded for another week, we returned to a garden overgrown with weeds. We hadn't coordinated with someone to help while we were gone and only the comfrey and amaranth had enjoyed the neglect. Given that we would be gone a month, the garden would have a major setback if someone didn't take care of it. We were lucky to have Tomás Perez and several other community gardeners now actively involved in the day-to-day work in the garden, and they volunteered to keep it up while we were gone.

We packed, bringing film and some records of what we had planted, hiked to Mayalan, flew out on an Arava, and then flew to San Francisco.

It was hard to adjust to the noise, smells and weather back home. I was still in culture shock sitting in the community room of the new DID training center at Camp Joy in the Santa Cruz Mountains in California.

My days in Centro Uno had a pleasant sameness. I looked forward to the small successes of seeding, plants growing and harvesting or completing several inches on my weaving projects. I didn't look forward to traveling. But here I sat in the big indoor/outdoor redwood and glass room, off of the hippie-cool vegetable garden, feeling uncertain and separate. It was as though I didn't remember how to communicate with people here in California. At a loss and not at all cool or quick, I became agitated by the urgency of life here I'd forgotten about.

Stephen Kaffka, a tall thin protégé of horticulturalist Alan Chadwick, master gardener and the originator of the French Intensive Biodynamic movement, was now the DID horticulturalist. Our teacher, Warren Pierce, from Santa Barbara, had disappeared. We were never told what happened to Warren. All of our correspondence with him and questions about how to handle insect or fungal situations went unanswered. We were relieved to have Stephen respond eventually but so much time and research had passed that we had figured out many of the issues on our own.

Stephen visited us in Centro Uno in December 1977 and wrote an evaluation of the garden that told the story well. It was not an easy place to garden. Surprising challenges like the nematodes made planting anything completely different than doing so in a temperate garden.

It was great to have an expert give us tips and also acknowledge the difficulty of the humidity and heat with an organic approach. In his report he reduced the name of our practice from French Intensive/Biodynamic to just French Intensive since there were no Biodynamic elements in our practice. He recognized how hard it was to garden in the heat and humidity, and which elements of the practice made sense and which were not feasible. He applauded our little cane corrals with the palm roofs to maintain moisture during mid-day, documented the difficulty of daily attention to moving the fronds on and off, and emphasized the lack of close water and any watering system except hand carrying in the dry season.

The majority of those attending the talk and slideshow at Camp Joy were with the DID program, curious about how French Intensive/ Biodynamic organic gardening would work in the jungle, but a few other gardeners also attended.

Preparing to show our slides, I took a breath and a step back. Ernesto was the presenter. We were solidly committed to our cause, but my background in agriculture and horticulture, including courses on insects, fertilizers and overall planting at Cal Poly San Luis Obispo, made me more of the agricultural expert than Ernesto. However, from the perspective of the culture of our Maya community in Ixcán, I was not the expert. There, I accepted my role as the expert's woman partner, silently seething. Even though he was our "site director," there were just two of us. My frustration came to a head at the presentation.

We had taken quite a few slides of the people and the garden, from clearing to composting to garden beds, to showing the challenges of following the program without tools, running water and the severe nematode problem. We were excited about a crop, Crotalaria, that helped reduce the nematode problem. As a legume it could fix or collect nitrogen in its root nodules and had an added benefit of providing healthy hollow stalks that we used as part of the vegetable bed building process.

Ernesto was presenting, standing to the side of the screen at the front of the room clicking slowly through the slides and discussing in his methodical, and in my opinion, slow and plodding way.

"As well as incorporation into the garden beds, Crotalaria's great for the compost pile. It's been grown as a companion with coffee for many years, and it's this new information that we want to share."

"Ernesto, maybe we can move through these a bit more quickly?" I urged.

"*I* am doing the presentation," he snapped.

I gritted my teeth and stepped to the back of the room. We were completely on our own but also dependent on each other in Ixcán.

Although the joy of sharing books and working together in the garden had sustained us for a while, the rising tide of fear had begun to affect our relationship for the worse. Our inability to discuss our fears only exacerbated it. Given the day-to-day struggle for survival, I hadn't had the time or energy to think about it while we were in Guatemala. Here in the U.S., it was different. I was still reeling from infection and stomach issues but especially chafing at the continued lack of acknowledgement of my skills. Even in the U.S. I wasn't the expert, but the girlfriend, a status with no purpose. Living in Ixcán left no room for thinking about these kinds of distinctions, but in the U.S. I began to think differently about it.

The new volunteers and other gardeners at the Santa Cruz Training Center had been studying the method and were purists. I was now a realist. The method was not technically open to interpretation, yet we had modified it to meet the demands of the environment and the people we were living with and teaching. Our interpretations were not well received by the group. Even with the slides it was hard to explain the difference between gardening in the jungle vs. the temperate hills of California.

In addition to changes in the horticultural method, Ernesto and I had changed. I was becoming more and more hardened to the sweltering weather, the omnipresent jungle insects and animals, my actual and potential health problems, the sheer isolation, and the unrelenting fear that we lived with. On some level, the challenge of just surviving became my reason to exist. Thousands of miles away, I missed the community that I had found in Centro Uno and the children and women, my friends, and the simplicity of life.

Although we both had thought it would be good to have some time alone on our visit north, years later when I was going through my parents' effects, I found a letter from Ernesto to my father sent from one of his trips to Huehuetenango, saying that I was driving him nuts, and he needed to get away. Leaving me alone in the middle of the Ixcán, albeit with my friends in the village, was apparently one way to mitigate this feeling. I never knew about this clandestine correspondence and never considered sending his parents a letter, much less one in which I so blatantly described our problems, so this discovery gave me some clarity. It helped me see that I didn't just feel alone, I *was* alone. I can only think that neither of us understood the credible danger that we were continually under, and that he didn't understand my loneliness.

As I look back, however, I'm not sure that I told him about the nightly terror. How I struggled to fall sleep until morning, continually vigilant. I didn't share the terror that I continued to feel for years after, either. Instead, I just accepted it as a part of my life.

After the garden talk, I visited my mom in Sebastopol, and we went to Longs Drug store. The sound of the fluorescent lights buzzing and row after row of plastic bottles in pink, green, blue, all holding the same thing, shampoo, was overwhelming. I thought about the one glass bottle that we used to get milk in Ixcán and the fabric scrap that we used to get warm fresh tortillas to wrap up to take home. There was no waste, no overabundance. I had been warned that it would take me a while to acclimate to the Ixcán jungle but did not realize that being back in the U.S. would be so stressful and hard to comprehend. "Why do we think that we need all of this?" I gesticulated to the shelves.

After her visit to Ixcán, although challenged by fear and abandonment, she understood my bewilderment, "Good question."

I had not anticipated the shock of returning for this brief stay. The intensity of life outside of Ixcán, particularly the multitude of things and people, shook me to the core.

My cat Flo, the beautiful Himalayan, had been run over by a car while I was gone. The solace that I always found with animals and her sweet presence was missing. I had been looking forward to seeing her much more than I realized, and no one had written to me about her death. Maybe they were trying to save me worry or were just unsure how to share such sad news.

In Centro Uno we had gotten a small tabby a few months before. We named her Books because you can never have enough books! Everyone called her Mish after the cat on the package of the weaving thread— all cats were called Mish. Elena was taking care of her while we were gone. It was so wonderful to have such a good friend. I missed that community, Books and Lugnut.

Thinking about our return to the Ixcán together was mixed. I really wasn't sure how our relationship would continue when we returned, and I also couldn't imagine going without him. I longed to return to where I felt valued and had a reason to exist, and I think that he did too.

In Ixcán, each instant required complete attention and undiluted presence. The clarity of that minute-to-minute experience, and perhaps even the fear, was intoxicating. I realized I'd come to crave that heightened level of awareness; my pulse quickened with anticipation of our return.

# CHAPTER 27

Spring 1978, Mexico and Guatemala

When I was sick with e-coli, the doctor in the city prescribed fluoro-quinolone. I took both the pill for e-coli along with chloroquine, the prophylactic antimalarial drug, daily.

One morning, I woke up panicked, "Something weird is happening, the edges of my vision are getting dark, like my peripheral vision is narrowing." I went outside, and it was more pronounced; my vision had narrowed to the front only, like a horse wearing blinders.

In addition to *Donde No Hay Doctor*, I had brought a copy of the *Merck Manual*, the sum total of my medical knowledge. I reached up to the top shelf of the bookshelf and hefted down the thick red book that to date I had only tried to use once when baby Eric was so sick that first week that I arrived. Several hours later I deduced, after reading some compelling evidence from Japan about chloroquine, that there was an interaction between the two medications that was causing my visual problems. I stopped taking the anti-malarial medication to see if my vision would improve. Gradually my vision returned to normal. It was the dry season, so there weren't a lot of mosquitos and I stopped taking the prophylactic and forgot about it.

Returning to Guatemala from the U. S. we flew to Mexico City because it was cheaper and took the bus south to Tuxtla Gutierrez, in the state of Chiapas. We waited for about an hour outside in the open bus terminal for the connection to the Frontera of Guatemala. The white plastic chairs lined up on the dirt were all occupied, and we leaned against the wall for what seemed like an interminable period of time. I spaced out, the diesel buses idling, filling up the corrugated translucent green overhead canopy with rank blue gray smoke.

And then, starting with the tips of my fingers, I became colder and colder, very odd because it was easily 85 to 90 degrees, with equal parts humidity. Suddenly I started shivering uncontrollably, but then the shaking ended as mysteriously as it had begun.

Our time together in the U.S. had devolved into a level of irritation that transcended all except our mutual decision to return. The snarky conversation at the presentation was just the tip of the iceberg. Even though I was uncomfortable with Ernesto, Centro Uno was pulling me, and I yearned to get back to the place where I felt valued. But we were not focused on each other or particularly thoughtful of each other, and I am sure my continual illnesses had become irritating. I shrugged this new symptom off as yet another health issue I would deal with in time.

Our bus pulled up, as usual over-packed with campesinos carrying machetes tight to their legs, women with babies wrapped in rebozos, chickens, and a couple of dogs. We squeezed in, and I momentarily forgot the odd freezing cold moment. The bus slowly pulled out onto the narrow highway, making its way through the tropical forests and small cane ranchos with twelve-foot papaya trees, loose mangy dogs, pigs and chickens running wild, inching up to the slightly cooler more temperate highlands and the northeastern border crossing into Guatemala.

About an hour into our trip, after letting out a guttural bang accompanied by a thick cloud of black smoke, the bus came to a grinding halt. We all climbed out to check the smoking bus. It didn't look like it was going to be an easy fix. Still stranded two hours later, sitting on the ragged asphalt edge of the two-lane road, I developed a sudden, terrible headache, then heat washed over me followed by a wracking chill. Unable to think, much less try to make sense of what was happening, there was nothing to do but remain still, cross-legged on the hot asphalt, in the shadow of the bus with the fever moving in waves from hot to cold and then hot again.

Three hours later a replacement bus came to pick us up. The entrance to Guatemala was closed at night, and there was only time left in the day for the bus to cross into the no-man's-land border zone between Mexico and Guatemala. Stopping at a cantina, the driver yelled above the ranchero music, "¡Nos quedamos aquí por el noche!" The idea of sitting in a bar all night was not remotely appealing, and I was now in an altered state, not comprehending the ebb and flow of my fever. Ernesto and a couple of the other passengers decided to make the best of it and drank Cerveza Gallo and played poker with the bus driver all night.

At the back of the cantina was a small room with a cot through a door next to the restroom. The cot had seen better days and was probably rented by the hour, but the cantina waitress saw that I was pale and clammy and asked, "¿Esta bien?"

"No, no sé qué pasa estoy fría y tengo mucho calor." She looked at me knowingly. I had no idea what I had but she said that I could rest there for the night. It was a godsend as the fever returned with a vengeance. As I lay back, the headache returned. I closed my eyes to rest, but almost immediately heard a rustling sound. At the corner of the ceiling, hanging onto the rough white plaster above my head, were two four-inch scorpions, their twitching tails curled over their backs. They scurried over and then paused dangling above my head. I froze. I feared any slight movement would excite them and they would fall, whipping their tails back and forth. I anticipated their stings, the possible searing pain, as their tails tracked across my forehead.

The voices of drunk gamblers on the other side of the wall rose to a crescendo, the thin wall shaking with music and laughter. The scorpions moved to the wall away from the sound and slightly away from my head.

At 7 a.m. the exhausted, still drunk bus driver staggered out to the bus, pulled open the door and called out, "Vamanos!" We all climbed back on. Phasing in and out of consciousness, cold, hot, then shaking, the 14-hour drive along the precipitous narrow roads and passages of the highlands to the Guatemala City central bus station was interminable.

Once delivered to our destination, we staggered with our luggage from the trip to the U.S., and took a taxi to the hangar, a good 30-minute drive.

Still unsure what was causing the fever and chills, I was beginning to suspect malaria. The next morning, I searched the phone book and found that there was a malaria testing station in Guatemala City. I asked Ernesto to go with me because I was feeling pretty out of it. He said, "You can't possibly have malaria. We've been in the U.S. for the past three weeks. It's a waste of time to go to the other side of the city, it takes forever on the bus."

I ignored his dismissive tone and called the testing station. "¿Hay pruebas por malaria?"

The man who answered the phone said that yes, they did have the test. He told me the test would only detect malaria if I had a fever, and that the tests were conducted on Tuesdays and Thursdays. As luck would have it, it was a Tuesday and my fever was active. I took the first bus that passed by the hangar, and in another lucky coincidence, it was going out to the area of the city called La Corona, where the testing station was, so I wouldn't have to transfer.

I was wearing a light pink, short-sleeved T-shirt that I had bought when we were in the states and a new pair of faux linen yoga pants. I pulled myself up the steps and made my way slowly to the back of the bus, tripping over the ridged black rubber mat running down the center of the bus to the torn, dark green Naugahyde seat. The bus moved methodically through the city, doors opening and closing, more people getting off than on and then slowed and zig zagged as we moved onto rougher, pot-holed streets.

Out the half-opened, thickly smudged slider window were rows upon rows of cardboard, newspaper and lamina shacks with no roads between them, just narrow dark pathways. In the middle of a walkway was a pila, a central water source with a faucet, with women gathered around filling blue, pink and yellow plastic jugs with water. We rode another quarter-mile, passing miles of shacks reaching up the low rise to the horizon. The bus driver pulled over to the side of the road finally and said, "Aquí estamos." We had arrived.

I had heard of La Corona, but I hadn't put two and two together. The Crown of Thorns neighborhood had been devastated by the 1976 earthquake, destroying adobe and tile-roofed houses of the poor throughout Guatemala and leveling entire neighborhoods in the city. Replacing the adobe was cardboard, any metal sheet available, but mostly rusted and mangled lamina, corrugated metal and large pieces of yellow or blue transparent plastic sheets. There were no doors. Children ran wild through the encampment since school was out of the question.

I asked the bus driver where the malaria testing location was, and he pointed down the street and said, "Dos o tres cuadras." Two, maybe three blocks. I got off the bus. At the corner between me and the testing center, a group of men approached me, calling out, "Hey mamácita." There were six men. I hadn't thought about what I was wearing and what I looked like until now. My pink T-shirt was clinging in the humidity and heat of the bus. As I grew closer, I could see them clearly, in stained and ripped blue pants, filthy, sweaty T-shirts, and scuffed and worn black shoes with pointy toes and no socks. They moved closer and closer. I was too tired and feverish to think clearly and didn't scream for help or yell at them. Instead in my exhaustion, shaking, I said in soft Spanish, "What would your mother think of you assaulting a sick woman just walking down the street? No tienen education."

"No tienen education," is the equivalent of saying, "Are you not an educated person?" I'm not sure if it was that or the threat of their mothers, but they apologized and let me pass. I feebly walked the block-and-a-half to the malarial station. Opening the door, I found an efficient nurse who promptly took a vial of blood and told me to call in two days.

The bus was not there when I got back to the parada de autobus. The men on the corner were no longer there, either, however; perhaps they'd gone to look for another less prickly victim. I waited five minutes for the next bus, got on, and rode back to the hangar shaking. Waiting for two days seemed forever while I lay in the lower bunk in the hangar. Without a clear díagnosis it was hard to know what to do and how to treat it. I just lay there on the bunk listless.

Two days later I called them up again. "Si, tiene malaria el tipo se llama plasmodium malariae, hay que ir al doctor."

I had malaria, Plasmodium malariae. Only after the díagnosis did the gravity of my illness strike Ernesto. He said, "Oh no, let's go to the doctor right away. I am so sorry I didn't believe you ..." By that time, I had lost some trust in him; his concern meant little to me.

We took a taxi together from the Maryknoll hangar to the doctor's office in Guatemala City, not expecting that I would need to go to the hospital right away. The doctor scolded me for not taking the malaria-preventative medication, chloroquine. I explained about the drug interaction that had affected my sight. The doctor directed me, "Vaya al hospital imedíamente."

We did as told. I checked in and they gave me an IV and another stronger chloroquine drug to curtail the virus. The room was fine and the food much better than anticipated. At $25 it was a pricey place, but I was comfortable and stayed several days until I got a roommate, who was dying from cancer and called out in pain day and night. It was sad to watch, and I just couldn't take it. I checked myself out against the doctor's orders, and we stayed in a five-dollar-a-night hotel with a bathroom just down the hall, which was easier and more private than the hangar.

Ernesto thoughtfully bought me some books and magazines at our favorite English language bookstore. As I was emerging from a bout of violent shivering, followed by a viciously hot fever and profuse sweating, I opened my eyes to find on the bedside table a cold bottle of Coca Cola and Time Magazine. The cover screamed in bold red letters: "Malaria, World's Number One Killer."

I chose not to pay attention again to the increasing number of coincidental roadblocks to my return. Following my week or so of recovery, we moved back to the hangar where we waited and then flew into Mayalan with the army. Even after contracting malaria, I still didn't realize what danger I was in. I had braved infection and e-coli, what was a little malaria. At least I hadn't been bitten by a poisonous snake! I viewed this latest bout as just another minor impediment to get over quickly, so I could return. In retrospect, I realize now that I had become lost in the fallacy of my own strength, both physically and mentally.

Searching through boxes of correspondence in 2023 I came upon letters in progress and not sent, still flat, clean except for the even blue ink hand printing. It's so surprising, how did I bring all these things home? How did I bring this history with me? I start reading and realize I was writing a letter to Speed, the new Director of DRF/DID, and it didn't make it to him. I take a deep breath. I know these recollections of my time in Guatemala are not the best bedtime reading. I have struggled with sleep for years and still for some reason, I reach for the very things to read that unsettle my psyche. Somehow, I feel that without this still present anxiety, terror and intensity I will forget it.

*June 1978*

*Well, we got back to Guatemala in pretty good shape only to find out that in retaliation to the incident (Speed, the new director, showed me the clipping) where 100 campesinos were gunned down, the EGP had blown up an entire truckload of MP's out by the airport. Needless to say the atmosphere here is a bit strained. The army hasn't been very interested in flying to Ixcán due to all of the violence. We are hoping for next week.*

*Guy has taken an extended 2-month vacation that began, of course, the day we got here, so I guess he is out.*

*About a week later after having malaria treated ...The political situation here is getting extremely hot. The new president takes office this Saturday. Already the demonstrations are starting, we are hoping to fly in tomorrow however one can never say for sure & considering the explosiveness of the situation right now, it's hard to say.*

*Tomorrow, we have arranged to speak with Don Doñaldson about starting a flight service mas o menos. We feel that though this might be more expensive, even $50 a trip or so, the price is far cheaper than 2 people waiting in the city for a week at $10 per diem.*

Planning, organizing, looking for other transport, never questioning, never even considering if we should be going into a military zone that even the Guatemalan army and air force wouldn't enter, much less any private planes. I lay awake again trying to put the pieces that didn't make sense together.

# THE ESCALATION

The Escalation large photo of army in Mayalan

# CHAPTER 28

Early Summer 1978, Ixcán

The sound reached me long before I saw its source. Echoing off the mountains, the thwop-thwop of the blades and the high-pitched scream of the rotors were so loud and piercing that it was hard to tell where the sound was coming from.

I had left Lugnut tethered below the house on a long rope tied to a stake driven into the hard ground. I was concerned about him walking to the river in the night and slipping on the rocks. But I never expected a plane or helicopter to land there. The pista didn't even resemble a grass runway anymore.

I yelled to Ernesto, "I have to get Lugnut; he's tied on the pista!" I didn't hear his response as I ran away from the house toward Lugnut, down the narrow muddy trail I knew so well, leaping from rock to rock, glancing up in the sky to see where they were headed. The echo amplified—there was not just one, but *many* helicopters in the sky. All of a sudden five huge camo-gray transport helicopters hovered above the Centro Uno plateau and prepared for landing on the now three-foot high grass pista.

Circling the village, they accelerated, dropping toward the pista. Running to rescue Lugnut, I slid, falling down the last five feet of the trail. I still needed to make it to the other side of the pista. I ran tripping and jumping over the thick grass clumps to him and grabbed his rope.

Months before I had mistakenly used a slip knot around his neck, and he had cinched it overnight when he had pulled against the rope. We found him the next morning with his head and neck so swollen that we had to cut the rope off, patiently sawing it with a machete and massaging his neck to get the blood draining out of his swollen head.

My focus on saving Lugnut distracted me from what the helicopters might mean. When I reached him, he was pulling on the rope, straining to get away from the terrifying noise. I grasped the rope and pulled, releasing the knot from the bending wooden stake. "¡Vaya Lugnut!"

He launched down the pista at a full gallop, wrenching the rope from my hand and ripping my palm raw.

Scrambling up the hill, I leapt from rock to rock before they landed. They were hovering just above the ground, the grass laid flat in giant whorls as they jumped and jumped and ran up the hill, their heavy boots landing hard on the rocks I had just navigated. Weapons locked and loaded, they pounded up the hill and passed the house. I was now inside, my breath straining in my lungs, but safe in a house. As safe as I could be with just screen walls and no lock on the door. Where was Ernesto? I wildly looked around for Ernesto and found him hiding in the bathroom. I too crouched in the bathroom, the only room in the one room house with a door…no lock. Our hiding was unconsciously absurd.

The village was surrounded. They yelled as they searched the entire village, looking for evidence that the guerrillas had been here recently. "¿Hay guerrilleros aquí?"

Their boots stomped on the concrete stoop.

"Abra la Puerta," they yelled now, and their voices were close. Too close. Trembling, we rose from our crouch and opened the door. They were yelling directions.

My heart was racing as I searched the field below for Lugnut and didn't see him. I did see five helicopters, however, hovering above their whorls. Shaking, I knocked papers off the desk looking for the letter from Colonel Castillo saying that we were working as agronomists. When I finally found it, they looked at it and passed it around, their guns pointing down.

The soldier standing straight with authority, clearly the leader, demanded, "¿Han vista guerrilleros en las montañas y cerca de aquí?"

"No, we haven't seen any guerrillas here. Everything is tranquillo."

This didn't appease the leader. He shoved open the door with his foot and marched in, looking through everything and demanding, "¿Qué es esto?" "What is this? Why do you have so many books?"

Ernesto and I had burned all incriminating books after the visit by Jean the "French tourist," so they found nothing that qualified as evidence of sympathy for, or collaboration with the guerrillas.

Just as quickly as they came, they left, ducking and jumping into the gaping helicopter doorways. The slow-moving rotors picked up speed, whirring and shrieking as they lifted off. Flying toward Mayalan where the military installation was growing daily, they circled over the village, the darkness of their shadows blotting out the hot midday sun as they thundered overhead. We looked at each other as the sound receded, and Ernesto whispered, "I don't know what came over me. I just lost it. I was so terrified."

Years later, Ernesto's decision to hide in his terror made me wonder about my response to the helicopters. Why had I been so reckless with regard to our safety? I had been more concerned about Lugnut than I was about my life or Ernesto.

Another terrible fact I wouldn't learn until later followed just a week after the helicopters arrived. On May 29, 1978, the Panzos massacre shocked Guatemala when the local finqueros called in the army on unarmed Maya villagers in Panzos who had come to protest that their land was being taken. A sixty-year-old grandmother, Adelina Caal Maquín, known in the community as Mamá Maquín, led the protest. She was one of the first to be shot, and then the army opened fire on the entire group of several hundred Maya families with fathers, mothers and children, indiscriminately killing.

We knew nothing of this. The Centro Uno and Ixcán villagers shared, "Ya no nos saludaron." The soldiers are not greeting us now. We knew only that tensions were rising. The violence erupting in the highlands portended the escalation of violence in Ixcán.

# CHAPTER 29

Summer 1978, Ixcán

Tranquillo, what a beautiful word—peaceful. That's how we had described our village to the soldiers and how everything felt after the helicopters were gone. Their departure felt like an exhalation, it was a peace that came from quiet, not from joy. The next few months passed uneventfully as I turned to gardening. We weren't the focus of the army or the increasing activity of the EGP. At least I didn't think so.

We all just kept our heads down, Ernesto and I in our garden and the community in their milpa and crops and the community garden. This was a brief period of complacency. As the hot and muggy days of July 1978 came upon us, the rainfall increased and the garden flourished. The dry season just one month behind had given way to rampant compost opportunities, and growth exploded.

My agreement to spend two years in Ixcán was tied to Ernesto's contract time, and our two years would end in four months. The next group of volunteers, who had trained at the Santa Cruz Garden, would be coming down in October. I could not bear to think about the transition; I was so close to my friends in the village and the overall community. I wondered if Susan, a new volunteer, would be interested in weaving and how she felt about horses. My manure picking up was a daily process and I wasn't sure it would be taken up by a new volunteer. And what about our neighbors; Pabla and Luisa? Would the new volunteers love the scent of crushed cardamom in the large bultas sitting by the door at night? Or would they be more fastidious?

Looking around the garden and the village in Centro Uno, I realized how much we had been able to achieve, touching hundreds, perhaps thousands, of people across Ixcán. Being the first stop on the trail allowed us to supply seeds and gardening information as well as teach forestry practices to anyone passing through Centro Uno. The demonstration garden was thriving and lush. The Jamaica hedge survived the leafcutter ant attack and was now full and interplanted with luffa cylindrica to make scrubbing loofahs, a useful potential cash crop. There were so many things that made Centro Uno my home. The simplicity of life and the daily rhythm was now comfortable. I didn't miss Hercules flips; in fact, I couldn't remember what if anything I missed about the U.S.. I was at home every day in Centro Uno without yearning to be someone or somewhere else.

Mish was growing into a big cat, bringing the smallest of the coral snakes into the house as gifts and dropping them by the foot of the bed in a black and orange pile. Although venomous, their tiny mouths were too small to get a good purchase. Lugnut was doing well in his training, and I was finally able to teach him a nice comfortable, although tipped to one side, lope.

I was glad that our work would continue after us, but also uncertain about how the team we met in Santa Cruz could replace us. They were scheduled to meet us in Guatemala City. We would spend a month or so going over all that we had done. Initially we'd show them how to negotiate the challenges of long-term visas and then traveling to Ixcán and our village. Once in Ixcán, we would go over the basics, Centro Uno 101: who was who, where to get water, and how to continue development of the garden for another couple of weeks. I hoped we could articulate our work clearly, so that the new volunteers would understand the importance of the research that we had done, including the pamphlet on how to grow vegetables, the daily documentation of the plantings, and our notes on planned and spontaneous workshops and educational opportunities, a process that we had set up and meticulously documented in the small notebooks that we kept on the desk.

But that was in the future; for the next few months, I would just work in the garden and get things organized for the upcoming transition and prepare for the Día de los Santos. I spent hours with Elena and Julia, learning to weave larger projects. I was working on a man's shirt, the slender threads taking hours to weave just an inch or two. My plan was to weave a pair of pants for Ernesto to wear for the fiesta. Starting two months ahead of the fiesta, I needed extra time because he was over six feet tall and most of the men in the village were five feet and under. I had another foot of weaving the red and white striped tela to achieve the length, easily adding a couple of weeks to the work.

At the same time, I was working on a small moral with designs worked into the face of the weft, a precursor for my next project, a man's Todos Santos shirt collar and cuffs. The days blurred into a comfortable regularity. I was often alone while Ernesto went out to get seed or plants or to teach gardening and composting in another town. I was more comfortable now that Juan was next door, and I wasn't completely isolated at the end of the village, although he was there only when school was in session and took off visiting for the weekend.

Armed with my mother's bird list and the bird book that she left behind, I engaged a few children to learn about the differences between parrots, trogons and parakeets. We also studied insects, but without a book we had no idea what they were, so we drew pictures and wrote down where we found them. My college entomology class didn't include the three-inch wasp that bit me in the shed or the beautiful fluffy venomous caterpillars.

# CHAPTER 30

We visited Centro Dos to see the molino de caña de azúcar and watch sugar cane being milled into large bricks of panela, an unrefined sugar. A thatch-roofed round pen enclosed oxen, pulling the huge grinding stones that the canes were fed into. The extracted liquid was poured into a large flat pan above a fire. It was very smoky and hot and fascinating to watch the liquid fill molds the size of a regular red brick. Not much cane was grown in Ixcán, but the mill provided local panela, a dark brown molasses-type sugar, at the Centro Uno market and beyond.

Years later, in 2022, I heard from Juan the teacher and then met with Juan's cousin, RoSales Ortiz in Stockton, California just two hours away from my home. When I showed her the slides, she stopped me and said, "That is my father-in-law. That was his mill, and those were his oxen." She called her husband and together they were able to show their son and explain a bit about their family. They had grown up in Centro Dos. I noticed that she was limping and asked what happened and she told me that years later when she had tried to return to Ixcán with a group she was shot by the army in the foot and it had never healed.

The photos and the meticulous documentation of the rainfall, planting and snippets about what was happening in the community, and when, provided me with the outline of our history there. Meeting with Juan's cousin made me realize that the history of the people in Ixcán had been obliterated and maybe I could help them to remember the beauty and a time when there was so much hope.

# CHAPTER 31

Summer 1978, Ixcán

Tranquillo again was temporary with the narrow trails and rainforest shielding us from what was ahead, all was hidden to us then.

The army had dictated that the Arava was the only method to transport crops out. An "all call" went out across the Ixcán Grande co-ops for everyone to come to Mayalan to discuss the hold that the army and air force had placed on private transport.

We hiked to Mayalan since we were scheduled to fly out and meet our replacements two days after the co-op meeting was scheduled. The trail was now just a trail, not the terrifying slog of my first hike. I was acclimated and feeling well: no e-coli, no malaria, no infections. Passing campesinos, we heard that the clashes between the army and the EGP had grown in intensity and frequency, and the EGP was increasing in numbers. When we crested the hill to Mayalan for the meeting, our eyes could barely take in the transformation. The pista was now triple in size with barracks for easily hundreds of troops, and concertina wire surrounding the encampments punctured with helicopters, moveable lights and generators. The bodega was dwarfed by the new construction. Hundreds, if not thousands of armed troops stood by.

A sea of men, most wearing the red and white striped pants of Todos Santos filled in the gaps. The colors striking against the wet green grass.

Speaking from the church dais, Tomás and the other co-op leaders demanded that the army either provide the transport or allow others to do so. The co-op leaders' speeches were bold. "We have power as a group. We are organized. We have made Ixcán Grande from nothing but pure jungle to a thriving community. We need to be able to transport our crops and our sick." Hand drawn signs were held high, "The president said that you were our friends. Behave like our friends. This is our land and our right."

Where previously some volunteer air transport had been allowed to fly in, like Wings of Hope, now only the army could fly. Hundreds of bultas of coffee and cardamom were left sitting to rot in the bodegas, the ability to market completely curtailed.

The meeting was tense. There was no accord. No agreement to allow for flights other than the army for occasional cargo.

The response by the army wasn't the peaceful assistance when President Laugerud had announced, "We are here to help you." Instead, there was a new President, General Romeo Lucas Garcia, who had transformed the light military presence almost overnight into an armed battalion intent on counter-revolutionary suppression.

The trail was narrow, deep with mud and roots and there was no clear path.

# CHAPTER 32

Fall 1978. Mayalan, Ixcán and Guatemala City

We spent the night in Mayalan, then flew to the city in the Arava after the meeting. The army had agreed to fly us but none of the crops. Impressed by the intensity of the meeting and hopeful in the strength that the co-ops showed, we hadn't realized how dismissive their attitudes toward the Maya landowners really was until then.

Our replacements, Susan and Jim, flew in from the U.S. and were to meet us at the hangar apartment. The hangar was, as always, a bit rough, with its unfinished concrete floor and bunk beds, nothing comfortable. Now, it felt more desolate, cold and abandoned with the pilots long gone and the radio infrequently monitored.

Our concern about the new volunteers' ability to take over our work was reinforced the minute they stepped through the open hangar's folded tilt-up door. It wasn't so much the suitcases and bags that they unloaded from the beat up green and orange taxi that made it look like they were going on a backpacking vacation; it was the aroma ... they reeked of fresh garlic. An invisible cloud enveloped them. We looked at each other slyly, mouthing, "Oh my..." And then out of the long blue zipper bag they pulled two spanking new machetes, the blades wrapped in cardboard. It was ludicrous. I whispered, "Oh my god talk about bringing coal to Newcastle. Why didn't they bring a decent Bulldog digging fork?"

Fresh from Santa Cruz and the French Intensive/Biodynamic course, they were interested but hesitant. Jim immediately said, "I'm in a relationship with another woman from the program. I don't know if I want to do this."

We were filthy and disheveled all the time by now. Our clothes had become unrecognizable rags, and those were our "going to the city clothes." The required mental and physical toughness to survive had changed me without my full understanding or agreement. The stern lack of fear and intensity that I'm sure I communicated to the new volunteers was now my persona, obscuring the day to day and moment to moment terror that I wouldn't even begin to understand until decades later.

I probably projected a sort of *Heart of Darkness* intensity about the project and what we were doing in the jungle. "Yes, that's a guard with an Uzi. We're going to fly out on the Arava. See that plane out there on the tarmac; it is a STOL paratrooper plane." The volunteers followed my pointing with raised eyebrows as I laid out the situation. "The EGP is the Guerrilla army of the Poor, and we've had a few visits to the village by both the army and the EGP in the past few months."

It wouldn't matter, however; although they had completed the five-month course and then been flown to Guatemala, Jim, the new volunteer, decided within a day that he would not go to Ixcán, stating, "Clearly it is too dangerous, and I hadn't planned to fall in love with someone in the class, but there it is."

Given his decision not to go, Susan, the only realist in our group, decided as well, "I should go back to the U.S. this isn't going to work, and it really sounds as though things are going off the rails out in Ixcán."

A huge relief washed over me. I could return to our home and the project with the hope of extending for another two-year term!

We called the DID team in California from the Guatel, the central phone bank with little booths where you were charged by the minute to call the states. The first words out of their mouths were, "Things are not going well. The volunteers that came to replace you were not alone in their decision to not follow through with the program. No one from this class nor the previous class has agreed to go anywhere." Worse, he added, "The grant is being put on hold given the lack of program follow through."

Unclear about the future, we organized our return to Centro Uno with provisions for the next several months: cooking oil, gas for the propane stove, and seeds. Our visas would be up in two months, and we would need to return to the city to get them extended, but the extension could only happen as part of a recognized program.

Just as we were ready to fly back in, the Maryknoll house called us at the hangar and patched through Director Speed. "The program has been shut down completely, I'm sorry, but we don't even have funds to get you home. You will have to find your own way."

"Who are these people, and what is going on?" Ernesto asked. We would not even receive a plane ticket back to the U.S.? All our belongings were still in Ixcán. In shock we started brainstorming options hoping that some last-ditch effort would allow us to continue our work.

"Maybe the Peace Corps?" I floated. But I knew that they only placed volunteers where there was communication and transportation, or at least a road close by, so there was no way that Ixcán would be an option. It was all very confusing. We checked our bank account and had about $500, enough for two tickets home but nothing else. The main problem was our visas, which would be expiring by the end of November 1978. We couldn't extend those without a sponsor.

With all of this pending, we were both glad to return to Ixcán but concerned about how to stay. Meanwhile, the upcoming fiesta on November 1st beckoned. With measured hope I shared optimistically, "Just think, we can go back for the Día de los Santos, and by that time maybe there will be other options!"

Yet days later when we tried the phone number again, a recording said that the number was no longer in service. DID leadership was gone. The main staff had gone on to political jobs, and when we contacted the Direct Relief foundation (DRF), they were not helpful, saying that the program had folded.

Returning to Ixcán was bittersweet. I was happy to get back home to Centro Uno, but also unsure of how the next two months would play out and how long we could continue to live there. Although we didn't know it at the time, all of Central America was involved in conflict. It is only with the benefit of history and time that all the pieces have come together to enable me to understand how Proyecto Ixcán, Ixcán Grande, one of the most progressive communities ever developed in Guatemala, became so central to that fight.

# CHAPTER 33

September - November 1, 1978

The Día de los Muertos and most importantly, the Día de los Santos fiesta, was just a month away when we returned without new volunteers.

Our first stop was Elena's comedor. "¿Dónde están los voluntarios Lucinda?" she called out, hopeful when we showed up alone that this meant we were staying.

Julia was kneeling under the overhang with her loom and almost complete huipil tied to the support when I walked up. She had made a lot of progress while I was gone; there was no way I would be able to finish the collar that I had been working on in time for the fiesta. Weaving Ernesto's pants had been a big project and had taken a long time, but it was simple compared to working on a collar or a huipil; both involved intricate designs and painstaking attention to detail.

Santiago and Elena's rancho was the center of activity, especially with Viviano, the village tailor, as Elena and Santiago's neighbor. The foot-powered treadle sewing machine whirred constantly. Red and white huipiles and pants being tailored at Viviano's tailoring business, draped over the side of his machine, added to the joy and anticipation.

The village was alive with activity. Women and girls were madly weaving new huipiles and camisas with long collars; men and boys were cleaning, clearing the weeds and grasses down with machetes. Backstrap looms hung everywhere on the posts supporting every rancho roof in the small village center. The excitement was contagious. This was the most important time of the year, a holiday for the children and a deep connection to each other and history when the people from Todos los Santos celebrate their Saints' Day and their pre-Columbian roots.

In Centro Uno, drunken horseback riders were to gallop from the market to our house. The goal to reach up and rip down the live flapping chicken and carry it squawking to the finish line was time tested. Everyone was crazy with anticipation about who would win this year. Perhaps more than just one trago was needed for sufficient bravery to perform this incredible feat. The several-day festivities started in the graveyard on the morning of the Día de los Muertos with offerings for the dead and the building of floral altars. The jungle provided lush deep green elephant ears, orchids, bromeliads and other native plants to create spectacular natural altars.

Prosperous Centro Uno assured an event that rivaled the town of Todos los Santos. A marimba was hired to play 36 hours straight, starting on Día de los Muertos and continuing through the Día de los Santos. This was quite an expense but worth it for the fiesta.

In preparation, the men started at one end of the town limipando, cutting the weeds down low to establish the race course and then delineating it using long straight pieces of cane and sapling poles. It was important to create a clearly defined space for the race, so that no small children or onlookers were trampled in the drunken melee. This was the only time of year that alcohol was openly consumed, a key part of the tradition.

For days, mule drivers trudged into town laden with snacks, bottles of Gallo in wooden crates, cabbages, potatoes, and other specialties directly from Todos Santos and the highlands. In addition to food, new red and white cotton thread and colorful acrylic yarn were packed in for last minute touchups. And for the men's historical reenactment of the Spanish conquest, a frenzy of projects ensued, including building large papier mâché masks designed and crafted for a dance and drama of the reenactment.

The children on school vacation were actively involved in the fiesta, from helping cut the grass and weeds with machetes, to weaving and taking care of their younger sisters and brothers while their parents worked. The boys had dreams about when they could ride through town and compete, and two boys who were not old enough to ride camped outside the house with the hopes of convincing us to let them ride Lugnut.

"Don Ernesto, por favor podemos montar Lugnut. Va a hacer más caro antes de salir si el gano." They just knew that they could come from behind, the underdogs, and win. Then they followed up with, "¡Cuando salen se pueden vender Lugnut por mas!" Lugnut would be more valuable when we left, and we could sell him for more if he won the race.

Roberto, Mariano's son who was one of the eldest boys, asked politely, "Prestame Lugnut por favor." Lugnut had not filled out much but was rideable though he still cantered to the right, so you were always off kilter. Astride him, it would be tough to grab the writhing and flapping chicken. I certainly couldn't see him competing against Tomás's big appaloosa or Viviano's new horse, but apparently any horse was better than none.

One time Ernesto had ridden him to Mayalan, and Lugnut had slipped on a root and fallen over in the mud. We were lucky that he didn't break a leg. His footing was, at best, marginally okay for just a short jaunt on flat ground, certainly not a race.

The day dawned hot and clear. The construction of the altars was now fully underway. This day of sadness and remembrance was becoming a beautiful and lush acknowledgement of those who had passed on. The graveyard, small but large for the young village, was abloom with tropical flowers and large philodendron leaves. Families gathered at the grave sites sharing food and cusha with the dead. The day extended into night as they continued to set up the race course for the next day and the performance area for the reenactment.

The next morning eight horses of varying sizes, shapes, ages and health stood at the starting line. Lugnut was not one of them. We lined the cordoned off track. The race started with a whistle; horses thundered down through the market stalls galloping at full speed, their hooves ripping up the short grass. The riders gripped the reins in one hand to stand up in the stirrups to try to grasp the chicken. The gallery screamed for their favorite rider, "¡Corre, corre Viviano, Celestino, Tomás!" The terrified chicken, hanging by his feet, flapped to get away. Viviano grabbed the chicken by a hair, feathers flying, and galloped triumphantly back down through the crowd on either side. His horse, clearly the star of the show, pranced sideways back down the track to the start. Viviano's investment in a new, stronger horse had given him a clear edge this year, but there would always be the next year for the losers, the competition centuries in the making. It was a great relief that no one was maimed or killed. I had been holding my breath. At least by now everyone knew that I wasn't a nurse so they wouldn't call on me for help.

The marimba kept time all day. The musicians switched out to rest and have something to eat and drink yet never lost the momentum and cadence. As night quickly descended, they moved the large marimba from in front of Tomás's store to the clean swept dirt floor under the school/church overhang by our house. By now a level of exhaustion from the multiple days of activities was overcoming the crowd—several men were sprawled on the ground by the market stall and others staggered, some singing softly with an occasional cry, "Ahhahai!" The connection to Todos Santos in the highlands and their collective centuries' old traditions of weaving, performance, and the race were being passed on to the children of Centro Uno as well as their language, Mam, and the ability to throw quite the celebration.

Dressed in my new huipil that Ernesto had secretly asked Baudillio's mother to weave for me, I felt so much a part of the community. I joined in the slow shuffling dance beneath the school overhang, holding a bottle of Gallo beer, my skirt wrapped tightly around my hips. We all danced with each other, women, men and children, slowly and peacefully intoxicated. The day-long celebration took us away, for just a while, from the hard work of surviving in the jungle and the triste, sadness, of the Día de los Muertos.

At last, the dancing started to wind down and we walked to our dark house just next door, the happy and slightly slurring voices of our friends following us across the garden and above the slowing marimba beat. "Adiós, adiós, Don Ernesto y Dona Lucinda, pasen buenos noches."

We held hands as we stumbled down the narrow muddy path to our house. "I can't believe we are leaving soon." I choked out. "How can we leave this?" gesturing toward the dark garden and the dancing and light in the school.

"I know, what a day!" Ernesto slurred.

Tired and happy, we had no reason to anticipate what lay before us.

# CHAPTER 34

November 1, 1978

When we reached our house, the door was ajar. I reached for the Aladdin lamp that was usually on the low mahogany counter by the door, but it wasn't there.

"Oh, where did I put the lamp?" Swaying I stumbled over something on the concrete floor. Ernesto grabbed my arm. "Steady!" he laughed.

I pushed whatever was on the floor with my foot and felt my way to the counter and the box of candles. "What is all of this stuff on the floor?"

Striking the gas burner lighter I lit the propane stove and dipped the candle in to light. As the flickering light from the candle illuminated the small room, I could see that things were different than when we had left just a few hours before.

We had packed our books, logs of every day in the Hortaliza, and all of our belongings and stacked them on the desk. I walked in to reach for the counter and stumbled. The books that had been piled neatly were now littering the floor. Ernesto walked around me and started to pick them up and remake the pile.

"What the hell?" he mumbled. "Did a dog get in here? A drunk from the fiesta?"

In the light of the candle nothing made sense; there were very few books, and things were missing. Confusion took over along with exhaustion from the long day. I just stood for a moment and stared, trying to reassemble the scene. "What's going on?"

"Where are the record books? And the binoculars? And wait what is still here? Almost everything is gone!" I grabbed Ernesto's arm and pulled him towards me.

The flame flickered as we searched for all of our handwritten records from two years of research— tracking the climate, planting records and testing varieties, and reforestation work. Also missing were rolls of film and our two cameras—the 35 mm and the box camera. Books on medicine and general health, *Donde no hay doctor* was gone. The *Merck Manual* was gone. Our fishing net and binoculars, clothes, packs and almost everything that we had ready to take back to the U.S. was gone.

In the flickering candlelight I saw a ripped piece of paper on the counter. A note written on paper ripped from my own journal using a thick orange felt pen that had been in the battered white metal cup cut that was now pinning it down.

Ernesto started to read but the writing was irregular and hard to decipher and we were still woozy.

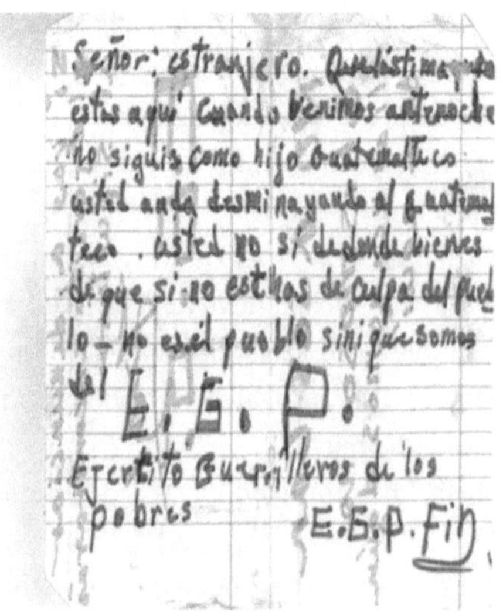

Guerrilla note

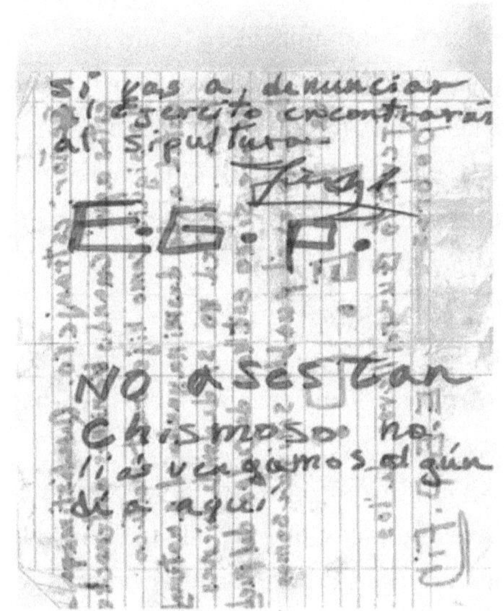


Guerrilla note

"Señor extranjero. Qué Lástima que no estás aquí cuando venimos antenoche no siguis como hijo Guatemalteco. Usted anda desmayando al Guatemalteco. Usted so si de donde vienes de que si no astillas de culpa del pueblo- no es el pueblo sin que somos del E.G.P. Ejército Guerrilleros de los Pobres.

--E.G.P. Fin.

On the other side:

Si vas a denunciarnos al ejército encontrarás la sepultura.

Fin

--E.G.P.

No asestan chismoso no lias vengamos algun día aquí."

"What is sepultura oh my god where is our dictionary? What is a chismoso?" I sorted the books on the floor looking for the yellow and red English to Spanish dictionary tossing the few remaining books to the side. "Can you try translating? Ah I found it!"

"Mr. Foreigner, what a shame that you were not here when we came the night before last. You are not a son of Guatemala. You have come to Guatemala to exploit the people of Guatemala; you do not belong here...this is not the village's fault; we are not of the village. We are the E.G.P. The Guatemalan army of the Poor.

—E.G.P.

On the other side

"If you report to the army that we have been here, you will find your...what was a sepultura?

I found the s's and scanned down. "It says grave or internment."

Gone now was the pleasant buzz, shocked into cold sobriety we stared at the note. I hugged Ernesto as he continued to translate.

"End

—E.G.P.

Do not gossip, I think that is what it means or this is not a joke... or we will return one day for vengeance."

The night had started so well, with everyone alegre. The dark, earthy, hollow marimba beat had resonated, hemmed in by the jungle edge. Dancing, shuffling, beer in my right hand, I had danced with everyone and fit in here in a way that I never would have thought possible.

I shut the door to our house quickly, as though closing it to the dark jungle would keep us safe that night. The thin ripped screen windows were black as pitch. We dropped down on the steel-framed cot; the only familiar thing in the now foreign room was the moldy mattress, its dank smell somehow comforting.

I reached out to Ernesto, and he struggled to say, "Don't they understand that we are here to help?"

"I don't know, I don't know," I sobbed.

Maybe in daylight we could make sense of it.

We awoke the next day to find the torn sheet of paper still there and our things still gone, the scarred mahogany counter and concrete floor, barren. The cicadas transitioned from their night calls to the raucous morning buzzing and clicking, slowly speeding up to a continuous crescendo across the jungle. The buzzing interrupted all thought. With a week or two left in Centro Uno we now had no purpose, and the continuous noise felt as strange again as it had that first day flying into Xalbal.

With coffee in my speckled metal cup, I moved to sit on the cracked concrete stoop in front of the house as I had for almost two years. Looking out across the jungle to the Río Ixcán, I said to Ernesto, "We worked at being as apolitical as possible, after realizing that family gardens weren't the only thing that the community wanted. We just did whatever was needed."

Ernesto nodded. "Maybe the time has come to not be apolitical."

We had constantly walked the edge between the right-wing Guatemalan army and the unknown guerrillas, realizing that at any turn we could easily disappear into the jungle with no trace. The disappointment that the guerrillas, the EGP, somehow did not understand who we were was crushing, since our focus was to help the people. Now we felt exposed and watched.

We had met the Guatemalan army many times, but this was our first experience with the guerrillas, however indirect. I could not stop from wondering what would have happened if we had been there when they ransacked our place. From the tenor of the note, they considered us enemies of the poor. There were many people, families from other pueblos, from Tercero and Piedras Blancas as well as others at the fiesta. There was no way to know who could have slipped into our house while we were dancing next door. We had made it very easy to take everything important with our records and journals, the cameras and our books stacked up by the door and ready to go.

We were stranded in the middle of Ixcán Grande with no money, our visas and letters gone with the guerrillas, and not a sponsor or even a plane ticket home. The days were running out for us to stay legally in Guatemala. Yet we were most distraught to lose the two solid years of data on the climate and the garden, so important in understanding how best to help families grow gardens in this land that had been untouched for centuries.

The Ixcán was now an active war zone. No one was allowed to enter the area or leave without having their identification and documents checked multiple times. There was no easy way out of Ixcán Grande. We had been aware of the tensions gradually building and then more clearly delineated at the last reunion in Mayalan. But Centro Uno was so far from the other co-ops, we'd felt safe day to day. Like all the other challenges of living there, we had become inured to the searches, the weapons, the bombings.

The next few days crept by. We continued to plant, weed, and water but everyone and everything grew tainted with suspicion. I went to the comedor and asked Elena, "Who are the guerrillas, and why didn't they know about us? They must have heard that we've been living in Centro Uno for the past two years."

"No se." She didn't understand either. There weren't any gringos other than us this deep in the Ixcán jungle. How could they not know we were decent people just trying to help people become more self-sufficient?

I didn't know what to think.

Several days later, soldiers swept through again. We heard them before we saw the helicopters bearing down on Centro Uno. This time they came with a purpose—to our house, first on the trail from the pista.

The soldiers demanded, "¿Ustedes han visto el EGP, los guerrilleros han visitado aquí?"

I replied, "No los vistamos." We had not seen them, which was true. The letter had said: if you tell the army about our visit, you will find your grave. Was this a test? Did the army take our things and pretend to be the guerrillas? The shock of the army arriving seemed too coincidental. We remained quiet.

The next week passed slowly. Since the army didn't kill us, we figured that it must really have been the guerrillas who took our things and left the note. We would see if the guerrillas thought that we had contacted the army. Our internal confusion and conflict mimicked the external.

As the days passed, random visitors came to our house. Sitting outside on the concrete stoop, we were assessed through an informal court hearing by men who looked like ordinary campesinos, but who we thought must be guerrillas since we had never seen them before. The questioning began, "I heard about your garden, why are you here, what do you sell?"

"We are testing a new gardening method to allow people to grow intensive healthy gardens not dependent on expensive chemicals, so that they can provide fresh produce for their families and..." Ernesto started.

"It is easier for us to travel and bring new crops and ideas back to the people," I added. "Our goal is to help people to be more self-sufficient and live healthier lives. Ernesto travels to the Costa to bring back seeds and has learned how to graft, so he can teach classes. I teach a bi-weekly class in health and sanitation, pretty much whatever the women want to learn about."

We explained our belief that the people needed to be strong, healthy and well-educated to be able to compete against the increasing pressure from the big, traditional landowners. We found ourselves more outspoken about how gardening and self-sufficiency was actually political. Anything that gave people title for land, education, hope and the ability to make their own decisions was political in Guatemala.

José, who lived at the edge of town, started visiting us, too. He was frequently absent and his home at the edge of the village was shoddy and unkempt. We knew his lack of work made life hard on his wife and family. His wife had come to the birth control class on her own. Now, in retrospect, we wondered if guerrilla activities may have occupied his time.

It had been a week and a half since the guerrillas had taken our things and a week since the army had searched us. We felt like we were under a magnifying glass. We finally had our last "interview," this time with a man who was taller than the average campesino, maybe Ladino but still wearing the ragged clothes of a field worker. He was well educated and emanated an internal strength of purpose and vision different from the others.

Did he think that we had contacted the army? The timing was too close. Would we find our grave? He didn't question, instead he congratulated, "Gracias a ustedes a venir y ayudar la gente. Mis amigos han dicho que ustedes van a salir. Por favor quedarse aquí y siga que están haciendo." He congratulated us on the garden and what we were trying to do. He told us how important our work was to the village and the overall Ixcán. He said that he understood we were leaving but asked that we stay and continue our work.

"We don't have a choice about staying, our program is done, and our visas are expiring in two weeks." Ernesto told him. "We are sorry we have tried to stay."

With that he stood up and brushed off his pants saying, "Gracias a ustedes, Adiós y qué vaya bien."

After he left, we looked at each other, and I said, "How can we stay?" We were scheduled to leave the next day, walking to Mayalan. Our visas would run out at the end of the month. We had given up on finding our things, and the time had come to leave.

"We're out of options; no organization wants to place volunteers out here. Two years ago when it was much safer the Maryknolls didn't want us to come here. You just need to let it go." Ernesto looked toward the garden…and muttered, "so much work." Shaking his head.

That night we went to dinner at Elena's comedor. I savored every moment of what was once just a regular part of my day but would now be the last time we shared la cena. Slipping onto the well-worn bench, touching the familiar mahogany table worn smooth with use, I waited for my blue speckled enamel bowl of frijol. Elena slid the bowl across the table and I reached for the salt in the small terracotta bowl with grains of rice to keep it a bit less damp.

I choked out, "We have decided to leave tomorrow. We don't know if we will be able to get out of Ixcán before our visas run out." The significance of all our belongings being stolen weighed heavily on our friends as well as us, and they were concerned for our safety and growing more anxious about theirs.

We hoped to get our things back, but we were in the middle of something much larger than we had realized. The guerrillas distrust of our motives and the subsequent arrival of the army was terrifying. We'd once felt like we could trust the guerrillas, but now nothing was clear.

Elena deftly turned the tortillas, sighed and said, "Como Dios quiere."—"Only god knows…"

Returning from dinner, tired and disappointed to be leaving, we opened the door slowly. Stepping in through the door I tripped over something and in frustration kicked out knocking something over. I struggled to light the propane cooktop in the darkness, and grabbed the last remaining candle lighting it.

As the candle sputtered, new shapes and forms began to emerge, filling the previously empty space. In the candle's illumination our missing belongings came into view, a pile of books strewn across the floor and on the desk: more books, our handwritten research and the cameras and film.

"Oh my god it's all here!" I sank on to the chair by the desk shuffling through everything. At first glance it appeared as though all had been returned, but on further review our binoculars and the fishing net and the *Donde no hay doctor* were missing—but we would have no need for those in the U.S. And then we saw the note, this time written on the back of a piece of paper wrapper for Mish hilo, weaving thread.

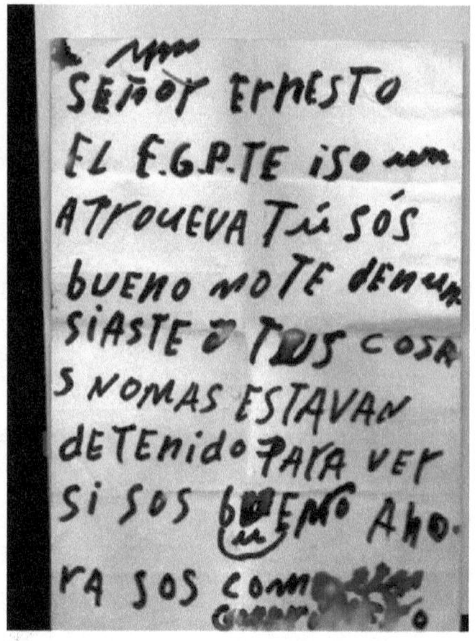

Guerrilla note

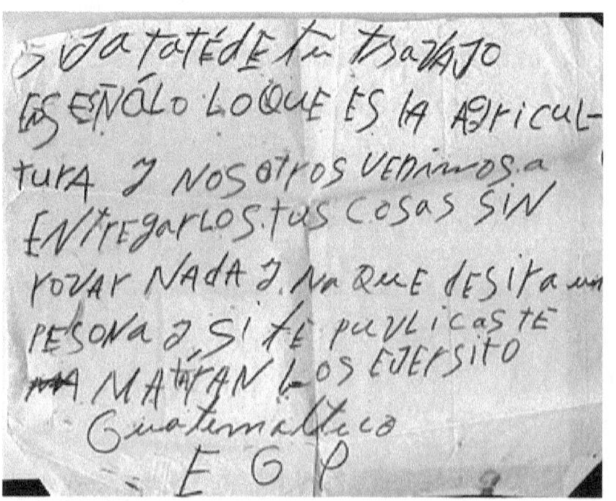

Guerrilla note

I fixated on the final line: "If the army finds out that you knew we were here, they will kill you ...The EGP."

# CHAPTER 35

November 15, 1978

It was a muggy but clear morning when we gathered on the front porch to get ready to leave. We packed everything into boxes or the big duffels that I had originally brought with me. The rubber tree was oddly still; there were no birds perched on the thick branches calling. The parrot tree, my favorite tree, stood as a sentinel in the foreground of the broad Ixcán valley just a wisp of light fog lifted from the Río Ixcán and hovered above the trail below. This would be the last time I savored this morning view as I sipped a cup of sweet cinnamon coffee watching the day awaken and feeling the heat of the sun rise.

Elena and Julia helped us since this would be our last time to meet at the house, and we left extra salt, oil, plates, cups and other things that they could use in the comedor. Our cat, Mish, was going to live with Elena so she had brought a striped mantel to wrap her home. Her tiny tiger face peeked out of the multicolored bundle under Elena's arm.

We followed Elena back to the comedor and sat down for our last lunch in Centro Uno, so hard to fathom. I knew that I would come back to Ixcán. I just wasn't sure when, there was no way that I could just leave my friends.

We entered the comedor with the polite, "Con permiso," a bit more formal than usual. The gravity of our leaving was hanging heavy. Elena had set a glass mason jar of flowers from the garden on the table beside the salt dish and the earthenware jar with the large tablespoons. It was a special meal, not just the normal frijol negro y tortillas but caldo de pollo con verduras y arroz, large chunks of chicken, a special treat, and vegetables from her garden. Steaming on the wood fire, the spicy and fresh scents of vegetables and chicken filled the comedor with comfort and safety. The tiny hot chiles were still beyond my tolerance to liberally sprinkle into my beans, but I figured this was my last chance, so I ate two of the chiltepin while fanning my open mouth. I told Elena between wild hand waving, "¡Tengo que regresar, porque lo necesito terminar el collar!"—"I have to finish weaving Ernesto's collar, and I will need your help. I can't do it alone." We all laughed.

As we were finishing our meal, a rustling commotion outside drew us all out the door. Even today, I have returned to what came next again and again.

Stepping out of the dark, smoky cane hut into the bright sunlight, my eyes adjusted quickly. A circle of my neighbors and friends clustered together. Kaibiles surrounded them. There had been no sound of helicopters. The only sound was a lone dog barking at the intruders. Circling behind and then around my friends more soldiers materialized, as if by magic, out of the tree line. A soldier stepped in front of me and held a machine gun inches from my face. The green, brown and black grease caked on his face, cracked, his lips exposed. Beads of sweat gathered on his brow and upper lip. His face, tight with menace transformed to talk, but I heard nothing.

My body grew numb.

The world around me stilled. Faded away. The heat, the sounds, the smoke and cooking smells.

With no change in his blank, cold, expression, he lowered the machine gun and focused it on my chest.

The villagers had been rounded up and gathered together. The leader of the Kaibiles rotated slowly, his weapon raised.

"¿Han venido los guerrilleros?" A single question: "Have the guerrillas been here recently?"

The other Kaibiles raised their weapons.

Viviano said, "No."

Mariano said, "No."

The soft no passed around the circle until it got to me. "Nnnno," I stammered.

They disappeared as quickly as they had come. The green jungle absorbing the green camo. The quiet broke with a start. The parrots and the cicadas resumed their calls.

No one spoke; I didn't realize that I was holding my breath. My neighbors turned and hurriedly left the clearing.

Slowly, the deep green of the rainforest, and the village edge came back into focus. First, the thin blades of bright green grass glistened with droplets of water from the recent rain. A slight steam rose almost imperceptibly. Everything around me was in incredible focus, crystal clear.

We left our bowls on the table and walked guardedly, scanning the dense bushes and trees at the forest edge back to our home to finalize packing. We knew one thing: we had to leave *today*.

Lugnut moved slightly off to the side of the concrete stoop, quietly munching grass. I swept the house clean and admired the flowering pink and purple fence that had rebounded after the leafcutter attack. The garden was lush and beautiful. Mustard and radishes filled the beds marching down the hillside. The compost piles cooked away under the shade of the tree, a thin mist of vapor above them. I took in the sights for the last time: the rocks where the coral snakes hid and the wood pile where the cantil had coiled, the cane and branch covers over the mounded vegetable beds, and the sign, La Hortaliza Anna.

We tightened the cinch on Lugnut and loaded the pack mules. All our belongings were now on the packsaddles, boxes and bags and securely wrapped in colorful yellow and blue nylo.

For the last time we walked slowly through the village, my chest heavy with tears I wouldn't let myself shed for years to come. By now the pista was carpeted with thigh-high grass. Juan's house stood empty; he was on vacation. The church/school was also empty. Rough mahogany benches lined up waiting, but no padre had come in a year. The market looked the same as always, a tattered cane and frond roof over the small clearing that grew lively every Sunday. I gazed at Tomás and Pabla's store and then their rancho, Faustino's rancho, the empty rented house of the Ladino family with Pinga long, long gone. The ranchos of Tomás, Mariano's brothers, Viviano, Celestino, Joel, and Santiago. Julio and Francisco's ranchos. Elena and her comedor. All stood quiet with fear after the Kaibiles sudden arrival and disappearance. The children waved goodbye hesitantly from the confines of their homes. My babies, my children. I could not believe that I was leaving.

Entering the dark trail shrouded from the world, we climbed the first hill and walked rapidly towards Mayalan. The mules and Lugnut carried all that was left of our time in Centro Uno every step in the four-hour slog through the hot red mud and tangled roots and rocks of the trail in the thick rain forest was uncertain.

The community had held us in such love and support. I knew the Kaibiles would return and even still, I could not imagine the horror that would follow.

# RETURN TO THE U.S.

Photo of Elena and Books

# CHAPTER 36

November 1978 – Present day

I have no recollection of how we returned to the U.S. Even now after years of reliving those almost two years, I can't remember the hike to Mayalan nor the flight out. All I remember of those last few hours in Centro Uno was sheer terror—the menacing faces of the Kaibiles and how time stopped. Yet perhaps that shock protected us from certain death. I imagine that for the entire hike I held my breath, afraid to make any sound at all that would clue in anyone listening in the trees, cane, and underbrush as we passed.

At some point, some dark pre-dawn morning, perhaps, I will awaken with the hike, the flight, the final goodbye to Lugnut, the sweetest of all horses, the pista in Mayalan, and the memory of lifting off and seeing the ever-stretching green below out of the window of the Arava or Guy's plane. It will come back to me with clarity so intense that I will feel the heat and humidity and recapture my memory.

# CHAPTER 37

Return to California, December 1978

Returning to the temperate climate of California was like receiving an IV after a bout of dehydration; all of a sudden I had energy and a sense of health that had been stripped from me in Ixcán. I had rarely stopped to reflect on what a hard physical life we'd led, from the heat and humidity to the never-ending parade of illnesses including worms and malaria. Now that we'd left that all behind in the moist greenness of the lowland tropics I was revived.

We took lots of photos and rushed to get them developed so we could send pictures back to Centro Uno. The photos I took were slides, so they required time to print and send south. This was before email and texting by several decades. Families posed wearing their fiesta traje in front of their house or the jungle. I received letters back thanking me for the photos with news about the village and how everyone was doing. The letters were guarded, and it was hard to know if that was due to lack of language skills or the worry that any letter carried out would be checked and censored. I doubt that the army was really capable of that, but I knew my friends feared that writing anything that bordered on anti-government concern could be interpreted as support for the EGP.

The last few days we were there, everything in our Ixcán life that had been rumbling in the background came to the forefront. Since the Community had been established for so long, the citizens of Centro Uno were used to being partners, decision makers, and role models to all of the Ixcán Grande co-ops. Yet when we left, they were uncertain and afraid and didn't know where to turn.

Ernesto, now Ernest again, and I, Lesley again, not Lucinda, had gone our separate ways. The uncertainty and intensity of what we had lived through together affected each of us differently. In Ixcán we were more or less a team, a family with a daily rhythm: rising early to cook the black beans, making coffee, surveying the night damage to the garden, watching the first rays of light blanketing the lush green valley, weaving and planting and teaching and researching. We had meaning.

The contrast of tranquility and terror and then losing our purpose and abandonment was hard to understand when we were back in the U.S. Together, every day was a memory of where we had been, who we had been and what we had lost as well as the realization that we weren't always a team. I lived life with an almost hyper-intensity, and he was more laid back or maybe just checked out, grappling with depression—it was hard to know.

Mariano, the father of Eric, the baby who almost died, sent letters to me at my mother's house, the one fixed address we had. He wrote about how happy he was to get my letter and that his family was doing well. His wife was taking the birth control pill (a legacy from my women's Cocina health class) without any issues, so no more children. The letter was dated August 4th, 1979. Mariano asked me to send photos of us, which I did, but I never heard a response. The letters from Tomás, our immediate neighbor, thanked us for the photos and said everything was tranquillo. His last letter was in late 1979. Years later I learned that he was taken from his house in Centro Uno and killed on January 1, 1982, ostensibly by the EGP but it was hard to know for certain as the army often masqueraded as guerrillas.

I also exchanged letters with Elena and Santiago. We sent prints of photos of their family and photos of our family and ourselves. I imagine that Elena told Julia or maybe paid Viviano's son to write since she couldn't. In her letters, she told me that Mish was fine and her garden was doing well.

I knew how much effort correspondence took. I imagined the scenario; the lined notebook paper and envelopes were carried in by mule or backpack, the content of the letter was probably discussed in detail, each person thinking and re-thinking about what to say. The cost of the paper and the cost of sending were not easy tasks. Before sending my letters from California, I visualized a response on our friends' end and how the letter might reach us in California. I could picture the envelope sealed and carried out to Barillas or to Mayalan and then sent from Guatemala City.

Soon, I started to hear concern and then fear in the letters. And then the letters stopped abruptly in late 1980. We had kept up our correspondence for not quite two years.

By 1980, I finished my degree in Horticulture at Cal Poly SLO and moved to a small town in Northern California with my new partner, Charles, and the intention of building a Waldorf school that had been our joint university project. A Vietnam veteran and architecture graduate, his intensity and anger gave me an opportunity to pretend that I was just fine, a "normal" woman and then wife, just struggling to deal with the ravages of a Vietnam veteran's disillusionment and anger. Never once did I see myself as equally damaged, even with continual anxiety and an odd humming sensation that thrummed through my body day and night.

The San José Mercury News, delivered daily, was thrown over the chain-link fence to the dirt and gravel road at the 120-acre goat ranch where we lived designing the school. The Mercury News Mexico City bureau first reported about the growing unrest in northwestern Guatemala in 1980. With the change in my relationship with Ernest, my direct connection to Guatemala and my memories had been severed. We weren't a team thinking about what was happening anymore and I didn't even contact him. I pushed down my worry and fear for my friends' safety and for the people in Ixcán. I had no one to talk to about what was happening but still tried to make some sense of it. I lived with a veteran—how would I talk to him about this place where even I could not venture in my mind? There was no one.

Still, determined to know more, I called the reporter in the byline who was in the field office in Mexico City and asked him, "What do you know about Ixcán? And particularly the area around Mayalan?"

"We have heard of repression, but I can't help you with individual areas," he said. He was focused on the larger picture and not interested in following up on the small village of Centro Uno, Ixcán, so I was unable to find out anything. Travel there was out of the question.

Jimmy Carter's presidency had ended, and human rights' policies that had supposedly been a standard of the administration had ended as well. Ronald Reagan's repressive diplomacy and counter insurgency measures were exacted in Guatemala and throughout Central America.

As of 1981, DID Program Director Edwin Thomas and one of the revolving door heads of the DID when I was a volunteer, was now a member of President Ronald Reagan's cabinet and Assistant Counsel to Reagan. By the early 80's, The Mercury News was reporting more frequently about Guatemalan unrest and thousands of refugees flooding across the Mexican border. How odd, I thought, that Thomas was now a member of the cabinet as the escalation of the Guatemalan army was increasing daily. I wrote him a letter asking him to remember the purpose of our work in Ixcán. I was hoping for a response, but clearly, I was naïve.

Central America was solidly in the crosshairs of the U.S. again with the Iran Contra affair, the CIA in Nicaragua, El Salvador, and in Guatemala. I ceased wondering about the model villages. It had been less than four years since we had had that chilling conversation with USAID in the high rise in Guatemala City about the Coronel, "taking care" of the situation in the Ixcán area. Now it was making more sense. Was he USAID, or was he CIA? It wasn't just chilling or terrifying anymore, it was horrifying.

Even with the brief uptick in information, the dearth of news was frustrating. At least the Mercury News had a bureau in Mexico City, but any other news about Guatemala was initially overshadowed by horrors from El Salvador and Nicaragua. The Sandinistas had been successful in elections in Nicaragua. There was hope for a more regional transition of power to the majority of the people rather than in the case of Guatemala, where only the upper 2% held power. The EGP had reigned in Ixcán for a brief period, with the army and air force pulling out of the jungle. But then, after two years, the army returned with a vengeance and engaged in a scorched earth campaign that mirrored, chapter and verse, the U.S. war in Vietnam.

Missing from the dialogue about the war and oppression was the ownership of the land in Ixcán. The Maya co-op members in Ixcán were characterized in the news as simple peasants, workers, or illegal homesteaders, not as recognized landowners. Father Bill Woods had been working on securing their land titles at the time of his death, so that the land would be their land. The Franja Transversal del Norte highway, deep into the jungle and moving toward the border of Mexico, had been stalled for years as the jungle was just too impenetrable and access through Proyecto Ixcán was not allowed. There was no easy way to move rocks, mud and huge trees in order for the construction to move forward. By late 1979 the clearing completed by the industrious Maya to develop their own properties was helping the vision of completing the road become a more realistic goal. Even though oil and other natural resource discovery was not going as well as anticipated, the opportunity to open up Ixcán to large scale investment, and ultimately development and completing the road through the project, was looking better for the wealthy landowners and multinational corporations. Land ownership by the rural poor cooperatives was anathema and the jungle was no longer impenetrable and ownership was not an issue.

Before Ernesto, Larry and Ann, the first DID group, had arrived in 1976, the El Tigre de Ixcán, José Luis Arenas, owner of the Finca La Perla, was executed by the EGP for his crimes against the people. The EGP held tribunals and asked people in the local pueblos on the east side of the Ixcán valley how they were being treated. Purportedly, Arenas had stolen over 10,000 acres from the Indigenous Maya native lands during the period that he had owned La Perla.

His evangelical sons conspired with the Guatemalan army, the Guatemalan government, and the Reagan Administration in retribution for their fathers' death to make La Perla a center for the armed forces and a new civil patrol. The focus was to terrorize and remove the local Maya population from their rightful lands. When Carter was president there was no obvious support for the right-wing ethnic cleansing; it was the Israelis who entered the picture and sold weapons and trained soldiers. Hard to know how involved the U. S. was. We had seen evidence and had witnessed the buildup of U.S. equipment, helicopters as well as Israeli weapons and aircraft and advisors.

We were farming almost half an acre in the French Intensive method in front of our rundown shack built of old boards from Army barracks in Morgan Hill, California. One morning in 1982, I went out to water the garden and picked up the newspaper. Setting it down on the stoop, I went in to make some tea. I came out and sat on the unfinished wooden plank steps and opened the paper to the world news columns. I lifted my cup of tea to my lips starting to blow gently to cool it down as I read the first few words, "Massacre Cuarto Pueblo," and dropped my cup burning my hand and splashing tea onto the paper.

It was a warm and beautiful day marred by cold dread as I spontaneously pressed my face to the paper. These were people who I knew, who had walked through our garden and in their excitement to start family gardens in Cuarto Pueblo, had asked Ernesto to hike 6-to-8 hours through Mayalan to teach them a gardening class. They had built garden beds following our pamphlet by the lamina bodega so that everyone in the community could see and learn.

I reached out to the Mercury News reporter again, "Can you tell me what is happening?"

"Tens of thousands of people are streaming across the Mexican border, and refugee camps have been set up on the Frontera, the border between Ixcán Guatemala and Chiapas, Mexico. No one is allowed in to see what is going on."

I wanted to go down to the refugee camps, swelling with tens of thousands in Mexico, to see if anyone I knew might be there and I could help. But the camps were closed to unattached do-gooders, and a surprise pregnancy with our first child and a complete lack of funds and support made the trip unrealistic. The Guatemalan president at that time, Rios Montt, an Evangelical Christian, with the U.S. as accomplice, unleashed a war of terror and genocide across Ixcán and beyond through the Maya highlands.

I was safe in the U.S. with absolutely no ability to do anything but imagine the horror. I had been there. I had met the Kaibiles and knew their vacant stares, their violent potential. The incomprehensible had happened. I had imagined the worst escalation of the army, but assumed their focus would mainly be on the guerrillas, never on defenseless women and children.

Little did I realize that no indigenous Maya were safe; all were to be exterminated in Ixcán and the highlands. Once the killing began it was merciless and without reason. Villages in the highlands were eliminated and the response to the counter insurgency nothing less than a genocide.

It wouldn't be until years later that anthropologists and historians were able to document what happened with anthropologist and Jesuit priest Ricardo Falla painstakingly documenting the atrocities in his book *Massacres in the Jungle: Ixcán, Guatemala, 1975-1982*. Others followed up later interviewing survivors and then exhuming large mass graves.

But I knew the people, they were not just poor homesteaders, they were my community, families with children and pets and incredible determination to build a new world. I couldn't let them be killed. I needed to stay in my memories of the time before but that wasn't working.

# CHAPTER 38

Summer of 1998

I was the Architect of Record for a large construction project at a local school district. I had passed my exams in 1996 and was a principal in our architectural firm.

At 6:30 a.m. I met with the team of construction managers in "the war room." It was really just the break room for the maintenance staff, furnished with a 10-foot table and assorted plastic chairs too old and crummy for the students. The project that we had designed, to be constructed over the summer, was destined to fail unless we met twice a day; there were just too many moving parts. It was not unlike a military operation, trying to ensure we weren't digging trenches in the wrong locations as we installed over 200 portable classrooms on 22 school sites over the short summer period of eight and a half weeks. Two of our team members had been in the army, so they brought an uncommon and helpful urgency and organization to the process and, jokingly, credence for us to call it the "war room."

As the architect, I was the team leader and also the only woman at these meetings. With so much going on and a lot of time spent together, the meetings became more intimate than a typical professional project meeting; there was a lot of sharing about what happened on this project or that, but every once in a while, someone would tell a story about something other than construction. Men in particular seemed to like to tell stories about their exploits in uniform.

One morning, there was a pause at the table, so I decided to pull a story out of my knapsack from Guatemala. I wasn't sure if I should share the one about the snake in the bed or the ubiquitous coral snakes that the cat would bring in the house, or the snake eating the chicken. I had shared it with my friend Carol and she said that was a story I had to write down.

I hadn't yet but I took advantage of the pause and said, "I've got a story for you. It all started with little Pepe screaming as he ran across the small village Centro Uno, Ixcán, Guatemala, where I lived for two years. 'The snake has eaten our chicken! Please come help!' Machete in hand, my boyfriend Ernest and I hiked quickly through the razor-sharp grass along this little jungle trail to where everyone was standing around the snake, an eight to nine-foot-long boa constrictor with a huge lump of semi-digested chicken about a third of the way down. Imagine those patterned tights that women wear with a big distorted bulge in the middle. That is what it looked like. Everyone was discussing how best to dispatch the snake: Beat it with a stick? Cut its head off? Can we get the chicken out and still eat the chicken?"

My colleagues' jaws dropped, but I continued, undeterred.

"There was a lot of discussion while we watched the snake absorb the chicken and a potential lost dinner. Finally, the group came to a unanimous decision to simply cut the snake's head off, but then Ernest suggested that we skin it. As you may know," I went on, "You need to skin a snake immediately following death or the skin sticks and rips. And with that Ernesto reached down and grabbed the headless head end of the snake, holding it up so that I could slit the underbelly skin. Then, as it writhed, twisting right and left, even though dead, I used both hands to pull. I started at the top and ripped the skin off in one long tug, and it sounded like tearing sandpaper, a gritty ripping noise. It was a bit rough when I hit the chicken area, it took some finesse and

I had to work around the lump…but all in all came off pretty clean!" It was my macho story.

The group at the table was quiet for once until someone cracked a joke, "Wow, do you have any other snake stories?" I guess the snake stripping at 6:30 a.m. was even a bit much for them, but then the real story came out when the guy across the table, big and strong with long blondish hair and a lush mustache, spoke. Usually, his voice boomed but instead he said softly, "I was in Guatemala too. I was an Army Ranger."

I asked, "When were you there? I was there in 1977 through 78."

He said, "I was there in 1981. Several of us Rangers were military advisers to the Guatemalan army," and then, more quietly, "We went into a small village and the Guatemalan army killed everybody in the village, including women and children while I stood by dumbly watching. When we got back to their base, I said that I am not going back out, the Kaibiles are savages."

As he spoke, a chill overcame me. I couldn't believe what I was hearing. It was one thing to read about it in the Mercury News, but it landed differently hearing it from someone who had been there. As soon as I'd returned home, well into the early 80's, I had tried to find out what had happened to my friends back in Centro Uno and the larger Ixcán, but the speed of my life—marriage, two children, dogs, cats, and being the principal of an architectural firm—had not left space to think or remember. I pushed feelings and fears down even fifteen years after I first read about the massacres in the paper, so I wouldn't feel the loss and the pain.

During my time in Ixcán, I had seen the seeds of a genocide. Though I had not seen the U.S. Rangers yet, here was proof that the U.S. had been involved in Guatemala in the early 1980's, and most likely the late 1970's as well. I needed to know what happened. In 1998 information was hard to find, and I hadn't wanted to know or imagine what happened. I was too still to frightened.

I gradually started writing down my thoughts, initially just short memories here and there like the snake story. The story that started out as funny but opened yet another window to the past. And then, weaving time, trying to understand who I was when I left, naïve and young, there with a mission and passion and a reason to live and to be of use, and who I am now.

I was ready to see the larger picture and I needed to know what happened.

# CHAPTER 39

On weekends, when the children were young, I sat in an upholstered armchair covered in a faded floral damask in the corner window of our upstairs bedroom unable to think or move, just staring outside, completely disassociated from thought. Every once in a while, I would be shocked into an even deeper level of sadness, a place devoid of feeling.

My children would be outside playing while I sat, but even they felt distant sometimes. My joy in being a mother and making sure that they were loved and cared for was so different from how I had been brought up. I knew that it was okay to cuddle, and occasionally I would remember Francesca's tiny voice asking me, "Doña Lucinda no quiere que duermo con usted?"—"Don't you want me to sleep with you, you must be lonely."

After 38 years, and 30 of those in psychoanalysis, one day that feeling lifted. Occasionally it still returns, but I've been able to recognize it and realize it for what it was: acute PTSD. Living in a state of continual fear, initially of the environment, and then of the creeping changes and escalation of the army and the guerrillas, and then so worried about what had happened to my community and friends, had altered me.

Meeting sometimes three times a week with psychoanalyst Dr. Angela Sowa to analyze my anxiety and depth of depression, the trauma began to heal, abate and allow perspective. I slowly stepped back and saw my life as it was and was able to separate myself from the continual overriding terror. Sometimes I would just lie quietly and rest for the entire session, a brief moment of relaxation. I had not spoken or shared with anyone what had happened and even in analysis my focus was on what was happening at work rather than my fears in Ixcán. Gradually I was able to feel the deeper, suppressed emotions. The day to day of life in Ixcán came flooding back, filling my subconscious often at night. I didn't know what had happened or how to find out, but I knew I was ready to learn what had happened.

The expectation of loss and tragedy around every corner drove me to work continually during the week, exhausting myself. I believed that everything had to be perfect, every line drawn on a plan, every specification correct; slip-ups had consequences. I really only became aware of living in a continual state of anxiety and fear when it was finally gone in 2011.

Although my days were spent being a parent, wife, and partner in our successful architecture firm, my nights were caught in remembrances of the color, vibrancy, heat and fear of Ixcán, keeping me from sleep. The voices: content, serious, lyrical, and sometimes silly, of the people in my village, emerged distinct, and I knew I needed to tell their story, the story of the beauty of the Río Ixcán, the colors of the traje, the friendly "Adiós" as one walked by and the happiness of children so hardworking, eager to learn, and with such joy for living. That is the story I wanted to tell, how Elena taught me to weave and how I would sit with Lugnut at the edge of the garden and how the children's joyous voices would carry over from the open school to where I was squatting on my heels weeding the garden bed.

My intensity clearly impacted our older daughter, as she wrote about my experience for her senior thesis at Claremont McKenna in Political Science. We spent days discussing it while I visited her in Southern California, but I was cautious; it was a lot to share. She titled it with irony, "Gardening in Guatemala," as she discussed the background and beginning of the genocide.

Anthropologists wrote books about the aftermath, the murders, and then the exhumations. I read many of them looking for clues and familiar names on the lists of those killed. I reached out to those who had written about the genocide, emailing and calling, sharing about my experiences there and asking if they wanted to know about the people in my small community before they had become a statistic. I pleaded, "I want to bring color, texture, faces and laughter to the people and their lives there. I can't bear for them to be forgotten as nameless uneducated peasants; they should be remembered as successful farmers and unique individuals, families and friends." I was met with resistance… these authors had already done their research and my story was past history. Even though I was a witness, I began to doubt the importance of my experience.

I called my friend Sydney Croft in September 2015 and said, "I've been thinking about doing a celebration to acknowledge El Día de los Santos, All Saints Day. I have a bunch of traje, my own weavings and a lot of photos that I took when I was in an area called Ixcán Grande, Guatemala, in the late 1970's. I want to do an exhibition, do you have any time? We can do it in a hallway at the Granary. It's in a month and a half."

My husband and I had developed and repurposed an old granary building in downtown Morgan Hill, that had a long hallway that I always thought would be great as a gallery space.

"I have a lot of boxes that I haven't looked at for over 30+ years. I can't even remember what I have."

"Yeah, that sounds interesting. Sure, I'll help," she replied.

I found six boxes with slides and textiles piled at the back of a closet. Given our timeline of a month and a half until we revealed the exhibit, we started immediately. Helping meant not just searching through bins of textiles but also looking through photos. I sent 250 slides to be scanned, so that I would have digital images. Looking through all of the huipiles, camisas and morales and mantas we talked about the places where I had gotten the huipiles and who they were from. As we shook out, organized and divided all of the traje and fabric into piles and ironed, a theme came together.

"Look at this. It's from San Mateo and embroidered, not woven. It's the only village that has a huipil like this. This one is from Chichicastenango, it's very old hand spun cotton and wool, easily 25 years old when I bought it in 1977." And then, "This is my work, I started with this tiny belt thing of thick thread, then I did a wider belt of fine thread and then a striped moral and then a moral with woven in designs, dibujos, dark brown cotton with pink and blue. I also wove a pair of red and white striped pants for Ernest. I hope he still has them. It took a really long time to make them. I also worked on a shirt for him, and this one, which is quite complex, was the beginning of a collar for his shirt. It's amazing to see now. I can remember how painstakingly I worked on it. Elena was a good and exacting teacher."

"Do you have a photo of Elena and you weaving?" Sydney asked.

"Let me see. Yes, I actually have a lot of the whole weaving process because I wanted to remember and document it from the initial winding the thread to…I think I need to stop for a moment." I sat down and said, "I think I need some time. Can we start again tomorrow?"

I opened Pandora's box of memories that now took on a life of their own reimagined terror.

The next day I took a deep breath, and Sydney and I looked in detail at the 20 huipiles of incredible color and texture, each one so unique and different. We spread them out on my unused drafting table, my desk, the floor and draped them over chairs in my office. At the bottom of a box, I pulled out the huipil from Elena, con patos, with ducks. It was as I remembered it, ducks waddling one way and then the other way. Right below it was a huipil that my weaving buddy and her stepdaughter, Julia, had woven. And then my huipil, my gift from Ernesto; it was beautiful and huge. Somehow my height equated with girth. It must have taken forever to weave.

"The Ixil area was the area of the most intensive genocide, and these are the huipiles from those pueblos, Nebaj, Chajul, San Juan Cotzal, Chichicastenango, San Mateo, Santa Maria, and Todos Santos," I explained. "Let's organize them according to language type as these are Mam speakers, and these pueblos speak different dialects. There was a museum in Guatemala City that had an incredible exhibit about the different styles of weaving and the language groups. I wonder if it is still around?"

Online there was a map with descriptions of the traje of the different regions. I ordered it. It came quickly. We organized all of the huipiles and hung them with small printed numbers and explanations of where I had gotten them and where they were from divided by language groups.

In an effort to tell the story, Sydney helped me to write short paragraphs accompanying a brief visual story. I wasn't sure what had happened, and I was just beginning to feel the depth of what I had spent years blocking. I didn't know what I was going to be telling.

We opened the exhibition in our office hallway and celebrated the story of the beauty of the Ixil area and of Centro Uno, Ixcán on El Día de los Santos, November 1, 2015. There was a brief blurb in the paper and people showed up for a mini reception. Over the following days, as I walked past the exhibition from my office, this unboxing of the past began to have an impact on me. Emotions rose up choking me as I touched threads that I had woven in Centro Uno and had not seen or touched in over 40 years. Visions of the lush jungle and my friends cane back as the colorful weavings filled my mind. Every day awareness of the work, el trabajo, intensified, looking for an outlet. Occasionally I would find someone from Guatemala lost in thought tracing the threads of a huipil, and I would ask them. "Do you know this place?"

Often the follow up was, "Yes, that is where I am from. My mother wore a huipil just like this every day. But now since La Violencia…" The people referred to the genocide as "La Violencia or El Problema," it made it sound like a minor issue but the massacres left entire pueblos with no knowledge of the past and no ability to remember how to weave as they had.

From 2015 to 2019 my search for people who had written about Ixcán and were interested in my story and photos was fruitless. I had started writing down my memories but was about ready to give up, when

I decided to contact Dr. Victoria Sanford, Chair of Anthropology and Founding Director of the Center for Human Rights and Peace Studies at Lehman College, City University of New York. Anthropologist, human rights activist and author of *Buried Secrets: Truth and Human Rights in Guatemala*. She wrote about the exhumation of massacre victims from a village on the other side of Ixcán in the Ixil area. She wrote of the women with such awareness and tenderness that I suspected I would get a response from my email. Indeed, she replied.

We set up a time for a call, when she was in her car waiting to pick up her daughter from school. Clearly, she was expecting a brief call, yet forty-five minutes later we hung up, agreeing that I would send her some photos and some of my writing, and we would keep in touch.

I continued writing and she recommended people to connect with and books to read. I read and found some evidence in *Massacres in the Jungle: Ixcán, Guatemala 1975-1982* by Ricardo Falla that gave me a hint of what may have happened in Centro Uno, but there were no names, just "a man 60, a woman 21, a man and an old man had been killed." It was proof that something had happened in Centro Uno, that people had died, although I still didn't know who and what had transpired.

Falla also described the rape and murder of the over 400 community members in Cuarto Pueblo, Ixcán, on March 13, 1982, with names and details not covered in the Mercury News. It was a Sunday, market day, the day when people gathered from the outlying aldeas. The army arrived. Flash bombs first, then the lead gray helicopters swooped in, dropping soldiers into the main market area. Soldiers from the campo surrounded the market marching in and rounded up women and children, forcing them into the church. I imagined them passing the small vegetable garden, the hortaliza that Ernesto had helped build near the co-op bodega.

Inside the walls of the church, the women and young girls were raped while the men were herded in and interrogated, beaten into submission and death. And then after three days when most were dead, the church was set on fire. Families with children all burned beyond recognition. Cuarto Pueblo, where Ernesto had taught a gardening class to enthusiastic men, had become the site of a massive extermination.

I couldn't hold the horrific brutality in my mind; I hung on to my memories of the hard-working friendly campesino families. Their faces flashed before me visiting the garden, getting seeds, asking simple health questions, neighbors and friends smiling and the always trailing gracias and adíos.

These stories and many more were *after*, but no one wrote of the before.

# CHAPTER 40

February 3, 2019

Charles, my husband and partner of thirty-eight years, answered the phone in our open plan architectural office and called out to me, "Lesley, there is someone on the phone who thinks he knew you in Guatemala! His name is Juan."

Struck dumb for a moment, I paused, transported out of my professional comfort zone of thirty-five years as the principal architect, the cool decision maker. Forty-one years is a long time. Forty-one years without knowing what happened. I thought that I wanted to know, but I was now uncertain when faced with the possibility. Juan was the teacher in the village who lived next door to us and was three or four years younger than me.

"He says he found you on Facebook," Charles added, while I was picking up the receiver.

I pushed the button, unsure of what or how to think, "Hola Juan, ¿Cómo estás?" We shared email addresses and set up a time to talk.

I wasn't sure how to think about the upcoming call. Everyone I shared it with had an idea, from just listening to suggesting that I should record it or going up with a video crew and capturing the moment of us meeting after forty plus years. I realized that once again, I was not an observer with some intellectual space; I was learning what happened to the people that were the closest to me in the world outside of my family.

We set up a call for a Saturday morning. Sitting upstairs in our bedroom in my chair, I hesitated as I dialed Juan's number. I didn't know what I would feel. But when he picked up the phone, there were no words. I just started to cry, the sobs coming from deep within.

"Don't worry, I understand," he said and patiently waited.

When I stopped crying, he began to tell me his story.

"I was in Huehuetenango on a school vacation visiting family when you left. I didn't understand why you were gone all of a sudden."

"We left because we had no organization backing us, no money, and a visa with limited days." I told him of the guerrillas taking our things, threatening to kill us and then returning our things with a note that warned of our silence. I told him of the day we left, how the Kaibiles came and surrounded the town and interrogated the villagers looking for the guerrillas and sympathizers. How no one in the village said that the guerrillas had come.

Juan recounted to me, "It was in the early 80's. I'm not sure when it first started but the army made their way across the Ixcán, the plan changed several times, but was focused on killing everyone they encountered. If you stayed in the village trusting that the army would believe you, then they would round up the community and accuse them of supplying the guerrillas with food and kill you either by burning alive or hacking the people to death with machetes. If you fled from the pueblo the army would track you into the jungle and find you and kill you. You were running away; you were a guerrilla."

He paused and took a deep breath.

"The army came closer—to Centro Dos then Piedras Blancas, killing everyone in their way, less than one half mile away. The community came together all except for Tomás. Tomás was taken and killed maybe a year before by the guerrillas. But I am not sure that is true as I also heard his sons were guerrillas and the army masqueraded as guerrillas."

"On April 9, 1982, we, everyone in the village quickly took their children, but no belongings, and ran into the jungle as a group, 15 to 20 families. My wife had grown up in a small village close to Centro Uno. She did not want to leave. It was all that she had known. Her family had moved there when she was three."

"We waited for a week in the forest, hungry, terrified and weak, and saw the smoke from the village burning. We took a chance and went back to the village to see if there was anything left, any food, anything of the life that we once had. Most of the houses had been burned. Now working as a collective, we scoured the town for food and pots and pans as we knew that this would not be over quickly and that we could never return. Centro Uno had been so successful, it was incomprehensible. As you know, the people had cattle, horses, pigs, and chickens. We left all but our hunting dogs and pets as we ran back into the thickest part of the jungle."

"The army followed us, bringing in reinforcements. A few people left our group and went to a new encampment that was started by the army with the intention of becoming members of the Civil Patrol, aiding the army. Safety was paramount to them. I don't know what happened to them when they left us.

"We ran, and kept quiet and didn't build cooking fires during daylight as the smoke would give us away. We cooked at night, but the dogs and infants were a problem. The dogs would bark at intruders, and they would lead the soldiers to us. We were terrified. We agreed that the dogs must be killed, or they would give us away. We dug a large hole three meters long and one meter wide. We placed all of the dogs in the trench and, sobbing, killed the pets and buried them. Discussion wavered to babies and infants, and how to stop them from crying. The discussion was wrenching, a few vs. the survival of the whole. But we couldn't do that, the most horrible thing to even contemplate."

No that couldn't happen, I closed my eyes tightly and held my breath trying not to imagine...and he continued.

"The days turned into weeks, fleeing the army always on our trail. Stealthily, we moved through the jungle. By now we had met other village communities that had escaped the scorched earth campaign, realizing that we were the victims of something larger, the actual genocide of our race. Ladinos in the communities were not being killed, only the indigenous Maya."

"For over a year, my wife and I and two children, one a nursing infant, crossed the northwestern jungle with the expanded community group. All wanted was to return home and hoped that the war and atrocities would soon end. But the army became more focused on finding the communities. We called ourselves communities in resistance and barely survived in the inhospitable jungle. Many children, particularly the youngest, died of hunger and disease. The lack of food and fresh water was a constant problem."

"Two families from Ixcán left the group and remained in the jungle in small groups with other families. Determined to return to their property, they spent the next 15 years hunted and on the run until the peace accords in 1996. The rest of our group moved north, realizing that they would not be able to stay in Ixcán."

Finally, Juan told me, "My family and the survivors of Centro Uno and the other small pueblos and aldeas came together just north of Mayalan. Mayalan, the original main co-op and the jewel of the Ixcán Grande co-ops, was burned to the ground, including the co-op buildings, the church, the school, the clinic and all of the stores and all of the homes in the center."

I had read in Ricardo Falla's book how after a year of running and being hunted through the jungle, the people gathered on the south side of the river, thousands of people waiting to cross the swinging, hammock-style bridge to escape to Mexico.

The people moved quickly across the bridge. I imagined Juan and his family were some of the last to cross. As they watched, a woman and child, fearful of the army waiting on the other side, jumped to their deaths on the river rocks. They continued across the swaying bridge to the other side and joined the almost 150,000 refugees in Mexico.

Juan told me, "Eventually we landed in the refugee camp Puerto Rico, Chiapas, Mexico, still thinking that this was just temporary and that we could return soon."

As I sat taking in what had transpired, listening without interrupting, hearing this story for the first time, I was transported back to a Centro Uno that now lived only in my memory. When we hung up, I sat for a while and then went downstairs to the kitchen where Charles was making dinner. Abby, my border collie, trotted up to me, sensing that I was upset, and pressed her body against my legs. I reached down to pet her and felt a bit more grounded.

Charles asked, "How did it go?"

"People died, but I just listened to Juan tell his story," I said.

"Did you ask about Elena?"

"No, I just listened."

It would be almost two years for me to have the courage to ask Juan what had happened to Elena.

# CHAPTER 41

Spring and Summer 2020

Sequestered at home during the pandemic, I found more time to do research and write.

Guy Gervais from Wings of Hope wrote a book about his travels and work around the globe, *Come Fly with Me: The Adventures of a Humanitarian Bush Pilot*. In the book, he described how Fabiano, the co-op coordinator in Quiche was murdered, shot multiple times in the back by soldiers, and how Guy and his family escaped in the dark of night driving straight through to Mexico.

In the book *Not Our Day to Die: Testimony from the Guatemalan Jungle*, by Michael Sullivan, I found testimony from Gonzalo Ross Hernandez regarding crossing the Río Ixcán. "We slept in First Center. There, we talked with the owner of a dugout canoe, but he said that he was not taking people across and that he had been threatened by the army and was not allowed to take anyone across the river. Late at night, he arrived, 'I will take you across, but leave early so that no one sees you. I'll just check the dugout and return.' We went down to the river and he took us across. They say that two days later, the army killed him and burned the dugout."

Who was the murdered man? Was it Santiago, Elena's husband? I could not imagine how Elena had survived without him. Equally gut wrenching, I could not accept that he'd been killed for just providing passage across the Río Ixcán. But maybe he didn't die. Others said that the family fled.

I searched for other survivors and found some on Facebook, and yet now I was hesitant to contact them. It was hard to understand who was who given the different directions chosen by the fifteen families. What allegiances were made with whom? Juan had changed his name on Facebook and told me, "I don't want anyone to know who I am."

I found a small book with another testimony from Victor, who was four at the time they fled Centro Uno. Was Victor Baudillio's little brother? Did I remember that correctly? His mother wove my huipil and planted a huge garden of giant red, yellow, and orange zinnias with seeds that we had given her. Her joy was beauty. And who could forget the snake incident? It was their chicken the snake had eaten.

In 2004, Victor José Perez Pablo, a college student at San Tomás University, remembered that horrible day to Laurie Levinger, and she transcribed it in her book, *What War*. "We fled, I was four and we made it into the jungle but my mother went back to get blankets to keep us warm in the mountains. She never returned, the army blew her up as my brother and I waited for her to return." He stated, "We were in the middle."

I considered the initial title that I had given my fledgling book, "En Medio"—"In the Middle." Neither side had the people in mind. It reminded me of the notes left to us by the guerrillas: "If you talk with the army, we will kill you. If the army knows that you talked with us, they will kill you."

My imagination took hold. I imagined myself one of them, fleeing the Ixcán, but still able to see the blue smoke curling up through the trees from the burning homes just a kilometer away. I felt their fear: *Shall we stay? We are not doing anything wrong! This is our land. Oh my god, we need to run and run, there is no time, the jungle is enclosed, we cannot see where we are. Which way to run? Where to hide?* I heard the sounds of rapid gunfire, of women and children screaming above the cicadas. The jungle noise accelerated, and the noise was around me now, inside of me. I ran, but there was no hiding. Victor ran on short legs, red and white striped rag pants flapping on his tiny legs as fast as they could carry him through the grass, dodging the cane, diving through to the milpa with his brother and mother hundreds of feet from their small house in the village. His mamá hesitated, "My sons, stay here and wait for me. Hide and don't move. I have to go back to the house quickly and get some blankets, so we can sleep. I love you, stay quiet."

And then I saw the explosion, the flames leaping high above the woven palm roof. I heard the scream above the crackling flames and the jungle upset. *Mamá doesn't come, we are being so good and quiet. Why doesn't she come?*

I saw the neighbors' cousins run by, yelling, "Come with us now! We need to run fast; we need to escape!" "But, my mamá, where is she?"

How could I not be there? I could see it, green, red and white, blue smoke a blur and red flames leaping from the burning homes to the sky, lashing at the top of the parrots' tree. Where would they roost? Where would the people live? Why did this happen?

Levinger dedicated the book to Victor, who was murdered the next year in 2005. He had told his friend he was afraid of the army because he had spoken out. I had foolishly not read the entire book with the description of his death and had reached out to the author Laurie Levinger asking about an address for him. I hope I didn't create more pain, but I'm sure that I did.

My fantasy of sharing photos of life in Ixcán when I first read his account without finishing the book was just that, an absurd fantasy. There was no safety.

Then out of the blue in mid-January 2020, I received an email from Ernest. It had been 36 years since I had seen or communicated with him.

He said in his brief email, "I am moving to Ireland, and I don't know what to do with all the stuff from Guatemala, but I thought you may be the only person interested in it and would understand the importance."

I replied in an equally brief email, "Yes, please send me what you have."

A large box arrived at my office. On top was the pair of red and white striped pants I had woven; below were letters and correspondence from him to his family and also newsletters and letters from DID mixed in with weavings that we had bought together on our travels. I felt the weight of the red and white pants that I had woven … two to three inches a day during the midday heat. The fabric was tight, and the pants had held up well, part of Viviano's work at making them into "jeans" on his treadle sewing machine. I wondered whether Ernest ever wore them again after El Día de los Santos.

Two weeks later Ernest emailed to say he'd found even more. Slides and a slide projector arrived soon after, archived from 1980 in the original box. I took a deep breath as I fitted the round carousel onto the projector. I turned it on and started clicking, faces and names came flooding back, filling me with joy and recognition and then the choking sadness. There is no way that all of the beauty and love could be destroyed. So much to share now with the families that had lost everything.

Days later, I was in Sonoma sorting through, tossing and packing up my 91-year-old father's house. I pulled out a large manila envelope from a pile of photos in the bottom of a cardboard box and opened it to find light blue crinkly airmail envelopes, one written almost every month from me to my mother and father and then to them separately after their split. I hadn't realized that I had trained Lugnut and written to my mother, who had a horse as a child, about doing so, about my error in using a slip knot and his head swelling when the rope tightened around his neck. I wrote about "the G's" hoping no one would guess that I meant the guerrillas. I wrote to her about her friend, the tiny birdlike girl, Francisca, with the sweet smile that my mother always asked about after her visit. I wrote about being alone, with Ernesto gone for three weeks or two weeks or overnight so many times. I'd known that there were several long periods of aloneness but hadn't realized how many. The letters also spoke of happiness: weaving, how the garden was doing, and I realized my aloneness was not loneliness; I was a part of the community.

I Googled Centro Uno Ixcán and saw a tiny speck by the Río Ixcán. I had never seen an aerial photo of the northwestern section of Guatemala. I had only seen the dark tree canopies from the small plane. The remoteness, even 40+ years later, was striking. I zoomed in and realized that the view was from hundreds, if not thousands, of feet above the tiny village. I was glad that it was still so remote. But it no longer looked as I remembered it—the miles of rainforest were replaced with treeless savannah and monoculture plantings of oil palms, and the sinuous meandering of the Río Ixcán was straighter and more engineered looking. I searched longingly for the jungle, maybe a tree that I knew, maybe the tree where the parrots roosted, my tree, the tree I saved from the campesinos' ax.

Now that sameness of my days was repeating with the pandemic. I was taken back to my time in Centro Uno when waking up to a new day was waking up to a day almost the same as the day before. I had not driven anywhere for a month and a half. There was something calm about the sameness, and I realized what I had learned subconsciously in Centro Uno as I looked across the narrow track of a road that we live on, through the tall 100-year-old trees to the homes of my daughters and grandchildren. I saw my granddaughter dancing along the narrow winding muddy trail through our field and knew that I would never miss a chance to be embraced by the love of a child again.

# CHAPTER 42

Still at home with few distractions I found time and space to think and write and one day I realized that I was ready and asked for Juan's help in finding Elena. I had to step back to a place where time moved more slowly, speaking was slow and in musical tones. Life was governed by a strict level of propriety and calm politeness. A time when there was no internet, no cell phones, little communication. We had been both hauntingly and blissfully in the dark. Impossible to reconnect or follow up without an arduous unsafe journey. But now it was different.

Juan suggested that I connect with Luisa, who was living in Ixcán and had returned to Mayalan, now Mayaland, the name anglicized. Luisa was sixteen to my twenty-two years old when I was in Centro Uno, still a young woman and I had kept her that way in memory. Her mother Pabla was in her late forties. Her father Tomás had been killed after we left. On May 4th, I sent her a message on WhatsApp.

"¿Buenas tardes, es Lucinda? Yo estaba tu vecino en Centro Uno en 1977-1978. Como estás?"

Her immediate response was filled with love that astounded me. "Gracias Lucinda Dios es grande que todavía nos dio esta oportunidad." It was so beautiful it was impossible to hold, as though no time had passed and how wonderful to be able to reconnect.

Juan gave me Luisa's brother's number, and I reached out to Roberto, who lives in North Carolina, with a message too. He called me and said, "Quienes este?"—"Who is this?"

I said "Lucinda," and he repeated my name over and over again, a mantra of remembrance. Back there, back there, back there, my own mantra of remembrance, my voice slowed and developed that sing-song lilt of a Todos Santos cadence.

I wanted to do something to keep them safe. My 93-year-old father had just died on Christmas day after just five days of being sick with Covid-19, and I knew that my fear of losing Luisa and her family was driven by that recent death. I could not bear to lose her after so many years of not knowing and assuming that she, and everyone in Centro Uno, was dead.

I bought masks from Amazon and sent them down to Luisa's family. Or I tried to. It was not so easy. There is no Amazon delivery service. Not even a real post office. The main delivery services only deliver to Guatemala City, not to the campo, the countryside. I reached out to everyone I knew to find out how to send this small box of masks. I found a man who flies to Guatemala City every week taking packages, delivering them to internal transports to drop at towns far from the city. The masks arrived in four days to Playa Grande, Ixcán. Luisa called me to tell me that they had arrived. We talked, and I asked how things were going and she told me, "Estamos bien aquí, Lucinda, no hay la enfermedad, pero no hay trabajo ni tampoco la escuela." I thought how crazy that I sent masks that were unnecessary particularly since all schools had been canceled and there wasn't much work. I realized that I didn't know what to do, and now in the midst of the pandemic, masks were the most valuable thing I could send.

And then I asked if she knew where Elena might be found.

"No sé pero yo oí que ella está en Centro Dos. Voy a buscarla, pero no hay bus ahora." She was not sure, but maybe she was in Centro Dos, but there wasn't transportation and life was hard right then. Given Luisa's concerns about the buses not running, I figured with Covid-19 escalating I would just wait until a better time. My last vision, my last remembrance of Centro Uno and Elena would remain a fantasy.

I was still imagining that day that I left Centro Uno. The beauty of the jungle and rainforest, the deep green, the humidity cloud rising from the thick-bladed grass along the sharp pathway edges, recently mowed by a machete. Elena posing against the wall of our house. The weathered mahogany board and batten a backdrop for Elena's striking everyday huipil as she held Mish our cat, looking sternly at the camera. It was my goodbye photo, following other equally serious photos of family and friends on the day of our departure before the Kaibiles arrived.

Luisa called me via WhatsApp. Sitting at my desk I saw the number and quickly picked up my phone, answering and not thinking, "This is Lesley…oops, Lucinda, my Ixcán name."

"Lucinda, Estoy aquí con la Elena." *The* Elena. And then, "Lucinda no tiene la camera?"

"No sé cómo usarlo," I said. Here I was a relatively tech savvy professional with Luisa in Centro Uno telling me to just push the camera button. My phone lit up. There was Luisa, standing in a rusted metal lean-to; she panned the camera to Elena standing next to her, her elegant beauty and bearing not completely diminished, but her sparkle and life gone.

I gushed, unable to follow the Maya calm greeting. Elena told me that she was well, but Santiago, her husband, passed away last year. I asked about her stepdaughter Julia and her stepson José, and they too had passed away. I asked about her son, Manuel, and she said that he was still living, but now it was just her and her grandson. She was in Centro Uno, working washing clothes and couldn't take much time to talk. She asked about Don Ernesto. I said that we split up after our return.

I told her that I had two of her huipiles, "The one with the ducks and …" A light came to her eyes …

"¿Los patos?"

"Si, los patos y también tengo el primer huipil que la Julia tejo." I also have Julia's first huipil. It had been hard to convince Elena to give me her duck huipil, as no one wove ducks into the intricate geometrical bodices. It was a funny creative take on her traje. She had said it was too old, but as I left, she laughed and gave it to me as a parting gift. "¡Los patos!"

Both she and Luisa had asked me how Don Ernesto was and to make sure and send him saludos.

I had only sent a few emails to Ernest about the boxes a year ago or so, and it had been pretty straight forward.

My husband Charles asked me, "Aren't you going to send the manuscript to Ernest? It would be shocking to go to a bookstore and find the book and have no idea about it."

"I'm writing it like it's just my story," I said, but clearly that was ridiculous; it was both of our stories. He didn't have a bit of a part; he was a main character. Over the years I had allowed his character in my writing to become unfeeling and cold.

I emailed Ernest and asked if I could send him a draft of my manuscript. I wrote, "I have been writing a bit about Centro Uno. Would you like to read it? I have talked with Juan, Luisa and Elena, and they all are thinking of you and wishing you best wishes if you would like to contact them." He replied to my email, "Sure," and I sent my draft.

Within a day, he wrote back. "This is really powerful. I don't remember all of this, but your memory is probably better than mine. Once my wife and I went to Guatemala and we went as far as Huehuetenango, but I couldn't go farther, it was too hard. Was I really that big of a jerk? If so, I am really sorry."

That took me a while to think about. It had been easy to cast him in that role. But as I look back and think about who I am now, I realize that he was probably not as bad as I had written. I, in turn, was probably just me, the proverbial dog with a bone. I imagined how challenging it had been to live with me in the middle of the jungle for two years. We emailed back and forth a bit, a story here and there.

He shared, "I never realized how traumatic the experience was for you—again, we were so young—I guess I assumed you were just

fine with it all...you always projected this strength and independence...
and probably still do. I remember the warmth of being accepted by all
the people in Centro Uno as such a gift and what happened there is so
heartbreaking. The part about the Kaibiles appearing after our things
being taken is still disturbing to think about. I remember looking off
across the forest toward Mexico and wondering if we could make it
there before they killed us. I was totally sure they had come to kill us.
Don't know if I ever shared that with you."

We had never shared our fears and now, these many decades later,
I wished we had.

# CHAPTER 43

Panajachel and Santa María Chiquimula,
Guatemala, June 2022

Juan asked me if I wanted to go to Guatemala with him. I hesitantly replied, yes. My family was concerned after googling U.S. travel to Guatemala, where the warnings suggested; Do not travel, particularly in the Northwestern part (Ixcán) along the border of Mexico and Guatemala. We discussed traveling only during the day and then bringing others along since there is safety in numbers. We made plans and changed plans and developed a clear and elaborate itinerary. I rented a four-wheel drive vehicle, and I booked hotel rooms in Playa Grande, Ixcán, for Juan, me and the two other members of our team. I still could not think of Playa Grande being anything other than a stockade. How would it feel to be there in a nice air-conditioned room with a TV where so many people were tortured and killed?

My "safety in numbers" group included an expert in the field of oral traditions and anthropology who was interested in Ixcán and wanted to visit some of the areas that I had known and where Juan knew people or had relatives. I flew to Guatemala in early June 2022, promising my family that I would not take my new iPhone and leave my jewelry at home and not travel at night and not go anywhere unsafe by myself.

I carried a copier to Luisa's daughter and son who were in college in Guatemala City. That her daughter was in college is a testament to Luisa. Concepcion, 24, has completed her work at the university and is taking her exams for additional course work. Carlos, 22, was studying chemistry. They both met me at the airport for the handoff. It was their one wish, since copiers are very expensive in Guatemala.

José, the brother of a family friend, Juan Carlos, here in California, picked me up, and we left at 8 p.m. at night, driving to Panajachel with my iPhone clutched in my hand. My plan was to spend two weeks in Guatemala. I was going to keep a daily journal. Though not something that I typically do, I wanted to understand what I was feeling and what each day would reveal. We arrived after midnight in Panajachel on the shores of Lake Atitlán. The bars were crowded with tourists. Sunday would be my first full day in Guatemala.

When I had told Victoria that I was going to Guatemala, she suggested that I visit Ricardo Falla. I was both excited and terrified to talk to Ricardo. I sent the 90-year-old Jesuit anthropologist and author an email with my itinerary, and he responded immediately. "Yes, come on Sunday, the traffic is safer, not so many trucks."

The next morning José and his son-in-law drove me to Santa María Chiquimula. As we entered the town, the road changed from asphalt to concrete and then to cobble. Santa María is not a tourist town and the people looked at us strangely, but I felt much more comfortable than in "Pana."

The houses and stores stepped up 18- to 24 inches from the road with a ledge just wide enough for a sleeping dog, and there were sleeping dogs of every size and color spread out in the late morning sun, the dog siesta.

We were searching for the Iglesia, but it was the Sunday market, and the church is located in the middle of the market. We couldn't find a place to park, much less find the way in. The streets were solid with vendors and women wearing huipiles of exquisitely beautiful colors and textures. The bright colors contrasted with the warmth of the cobblestone streets and baskets laden with squash, spinach, beets and lettuce. One woman stood at the corner, her huipil in varying shades of green with complex interwoven details. The baby on her back was wrapped in a striped woven green sling. I had never seen these colors and this coordinated and elegant composition in a huipil. I remembered what it would take to weave those intricate patterns. I didn't take pictures as I wasn't there as a tourist.

As we circled the market, rain arrived with a vengeance. We found a parking space, and I climbed out and into the street. Rotting vegetables, stagnant water and fresh flowers took my senses back as I carefully threaded my way through the tight market aisles. Covered with an ad hoc assemblage of sagging tarps, the torrential rains puddled above the stalls, straining the linking ropes. I ducked, anticipating a deluge of water falling onto our heads.

Unfurling my umbrella and clutching my iPad, photos and a copy of my latest manuscript as well as a USB key of hundreds of photos to share with Ricardo, I ran the last steps to the church courtyard. A high wall enclosed the immense white stone colonial church and the residence with the back of the church forming part of the wall. In the center, a stone plaza large enough for thousands to gather, was rapidly puddling. José and I walked quickly to a small group of cataquistas, all in traje, and I asked, "Buenos días dónde está la oficina?" Before we got to the door, out bounded Nacho (no fathers here) who welcomed me with, "You have arrived! Ricardo's guest, we have been waiting!"

Nacho, tall, thin and enthusiastic, ushered me down the covered walkway to Ricardo's sala at the end of an open passage past big terra-cotta pots and some planting areas. The door ahead was closed and rain pattered down on the roof. I felt spacey, as though I was not entirely there. I realized after reading his book *Massacres in Ixcán* that we shared lots of experiences, and I was curious but afraid. His experiences came after I left, during and after the genocide, and although I wanted to know, I was uncertain. The village and jungle still live with me in my dreams and memories.

Nacho opened the door, and I saw two couches facing each other covered with bright handwoven manteles. It was still in the time of Covid-19 and I wore my mask. Ricardo sat on one couch and waved me to the other couch across the room. Since I had just traveled on a plane, I was cautious, making sure that I kept my distance. Nacho left us, closing the door softly.

I sat for a moment, gathering my thoughts and feelings. I was not sure if we would be speaking in English or Spanish, and my Spanish was rusty. I was also slightly worried that my story would be just another story about Ixcán. I took a deep breath and Ricardo said in English, "I am so glad that you were able to come."

Something in me unleashed. I leaned forward and started talking. "Me too, you may be the only person who can understand my story." My story spilled out, splashing every which way. I realized that both of us were talking at the same time, sharing our memories of the place and people.

He asked me, "Did you know Tomás in Centro Uno?"

"Yes, I knew Tomás. He was my neighbor, and he had a tienda with, of all things, a propane refrigerator that he brought from Barillas down the 20-mile-long winding trail of mud and rock, and it crossed the river in the cayuco, and it didn't freeze the pink and blue bags of sweetened water, but they were cold…or did the army bring it in by helicopter and drop it off for him?"

We shared all sorts of stories. And then I allowed myself quiet sobs, relieved to share this previously unshared experience. I realized that I was still clutching my iPad and the photos. I took a breath, set them down and said, "Ernesto, my partner at the time and I took photos while we were there. Everyone in the village wanted a photo of their family, and we took a lot of photos of the vegetable garden and the jungle and then also some of the army in Mayalan."

"Did you know Coronel Castillo?" Ricardo asked.

"Yes. I don't understand if or how he could have been involved in what happened in 1981 to '82. He was a decent person...or so I thought."

"Would he know you?"

"I think so. He signed my papers, and we talked many times, and he saved me once or twice from being killed by his troops."

We spent an hour or so just talking about what had been. They were my memories of before that he had experienced. His curiosity and interest about who lived in Centro Uno and how it was set up led me to talk in detail about each family—their children, their homes, their crops and their horses and cattle.

I talked about how successful and wealthy a majority of the people were in Centro Uno.

"When did you leave?" he asked me.

"We left around the end of November 1978."

"Did you know el padre from Germany who was taken by the army in December 1978?"

"Maybe in passing, no padres ever came to Centro Uno when I was there...actually only one came once but in 1977," I said.

A brother poked his head in the door. "Lunch in five minutes."

We walked together to a comfortable and informal dining room with a long table and a number of chairs surrounding it. I sat on one side of the table and Katie, the cook, served lunch. I had mentioned in an email that I was a vegetarian. The meal was prepared especially for me, squash, carrots, guacamole with sliced egg on top and the wonderful small hand-patted round tortillas I remembered from long ago. I felt so welcomed.

I was introduced to the Jesuits, and three young men introduced themselves. There was lots of kidding around. I am sure that I looked slightly haggard from the trip and the tears.

David asked, "Are you a Maryknoll?"

"No."

"Are you an Evangelical?"

"No!"

"Are you anything?"

I said, "No," and they laughed.

"That's okay!" So, I was in, sort of. I waited for the pre-lunch blessing, but it didn't happen. These Jesuits were curious.

After lunch we walked back to the sala. I talked about how things had escalated and how the small village of Mayalan, now Mayaland, evolved from a town to a large barbed wire enclosed encampment for the army, and how, little by little, and then all of a sudden, there were installations everywhere and a huge stockade was constructed in Playa Grande, no town, just the army, and in balance how Ernesto and I saw an increasing guerrilla presence. Being in the middle wasn't possible for the people.

But none of it made any sense. Why would this testament to land rights and inclusion become the center of escalation? Where was the U.S. in this discussion?

"We were left in the middle of the jungle. Direct International Development closed, and we had no visa and no ticket home," I said as I showed Ricardo the notes from the guerrillas and their confusion about taking all of our belongings and then returning them with their request that we stay and continue our work once they realized that we were trying to help the people and that we were not the enemy.

Ricardo asked to see my slides and photos. I moved to the couch to sit closer but not too close. I turned on my iPad and pulled up all 200+ slides that I had scanned. They weren't as clear as the original slides, but told the story of what had been before Ricardo knew the people. He was surprised at how successful the original residents and co-op members had been, and how developed the communities were, seeing the photos of houses and cattle and the fiestas for the first time. We talked about Tomás, and Ricardo asked me, "The guerrillas killed him. Was his son a guerrilla?"

"Yes," I said. "I heard that he was killed but I am uncertain that it was the guerrillas since the army often posed as guerrillas. I don't know about his son."

We jumped around from topic to topic. There was so much to share. Then I asked a tough question: "How was it to live hunted in the dense underbrush of the jungle and the towering trees?"

Ricardo lived six years in the jungle with people that we think we both knew, but everyone changed their name in the selva. Most of the people he lived with wore pieces of the Todos Santos traje. The men wore ragged red and white striped pants, a tattered long collared shirt, and the women a navy-blue skirt and white striped huipil. They were most likely from Mayalan or Centro Uno or Centro Tres or Centro Diez. Those were the main pueblos the Todos Santos people had moved to.

I had been told that Ricardo was a member of the EGP, so I asked him.

"I wasn't a member of the Ejército Guerrillero de los Pobres, but I worked with them to give them spiritual help and write down their experience," he said. He was in the jungle during that first phase in late 1979 about a year after we left. Then the army left, demoralized, leaving the Ixcán region in the hands of the EGP. Guerrilla warfare in the impenetrable forest was working well. But the army promised to return with a vengeance, and they did.

The Reagan Administration provided not just funding, weapons and training for the Guatemalan soldiers, but the elite army Rangers as "in-country" advisors, like the construction manager that I had met in 1999 at the school construction meeting. The scorched earth killing began with a brutality that had no bounds, annihilating every pueblo across the Ixcán valley.

We looked at his books and the painstakingly hand-drawn sketches, showing arrows wide at the base, narrowing to the tip, swooping into the pueblos and aldeas—the path of the army. A sweep killed all in that tiny dot. Ricardo told me, "I interviewed the survivors, documenting in detail how and who was murdered." I knew how fraught the process would be. I imagined him hunched over crumpled damp paper making notes in the middle of the jungle. Maybe he was crouched between the flanks of a ceiba with a canopy a hundred feet above with rain pouring down, asking gently, "What happened to your mother, your sister, your brother, your father?" Documenting and correcting, he was able to give surviving family members and the community, an understanding of who was lost forever, murdered.

I had tried to read his books several years before, but I was just looking for those I'd known in Centro Uno. Now I understood the importance and the enormity of the work that he had done and also the personal impact. I wasn't sure what I felt or how to think about what I had heard. I had held so much together for so long. What I learned was even worse than I had imagined.

We finally said goodbye, both of us exhausted. I promised to organize my photos better and resend them to him.

José was waiting for me in the center of the plaza. The sun was out, and the plaza had started to dry. Disassociated, I wandered. We left the bright whiteness of the drying stones, and my glasses adjusted to the darkness as we entered the market, weaving through the stalls, working our way back to the car. I climbed into the backseat of the minivan.

I didn't know what to do with my thoughts. I turned my head to look out the window and watched the changing shapes and colors of the multitude of dogs now stretched out on the high shelves for their afternoon siesta.

# CHAPTER 44

Panajachel, June 2022

The day after meeting with Ricardo, I wandered the meandering pathways of the hotel garden, one foot in front of the other, following fish-shaped stepping stones, bricks slick with slime, crushed rock trails, finding birds and secret gardens, eventually totaling 10,000 steps. Given what I'd heard it was ridiculous to be checking my Fitbit but it added some normalcy.

Set on the shore of Lake Atitlán, the tree shaded paths looped the Spanish style hotel. The large pool with tropical flowers crowding the edges offered a view to the volcano that was elegant and soothing. It was important to be able to think. I was starting to understand what Ricardo shared with me. There was a lot that I had not known. His book was so concise, but also just a summary of a series of books he had written with even more specificity about where, when and how many attacks there were. He told me that the army had pulled out of Ixcán just two years after we left, unable to curtail the guerrilla attacks. The forest was so dense and the guerrillas so practiced in quick strategic attacks, they debilitated the army, who left with the ominous words, "We will return with greater force."

Walking slowly, pausing to look up, I saw a hint of blue smoke on the hill above me and clouds drifting across the lake. *I still don't remember our trip out of Ixcán. If I can't remember how I left, how can I go back?*

Then, thick bladed St. Augustine grass snuck quietly under the concrete. I had seen how fractures in the concrete slab had started as a tiny crack and then a mat, more grass than concrete in six years' time. How will it be after 44 years? Will the grass and vines have obliterated the foundation? Just like 600 years before when the jungle took back the plateau, the Maya empire lost to vines twining and squeezing the rough dry stone to fertile earth.

Digging in the garden, we had found rough clay feet from bowls long broken and pieces of obsidian worked to spear points. What survives this decay of almost half a century? Not wood but steel. Perhaps a doorknob or a hinge? A partially woven huipil tossed in a hurry to escape the flames, the red and white threads intertwined with the damp blades, would have dissolved into the earth years ago.

Juan, my neighbor and the teacher in Centro Uno from so long ago, would be coming on the bus to meet me the next day from Ixtahuacán, his original village in the highlands before Ixcán, so I took my time to look at my photos and think of all of the questions I wanted to ask him. My heart rate escalated as I nervously wrote my thoughts of my meeting with Ricardo and wondered how Juan would feel. We had been so young and so much had transpired since then.

He arrived in Panajachel in the early afternoon. It had been 44 years or so since we had last seen each other. We had planned to spend the five days exploring Ixcán and staying in Playa Grande as our base.

Juan was to lead our small group on day trips to visit different areas where refugees had returned. This included Centro Uno and Centro Dos to see Elena and her family; the place we had lived, our houses long since burned; Mayalan (now Mayaland) to visit Luisa, her mother Pabla, her husband and family; Cuarto Pueblo where Ernesto had taught vegetable gardening and later 400 people were tortured and killed over three days;

and then finally to Victoria 20 de Enero, a small community made up of people who fled to the jungle and lived there for 14 years prior to re-establishing a community after the Peace Accords in the 1990's.

Our emails and calls had reconnected us. No longer the young teacher, he was stocky and his still bushy hair gray, but I would have recognized him anywhere. He was tired but I could still see his enthusiasm. I hadn't realized that he had been ill. We got right into talking about our life in Ixcán as though no time had passed. Over dinner I showed him photos of the school children with him standing by the chalkboard. He remembered all of the children's names, their families' names and where they lived.

The open-air hotel restaurant had a view of the lake and the volcanoes on the other side. Puffs of smoke and clouds rested on the shoulders of the volcanic cones, obscuring the tops of the volcanoes. Tiny birds flew through the restaurant landing on the backs of chairs, perching and hiding in the bougainvillea wrapping the posts.

After talking about our children and grandchildren, Juan pushed his chair back, setting his banana smoothie glass on the table and said, "I have been sick for a while. I was hoping I was going to feel better, but I am feeling worse. I hope I can keep going on the trip, but my stomach is having problems. It is hard to be away from my home where I know what I can eat."

Worrying about his health and the impact of returning to a place that neither of us had visited had prompted him to set up a Fire Ceremony. He was studying the ancient Maya costumbre and had asked me when we had talked before the trip if I would like to meet with him and his Chiman, Don Jorge, for protection on our journey to Ixcán. I said, "Of course."

I had been curious about the ancient costumbre since reading Maude Oake's book *The Two Crosses of Todos Santos*. I was worried about our trip, particularly now that Juan was sick, so I said yes.

That next morning, we took a tuktuk, a tiny motorcycle-like car, up a narrow-cobbled road high above the lake to meet Don Jorge. The recent rains obscured the trail to the cave, and we took what turned out to be a narrow creek bed down the cliff. I felt wobbly as though my equilibrium had given up on me. A warning?

Juan and Don Jorge paused for me to take a photo. Don Jorge said, "Take it slowly. We are like the deer of the forest." He and Juan danced from rock to rock while carrying cardboard boxes and a mesh bag bulging with pine sticks.

"Today I am a cow in the forest," I said. I was apprehensive of what lay ahead. I am an uphill hiker, downhill is my anathema, but that day I was not even sure of that.

We paused and caught a glimpse of the lake below, placid and deep blue-green.

A narrow ledge led to the charred rocky edge of the cave, and blue copal-scented smoke wisped out before us. Juan frowned and asked Don Jorge, "Why are they allowed to make magic outside the cave?"

Two men on large rocks were watching as we climbed over the narrow precipice. I asked for a hand to pull me up. Later I would reflect that this was not the place to share energy with those we didn't know.

The cave was low and along the back wall there was a long altar with tall loose bunches of yellow, red and pink zinnias resting against the rocks and candles burning in glass containers. Arching over the ceremonial platforms and stretching back into a place beyond sight, the cave ceiling was completely blackened without a speck of rock showing through. Flickering candles led into the darkness.

Coming to a flat rock space and using a stick to push off the still smoking remnants of the previous ceremony, Don Jorge sprinkled corn-meal in a circle as the base then sprinkled a cross in the center to the edges of the circle. Balls of pine resin the size of oranges were placed in a pattern in the circle. We unwrapped short bunches of ocote, a very sappy wood full of pitch.

Next to us knelt a woman in the traje of Sololá intent on her own ceremony. She didn't look up. Raw eggs circled her fire, and when they heated up, they exploded, spraying hard cooked eggs everywhere, even into my hair. "Don't look at her ceremony," Don Jorge said quickly.

He spoke in Mam, fast and monotonously incanting and unwrapping the packages. The unwrapped handfuls of ocote sticks were laid in the emptied cardboard box, and we unwound the wicks of thin white candles and placed them next to the ocote.

Turning slowly to me, he asked, "Did you have a dream about being attacked in a car by two men who were dirty and ragged?"

Shocked, I said, "Yes, it was so real." I had never had a dream like that before, and had not told anyone about it. The fact that he could see it made me realize yet again the seriousness of our trip and that my dream was more than just a random dream.

We were each given a cigar and two small light yellow beeswax candles. For two or three hours, Don Jorge spoke directly to the ceremonial fire. Everything sputtered and then burned strong and bright with a beautiful pine scented heat as we sat watching and waiting while Don Jorge chanted in Mam. Every so often I could hear him say my name. Eventually the fire died down, and Don Jorge announced, "Lucinda Miles, you are protected and safe for your trip."

But Juan needed more. I watched and waited. When it was over, we stood together in the mouth of the cave, looking out over the lake far below. Blue smoke from the remnants of our fires snuck out around our feet and atomized into the deep blue sky.

On our hike back, I felt stronger and more balanced. The bus stopped at the side of the road on a curve, and we ran to catch it. We had dinner with Don Jorge at an open fish restaurant in Sololá. He ordered fish soup that featured a whole unscaled fish that looked like it had swum directly from the lake into the bowl.

When we parted ways, Don Jorge promised Juan that he would perform another ceremony the next day for him, but that Juan need not be physically present. Later that day, Juan felt sicker and more worried, "I think I'm going to die." I reflected on the trials of living with my own PTSD following my time in Ixcán and how deeply trauma affects us.

Juan was so sick that he was unable to sleep or eat much. There was no way that he could travel to remote areas in Ixcán for several days in a car. The other members of the group backed out, and I couldn't see how I could travel to Ixcán by myself. The anthropologist was going to Antigua so I thought that we could finally meet.

# CHAPTER 45

Antigua, June, 2022

I couldn't believe that I was alone again, a refrain I knew too well. My family and others were focused on the group's physical safety, but my real concern was my emotional safety. I had made sure that I wouldn't feel. I would be protected by a group. We would be interviewing people. The focus would be academic in nature. But really, how could it be?

Writing about Ixcán for the past five years had been bracketed by the constraint of my architectural practice. Compartmentalizing worked well.

In Antigua, I was again alone with fear, which returned after all this time. Unlike being in California working on projects, there were no pressing questions about a detail on a drawing that could pull me away from the feelings. How had I stupidly thought that this would be simple? That we could go and visit Centro Uno for a few hours? I had kept the people alive: the children young, the women weaving and the red and white of their traje vibrant against the green. When I left that last time, time was held in place like a wasp in amber, unchanged.

In all the years that I'd written about trauma and fear, I now realized that there was no way that I could have written any of it without the mental constraints of my work. The rhythm of work created safety. I was able to shift to a place where I had emotional control and a clear understanding of the process and goals.

All this was stripped away. I had nothing but time by myself and my wandering thoughts. Ghosted by the anthropologist, I was alone. The PTSD that I had thought had receded returned every minute, my heart pounding, my nerves on edge, my head crowded with intrusive thoughts. The hotel was empty and the dark tile corridors were barely lit at night. I slept poorly in the huge cold echoey room with two full beds. Who were the ghosts who roamed the hallways and sent drafts of cold air circling my ankles? How could I ever have thought I could contain this trip by relying on others?

I was angry and sad, and yet strangely relieved that I couldn't go to Centro Uno. Although strong, I didn't know if I was *that* strong. It reminded me of the suggestion to have someone video my first reconnection with Juan, like a documentary. But no, I didn't want that. I just wanted to be there. So, I sat with my feelings in the small lobby filled with lush green plants in large terracotta and colorful glazed pots with exquisite weavings of the local traje of San Antonio on the whitewashed stucco walls. Sitting on the hard wooden mahogany straight chairs, I sorted photos for three days, flicking quickly on my iPad, like a video of the past.

I cherished the time I had spent with Ricardo. With him, I allowed myself to feel the deep sorrow and pain. He was the only other person besides Ernest who could understand what I'd experienced. Juan felt it so deeply, it ate at him. Initially I was frustrated with Juan for not joining me this far in the journey, and then I took a step back and thought about what had followed him all the way to British Columbia. I know what followed me, and his experience was so much worse.

My hope at connecting with the anthropologist had not panned out either. So, what was I doing in this god damned tourist town?

I called my husband Charles.

"I can't believe that I came all of this way and that I won't see Luisa or Elena."

"Call Luisa and see if she can meet you. From what you have told me, she will respond right away. What town is the closest to Ixcán?"

I looked on Google and decided on Cobán. It looked equidistant from Antigua and Mayaland. The town of Cobán sits in the high verdant rain and pine forest at the intersection to Tikal to the east and Ixcán to the north. Based on Google, it was exactly the same driving time from Mayaland and Antigua.

I texted Luisa on WhatsApp. In a few minutes she responded that she would leave Mayaland in the morning at 8 a.m. and see me in Cobán! Heart lifting, I worked backwards. Hotel Gaia was available. I made a reservation. I quickly snapped into my familiar, decision-making mode. I wanted to have a quiet healing place, and according to the website, Hotel Gaia was a retreat located in a nature preserve with a few well-spaced rooms and a beautiful dining room where they serve all meals. It would be a perfect location.

I asked at the hotel reception if they knew of a driver, and they did. He would be there at 8 a.m. I was nervous about seeing Luisa and worried about not seeing Elena since I knew she would feel slighted. We had called and talked multiple times since that first call but I knew that the trip for her would be hard, she was older and so much had happened in her life that her health had suffered.

# CHAPTER 46

Cobán, June 2022

The rain was pouring so hard that the wipers couldn't keep up, but ahead the sky cleared, and the bus station in Cobán came into view. My nerves would not stop their jangling since the inception of the trip.

Now, it was just me. Not the naïve and scared me of 44 years ago, but a woman who had worked at analyzing that fear and the long stretches of blankness. Would those disassociated states return? I worried that this unaccompanied meeting would plunge me back into that time, that self. The fantasy of a trip with a "safe" group had evolved into something entirely different. It now felt as though the others were just bit players in this play as they disappeared one by one.

Ahead, bathed in a ray of sunlight, Luisa and her husband stood at the road edge by the bus station. I had not expected her husband. I climbed out of the car and crossed the street. My heart clenched—I'd never thought that I would see her again! Here she was, a late middle-aged woman, with graying hair—but then, so was I. She was short and sturdy like her mother, and clad in an exquisite huipil. It was different from my memory of a Todos Santos huipil. There were no wide red and white stripes. But when her smile lit up her face—she was my friend Luisa. Once again, we were neighbors.

We patted each other on the shoulder as is the Todos Santos custom, but then pulled closer to hug. Our joy, mutual at finding each other after so long, dissolved my shyness and nerves. Luisa and Miguel climbed into the backseat of the KIA. José, my driver from Antigua, drove us to the hotel that I had randomly selected. After briefly clearing, the sun was comfortably warm for a moment, steaming the pavement. Now it was raining again as we meandered through the narrow, steep, and windy cobbled streets.

The Hotel Gaia sat at the end of an unpaved muddy and rocky lane. As we entered the lobby the hotel manager dismissed us before trying to understand who we were.

I couldn't quite put my finger on what it was about the rudeness and unease. And then it hit me: Luisa and Miguel were not the typical clientele of a place like this and I sensed disdain from the manager. As though he was thinking: Who is this group of Maya indigenous people and this American woman? Why are they here? Rain thundered on the roof as we were enclosed in the small lobby, all slightly confused with what would happen next.

I dropped into problem solving mode. It was almost two p.m. and none of us had eaten, so I asked, "May we have lunch?" The manager hesitated and then said, "Si está bien pero ahorita."

We rushed to our rooms to drop our bags in the now light drizzle through an open park-like setting that stretched all the way out to the forest edge—a manicured jungle and rainforest both peacefully lush and friendly. Bromeliads and orchids draped the upper branches of the tall ceiba trees, floating in the misty rain. The cicadas' high pitched clicking and the wet thick bladed grass brough back visceral memories of Ixcán.

When we sat down for lunch the manager came by and I told him our story, how we knew each other so well 44 years ago and thought that we were lost from each other. The genocide of the Maya peoples in the early 1980's made this reunion unimaginable. His manner changed, and he asked a few questions. I showed him some photos of me at 22 and Luisa at 16, smiling broadly under a tall rubber tree with a view of the

Río Ixcán in the background. He looked at both of us and saw out tears and said, "Qué bueno se quedan aquí como ustedes quieren."—"Please stay as long as you like."

We spent the rest of the day and evening reconnecting, crying, laughing and looking at my now organized photos. In the oddness of my trip's solitude, I found meaning in sorting and resorting and re-naming photos of that life before.

Luisa remembered names that I didn't and told me where many members of the pueblo ended up while we look through the photos.

Luisa asked, "Was it Don Ernesto who used to get up before day-break every morning and go to the pista to pick up estiércol?"

I laughed, "Oh no, that was me! And I even have a picture to show you!" I flipped through the photos and found one with me and Lugnut, manure machine extraordinaire, my hands in sky-blue rubber gloves and a broad brimmed hat.

"Why so early?" she asked, and suddenly I could smell the stench of hot manure in the mid-morning sun, the moisture from rain and humidity creating a cloud around each steaming pile while the cicadas buzzed in the background.

"Because after daybreak it was so stinky and moist that I would gag at every pile!"

"And was it you who had the snake in your bed? We heard you screaming all the way across the pueblo, so we all ran to your house to find out what happened."

I pull out the photo of Ernesto holding the snake's body dangling from the bloody headless end. "Yes, and it was a long one! Your father said it wasn't poisonous, but Mariano said it was. My father and Ernesto killed it in our bed, cutting off its head while pinning it against that wood wall with a forked stick." We laughed, and Miguel, seeing and hearing about his wife so long ago, said, "Estos son nuevos cuentos!" He had never heard these new stories having only known Luisa from the refugee camps. He didn't know the serious but also silly girl from Centro Uno who laughed running through the pueblo to the river with her best friend Chaya. These silly stories had been left behind, ghosts of joy in the village after her father was killed and they fled to the jungle.

We were the last people in the dining room, and the manager stopped by to tell us they were closing. We wandered off to bed. There was so much to remember and so much I didn't know.

The next morning, we met for breakfast on a deck overlooking the park and forest beyond. As we settled down to omelets and beans, we talked more. "I will tell you the story of what happened to me and my family after you left," Luisa said. "I have not told anyone this story." Having lost her entire community, there was no one close that she could share what had happened with until this day.

"Mi finado papa was very strict and lots of time when he was gone, my mamá and I would have to take care of all the animals, the milpa and manage all of the cardamom and coffee plantings, including harvesting and curing as well as minding the store. Eventually, he brought Pedro back to Centro Uno who was in boarding school in Huehuetenango to help manage the cattle. That was a relief."

She described the history of the separation of Centro Dos from the Ixcán Grande co-op. It was a challenging period as the members of Centro Dos, who were from Ixtahuacán, wanted to hold their land titles individually and not be part of the overall cooperative. This had created a significant rift that took up a lot of co-op time and led to bad blood between Centro Dos and the co-op.

Luisa continues, "There still was some bad blood between Centro Dos and the co-op without Padre Guillermo to negotiate. But mi finado papa never talked about internal politics. One day when he was gone the EGP came to Centro Uno looking for him. But he wasn't there so they left. But everyone knew that the guerrillas came looking for him at our house."

"Yes," I said, "That happened when we were still living there. We had gone on a trip to Honduras, but when we returned, we heard that."

"I didn't remember that it had happened so early," Luisa said.

"Were you there?" I asked.

"Yes," she said.

I knew this was the time that the army had started to take control of the skies and the ability to fly in and out of Ixcán. Miguel paused and pushed his omelet with his fork. He frowned at this new information.

"He went to talk to the army to make sure that they would continue flying in, but then they stopped. In just over a year the army stopped flying in except for transporting more and more troops to counter the increasing guerrilla forces. There was a huge meeting in Mayalan, the president didn't come, but the people demanded action on restarting flights to move the hundreds of quíntales of cardamom, coffee and corn that were waiting in the bodegas. The bodegas no longer had space. It was much worse than the meeting in the fall of 1978 when you were here. The people were angry."

While the waiter came by to refill our coffee cups, a light rain started to fall, and we shifted our chairs to sit under the overhang. I unclenched my hands and waited.

"My father talked less, not more, and then one day he said 'one side is going to kill me. I just don't know which one yet. I hope it is the guerrillas because they will just take me and leave the family alone. The army will most likely massacre everyone in our family.'" Luisa's voice and face went pale and flat with the shock of recounting her father's words.

That made sense. I had seen the army, and there was no selectivity, no empathy there. I had also seen the EGP and met with them, and they at least seemed to have a clearer understanding of the separation of individuals from their families and their communities.

"So, Lucinda, about a year after you left, they took him. They killed him, just him, but why? And the army also masqueraded as the guerrillas so no one knows for sure which side killed him." She was shaking now, gently sobbing. I patted her arm, consoling.

I remembered Tomás admonishing me about eating too many cookies or huevitos and realized how little I knew or understood of what was really going on at the time.

We sat quietly as she collected herself. Luisa said, "I have never told anyone what happened. At the time I was still so young. I didn't really understand if it was the guerrillas or others. The killing was just beginning, and there was a lot that we didn't understand. But we were alone, just mi mamá, Pedro and me. My little brother was in Huehue at boarding school, and my oldest brother, Roberto, was in Centro Diez.

"We still had our milpa and all, but it was different. We were alone."

I can imagine how the fear and suspicion must have started dividing the community. The lack of any communication, roads or safety and fear for their families could drive a wedge even between the most focused communities.

"Then, we thought that maybe when the massacres started in Ixcán, the army wouldn't come. We thought that maybe the army would spare us."

This was in the early 1980's. The timing must have coincided with when I read the first article in the Mercury News about the streams of refugees leaving Guatemala and passing over the border to Mexico. I pushed myself back from the table and said, "I want to get up and get some fresh coffee." Truthfully, I didn't want to hear what happened next. Miguel looked anxious. After taking some deep breaths and refilling my coffee, I returned to hear the rest of Luisa's story.

"When all those people, over 200, were massacred just two hours away in Piedras Blancas, we thought maybe we should leave too. It was hard to do though. It was only my mamá, Pedro and me and we had all of the chickens, cows and horses. We felt responsible for all of the work that we had done and for all of our animals."

I thought back to Tomás's Appaloosa stallion, and Lugnut. I never knew what happened to him after I left. I held my breath.

Luisa continued, "That night we went to bed, and when we woke up most of the people had left in secret in the night. There were just a few of us left, maybe five families. Elena and Santiago and Faustino and others had loaded up all of their horses, mules, and took all of their belongings and their family members, including Andres, Santiago's helper on the cayuco, and left in the night. They just left us there, so we gathered what we could carry and fled with Mariano, Nicholas, who lived with his family on the outside of Centro Uno on the trail to Mayalan, the other Tomás, Celestino and his family. We couldn't contact my brother Roberto because he was too far away, and it happened so quickly. It was less than a day. We had to leave the cattle and horses.

"We were terrified, and we ran into the selva. The army came, but we were gone by then, and we saw the flames of our houses burning. We heard the shots as they shot and killed our animals and even some of our neighbors. They burned your house too, Lucinda...."

Miguel passed me a napkin, and I blew my nose. Anger, hatred and fear overwhelmed me. I had felt that coming the day we left. Now the terror and horror of families just barely escaping and being close enough to see the flames of the houses burning was a reality. For Luisa, it was all of her life's history consumed by death and the fire. I tried to imagine again our house burning. What about the garden where we had worked so hard?

"We didn't know what to do because the jungle was very thick. The army mined the main trail with land mines, so if you traveled on the trail, you would be blown up. So, we traveled only in the tangled trees and cane, but it was so confusing. We would go forward, and then we would realize that we had gone in a circle or backwards. We had our machetes, but we needed to be quiet. We could only cook at night because the army had made a base on the other side of the Río Ixcán. Helicopters flew all day long from the base to the main stockade in Playa Grande back and forth right over where we were hiding."

I had been told that they had hunkered in the jungle for months evading the army, unsure which way to go. It is hard in the jungle at night. So dark. The trees are so tall that you can't see the stars. It is impossible to navigate and understand which way is north.

"Don Nicholas decided to go ahead of us and check the trail with his daughter. She was about 13 or 14 then because she was three or four years younger than me. The army was waiting for him on the trail, and they took them both to Mayalan where they killed him and took her as their wife.

"We found him a week or so later when we arrived in Mayalan. Mayalan was all burned, but there were a few structures left with posts only, and he was tied to a post. His wife was with us, and we knew it was him even though his body was mostly gone. She had woven his traje. She recognized her work."

Once again, we shifted in our chairs and I thought about how, of course even a small piece of tela, fabric, would be recognizable, remembering how every pass of the beater compressing the threads was fixed in my mind and muscle memory.

"We asked someone what happened to their daughter, my friend, and they said that the soldiers had taken her as their wife, but they didn't know where. Don Nicholas had been tied to the post, and then stabbed. His traje was hanging there from the knife. It had only been a week or so but in the intense heat and rot, there was very little left of his body. His wife, she gathered it up, and put it in an olla to take with her to keep it safe."

I imagine Luisa cresting the hill above Mayalan, seeing the smoldering ruins of the large bodega and church, the scorched metal roofs twisted and convoluted with the heat. Blue smoke hanging in the sky, hovering, and for a moment, a remembrance of welcoming wood cooking fires, but then stumbling down the rocky hillside, getting a closer view. A view of complete annihilation.

She and Nicholas's wife, Josépha, searched for any evidence of their daughter, Yolanda, and Don Nicholas. Fear of the army pervaded every thought, but the main army installation had left Mayalan. It was quiet except for the cicadas, parrots, and the cracking boom of falling trees burned in the conflagration. Memories of her own father's death surfaced but were tamped down.

"We were closer to the border with Mexico at Mayalan, and we finally made our way across the border to the refugio, the place where we could rest. There was some food there, and some water, but they had not anticipated so many people arriving, so there wasn't very much. We finally found Roberto. He had traveled with Juan and a group from Centro Diez."

We had been sitting out on the deck for almost two hours, and the sun came out again.

"It would be almost 14 years until we returned to Ixcán, in 1994 or so. A group from the army had taken a large block of land from Centro Uno to Xalbal and made new parcels for themselves. When we returned, they said that we had abandoned our land except for a few small areas that my papa had bought from the young finquero who had left when the guerrillas burned his rancho. We kept those, so we got some land."

"Where did you meet Miguel?" I asked.

"We met in the Refugio." She looked at Miguel

We talked about me coming to visit when Padre Guillermo is celebrated every year on the day of the crash so many years ago on November 20.

"Now, there is a huge mass as a remembrance of Padre Guillermo but it is important to remember the history and Padre Eduardo as well. Centro Uno was called Belen for a reason; it was the birthplace of Ixcán Grande and it was a story of success."

I sat in a daze as I thought back to my conversation with Ricardo just days before and his drawings and maps of the massacres. Luisa and I shared so much. Her husband didn't know her then or know her father. I carry the history, the beauty of the pueblo, the richness of the ancient rainforest and wet jungle, the memories of this life before. Memories that evaporated in a nightmare.

Her words repeated in my mind, "It was a story of success. How could this have happened? Tell our story."

# EPILOGUE

## Send Them Back

Current immigration policies have encouraged U.S. citizens to chant "send them back." The chant focused on sending people back to their country, but what does that mean? I think back on that day I called into the radio station and hung up. What would I say today?

In 1979 it would've meant sending the people back to their own properties, their own cardamom and coffee farms, their own herds of cattle and horses on slightly more than 28 acres. It would have meant sending them back to a time when, due to their hard work, they had created a highly successful community with a cooperative governance structure.

It would've meant crystal clear, rivers, and streams, as well as jungles and forests teeming with toucans and trogons against the background music of flocks of parrots winging from one side of the broad Ixcán valley to the other.

It would've meant small farmers' children being educated in village schools with teachers who spoke their indigenous language Mam as well as Spanish. I know because I lived there.

Sending them back in 1982 would have meant sending them back to burned villages and death. The U.S. and Israeli advisors and weapons of the scorched earth campaign of the late 70's culminated in a massive genocide in the early 1980's. All the people were forced from their own lands across the border into Mexico.

Sending them back in 1996 would have meant sending them back after the peace accords to find others had taken over their land: army officers, wealthy Guatemalan owners, and multinational owners. Their productive and well managed 28 acres would have been a thing of the past. If they still owned some property their crops would have been gone and their homes destroyed.

Sending them back in 2023 would have meant sending them back to acres of a U.S. company owned oil palm finca. All of the primordial forests are gone, harvested for furniture and flooring or just clear cut and burned for agribusiness. Parrots and the huge bright blue butterflies are gone. The crystalline rivers dammed and rerouted. The clear almost turquoise waters muddied with pollution and debris from processing plants built at the river's edge. Sending them back is to no jobs or, if lucky to get a job, it is for pennies a day on unsustainable fincas that cover what was their land until it was coveted and then stolen. I know because I have seen the change.

There is no going back. There is no sending them back.

1977-78 photos by Lesley Miles or Ernest Cole

Crossing the Río Ixcán in the Cayuco

Lucinda standing in front of what was our home for two years

The view from our front porch across the valley and the parrot tree

The Garden Sign

The Sunday Centro Uno market

Boys picking vegetables in the school garden

The trail to Mayalan

President Kjell Eugenio Laugerud Garcia in Ixcan 1977

Community photo 1977

The garden beds

Ernesto with the snake from our bed

Gardening class in Cuarto Pueblo

School children Centro Uno

Centro Uno girls

Baudelio and his mom, sister and brother and the Zinnias!

Lugnut and Lucinda manure pick up

Elena and Julia teaching Lucinda how to weave

Carrying water from the creek

Día de los Santos, November 1, 1978

El Día de los Santos horse race

Lucinda walking the trail to Barillas

Author photo credit: Tara Sturtevant

# ABOUT THE AUTHOR

At twenty-one, Lesley Miles researched and taught French Intensive organic gardening for two years in the middle of the Guatemalan jungle at the inception of a military escalation. At twenty-nine, then a horticulturist, she started a business and became a mother. At forty, she became a registered architect and at fifty, she developed an abandoned iconic granary building with her architect/partner and husband into a thriving mixed-use development and the 25th LEED Gold building in the world. At sixty, she started writing. Her debut memoir, *All Things Hidden*, resurrects a time before and then the voices of those lost in Ixcán, Guatemala, and unfurls her own harrowing tale of survival.

# ACKNOWLEDGMENTS

Living in the remote Ixcán Grande corner of the Guatemalan jungle for two years 1977-78 and then reliving the jungle in my mind for forty-five years, I have many people to acknowledge.

My husband, Charles, an architect, long distance runner and Vietnam veteran, has spent the last forty-five years with me and my mind searching the first part of those decades unmoored and lost and then, the last part, writing this book. Thank you to the patience of my children and in particular, daughter Alicia, who wrote of the Genocide in Guatemala for her Claremont McKenna senior thesis, Gardening in Guatemala.

Unbeknownst to my multitude of architectural clients they provided a safe place as design and detailing came easy as remembering and writing did not. It is important to mention this as it is only with my ability to engage in thirty-six years of psychoanalysis that I could sit and write these memories. My Psychoanalyst, Dr. Angela Sowa, un-knowing what was hidden, let me and led me to understand how acute PTSD and anxiety can be resolved and changed by the analytic process. And she is responsible for the title *All things Hidden*.

I never would have ventured so far and to such a remote place if it had not been for Ernest Cole. And although I never met Maryknoll Fathers William Woods and Edward Doheny without their vision and herculean efforts to help campesino families with no land be able to farm their own land none of us would have been there and seen the glimmer of vision and hope. I am forever grateful for Ernest pushing me to this experience and then after forty-five years of no communication, reading my manuscript and sharing memories that I had forgotten and reinforcing memories that I wasn't sure of.

As a fledgling writer, I slowly learned to write. The need to share my experience overwhelmed my ability. Friends and family gave me encouragement. Carol Holzgraff was instrumental in helping me to get started by insisting that I needed to write my story and then graciously reading my early attempts. My friend Sydney Croft helped me unbox my huipils and memories. Haley Cambell, writer/teacher introduced me to dialog and sentence structure during Covid. Dr. Thomas Ogden and I worked together; me sharing my writings to him to mark up. Barbara Nichols engaged her Spanish reading group who read each chapter over several weeks and asked many questions that led me to make clarifications and corrections. Brady T. Brady edited an early copy before I returned to Guatemala and gave many constructive comments pushing me to add descriptions. Mary Jo McConahay, reporter and writer, helped review and I am sure I did not catch everything. I had beta readers who encouraged me to continue; Roderic Camp PhD, Professor Emeritus Claremont McKenna, Laurel Gromer, Kim Bush, Diana Craig, Roya Cruz, Katie Skurtowsky and many others who I may have coerced into reading what they thought was my travel journal.

Jordan Rosenfeld, author and editor, read my first attempts and encouraged me to continue and to also take workshops with Lidia Yuknavitch's Corporeal Writing. Lidia selected my manuscript for an in depth read and comment, encouraging me to change the format into three themes. And then, as I wrote over the next five years, Jordan provided companionship writing together in "the tin can" and finally providing essential editing.

I am neither a historian nor an anthropologist. When I lived in Ixcán Grande I was in my early 20's and had no goal other that testing out and teaching French Intensive/Biodynamic gardening, an organic vegetable growing technique, in what was virgin jungle just ten years before I arrived. My story does not pretend to be academic in nature; it is personal and even with the benefit of hindsight and the opportunity to review and analyze the background of my experience with additional study, it should be taken as just my experience and my story of my friends and neighbors. I did connect and rely on anthropologists and authors who I met during my attempt to learn what had happened.

Anthropologist, Writer, and Human Rights Advocate, Victoria Sanford PhD, *Buried Secrets Truth and Human Rights in Guatemala* gave me the encouragement that I needed to push forward when I felt that the story of Ixcán had been told and no one was interested. She saw the importance in telling the story of the before. Anthropologist and Historian, Sarah Foss PhD's research and book, *On Our Own Terms: Development and Indigeneity in Cold War Guatemala (UNC Press, 2022)* helped give me the background of the Proyecto Ixcán and the original intentions that sometimes deviated from the implementation. Anthropologist and Jesuit priest, Ricardo Falla's book *Massacres in the Jungle Ixcán, Guatemala, 1975-1982*, documented the period of time that I was in Ixcán and what happened after we left. When I met him in Santa María Chiquimula, we shared memories that that no one else in the world other that Ernesto could have. I am eternally grateful for his work in the jungle hearing and then telling the peoples' stories.

The Maya people in Centro Uno Ixcán Grande included Ernesto Cole and me in their community as neighbors and friends from 1976-1978 trusting us. The joy of children, the responsibility of making sure that they were well educated and the work and hard life of a campesino family taught us so much more about survival. The living culture of Todos Santos Cuchumatan in Ixcán Grande and the individuals and co-ops achievements needs to be acknowledged not lost in the violence.

Many years and iterations later the manuscript changed when Juan Felipe Garcia, the one-room teacher and our neighbor in Centro Uno, Ixcán Guatemala in 1978, found me on Facebook. With his help I was able to find others who I thought had been killed forty-five years ago changing the trajectory of the story. In 2022, Juan and I traveled together to Guatemala. He shared his story and reconnected me with Luisa and Elena and others and their incredible stories of horror, terror and resilience. Without his curiosity and goal to find me, this story would have ended the day we left Cento Uno. Thank you to Juan Felipe Garcia, Luisa and her family and Elena and her family. Luisa your story from the beginning until the end of Proyecto Ixcán is incredibly tragic and yet so inspirational. Sometimes the stars just line up. When I sent my manuscript to Julia Park Tracey in 2022, I had no idea that she had lived in Central America at the same time as I did. Her interest my story was encouraging, pushing me to continue writing. Now, as the world has changed, I am incredibly grateful for her support and that of Sibylline Press in bringing my story and the account of the incredible success of campesino farmers in Ixcán Guatemala—including the destruction of their lives, livelihoods and the forest around them. A paradise lost.

# STUDY GUIDE QUESTIONS

1.  Were you aware of the early 1980's history of Guatemala and Central America? The location of Guatemala?

2.  Did you find it surprising that the indigenous Maya in Guatemala weave their clothing and speak distinct dialects? Although their life was very different were you able to feel the depth of the community? Did the book generate interest in searching out Todos Santos Cuchumatanes or the Ixcán area?

3.  Was it shocking to realize that the US was involved in covert military action in a country? How does that compare to now?

4.  The story is told principally in just two years, when the narrator was in her early 20's. How did her understanding of what was happening and happened change over time? Was there a time in the story when you would have packed up and left before Lucinda and Ernesto did and why?

5.  Were there inherent site, political and functional issues that impacted the co-ops ability to prosper?

6.  How can we help others in developing countries who are now experiencing the effects of a changing climate understand the importance of sustainable agriculture and be conscious of our impacts that then force people from their land? Were the original goals of Proyecto Ixcán viable?

7.  The setting of virgin jungle was rich in biodiversity. Some of the campesinos were able to see that their actions were changing the

climate and the environment. How did their form of agriculture benefit the jungle and forest and what were the negative impacts?

8.  How did communication or lack thereof play a part in the gradual increase of militarization? How did the changes manifest and how is fear a principal component of the escalation?

9.  How did the outcome of reconnection and hearing the stories of those who lived in Centro Uno influence your understanding of the people? How can we better understand the impacts of genocide and violence on individuals and the community as a whole?

**Sibylline Press** is proud to publish the brilliant work of women authors over 50. We are a woman-owned publishing company and, like our authors, represent women of a certain age.

www.ingramcontent.com/pod-product-compliance
Lightning Source LLC
Chambersburg PA
CBHW051134130726
47988CB00005B/1829